advance praise for
itsabelly's guide to going green with baby

"I wish I'd had a parent-based resource like this when I had my children. It would have helped me get a "real-mom" perspective on the endless collection of baby products to decide which were safe, which were better for the environment, and which were simply unnecessary."
—Brenda Berg, Founder, CEO, Scandinavian Child

"Going Green with Baby *is a very complete and informative collection of practical advice to help families live a greener lifestyle. The information is compiled in an organized and easy to read format that allows the reader to make immediate choices to improve the impact they and their children have on our planet. Whether looking for basic purchase options to support environmental efforts or making plans for true sustainability* Going Green with Baby *sets out a clear blueprint and allows you to make choices that make the most sense for you and your baby.*
—Pete Myers, President and CEO, Baby Planet

"This is a fantastic guide for helping consumers make environmentally conscious decisions when buying baby products. We, as manufacturers of these products, should take note!"
—Ryan Fernandez, CEO, Boon Inc.

itsabelly's guide to
going green with baby

● ● ●

MOM-TESTED TIPS FOR A HEALTHY BABY AND HAPPY PLANET

JENNIFER LO PRETE & MELISSA MOOG

Dear Dr. Greene,
I'm a huge fan and
so excited to hear you
speak @ ABC today!
Keep sharing your wonderful
information!!
Best,
Melissa

ib

itsabelly press

Disclaimer

Products, tips and recommendations have only been included in this book because the authors have actually tested them or received valuable feedback from other moms who are living green. We did not solicit freebies or accept promotional fees from manufacturers in exchange for inclusion in the book. Based upon our research and product information available at the time of publication, the authors and Itsabelly have attempted to identify products that are consistent with our desire to promote an eco-friendly lifestyle and social responsibility. You should always make your own choices regarding the safety and health of your family.

This book is designed to provide information only. It is not intended to be complete or exhaustive, nor is it a substitute for the advice of your doctor or other health care professional. Matters regarding your family's health should be discussed with a health care professional.

All efforts have been made to ensure the accuracy of the information contained in this book as of the date of publication. The authors and publisher have also made every effort to provide correct contact information at the time of publication. Neither the authors nor publisher assume any responsibility for errors or changes in such information. The authors and publisher expressly disclaim responsibility for any adverse affects arising from the use or application of the information contained herein.

If you have any questions about the products, services or businesses in this book please contact the appropriate professional for advice. Neither the authors, nor the publisher, nor Itsabelly shall be responsible if for any reason you are dissatisfied with, or you or your child are harmed by, any of the products, services or businesses shared in this book.

All trademarks and copyrights found in this book are owned by the respective company or manufacturer. All references are for informational purposes only and are not intended to imply any endorsement by or affiliation with the particular company or manufacturer.

Design by Lisa Elliot of Elysium, San Francisco, CA, www.elysium.com.
Editing by Nancy Grossman, Back Channel Press, Portsmouth, NH, www.backchannelpress.com.
Index by Nanette Cardon, IRIS, Anacortes, WA.

Printed in the USA.
ISBN-13: 978-0-9820741-0-7

Itsabelly Press
10940 SW Barnes Rd, Ste 237
Portland, OR 97225 USA 503-799-5719
www.itsa-belly.com

contents

• • •

foreword

"The creation of a thousand forests is in one acorn," Ralph Waldo Emerson once said. When it comes to little acorns, Mother Nature's wisdom doesn't fall far from the tree. When it comes to building healthy babies, however, a mom awakens to her own Mother Nature and to the immense responsibility of creating a safe environment for her child both inside and outside the womb. Suddenly everything around her, from the food she eats and the cleaning products she uses to the baby gear she purchases, becomes not just the landscape of her life but the friends or foes to her child's well-being and future. It can be overwhelming and time-consuming to research.

Going green means more than just buying organic vegetables (although that's a great start!). It means taking a look at the impact the environment will have on the baby, a highly sensitive being whose foundation for health starts with it's source surroundings. That means everything from revisiting the lead content of your lovely old house and the chemical cleaners you use in the sink to the paint you use in the baby's nursery.

It also means understanding the impact that a baby has on the environment (a baby generates three times more garbage than grown-ups). Multiply twelve diapers a day times 365 days times three years for starters. And consider the huge investment you will be making in toys and gear in the years to come, and how much energy it took to create those high-end gadgets, strollers and wipe warmers. These are just a few of the issues parents face as they become aware of their choice to bring a child gently into the world.

And of course, there's the birth itself—a new mom needs to educate herself about and prepare for that, too. More studies appear every day supporting the concept that a gentle birth is made more possible when a woman enters the laboring process as healthy as possible—well-nourished and in a safe environment, free from physical and emotional hazards—a good reason for her to consider the health of the baby as her own. The two are intertwined . . .

Of course, the idea of going green sounds wonderful in spirit and the new mom may be more inspired than ever. But she is also in a state of complete and utter transformation of her own body, lifestyle, partnership, job and identity. Turning inspiration into determination is no small feat in the face of such changes in a woman's life. As doulas, we support families every day who are struggling with making the most nurturing choices for their child and for the environment. Providing support for families in the childbearing years, we ourselves struggle to keep up with the latest and greatest innovations

And then, at long last, along came *Going Green With Baby*, the green-friendly baby guide that can give families the resources they need to make those choices with a peaceful mind, knowing their babies are being received gently as Mother Nature intended.

Going Green With Baby is like one of those little acorns with a thousands forests inside it! A must-have for every parent whose hopes lie in our newest generation of little ones.

—*Jesse Remer Henderson*, CD, CDT, LCCE
  Mother Tree (DONA) Certified Birth Doula
  DONA International Doula Trainer, OR
  Lamaze Childbirth Educator
  Mother Tree LLC, Director

acknowledgements

From Melissa: This book wouldn't be possible without Randy, my wonderful husband, who has gone above and beyond to support my passions because he truly believes in me. Even when he was diagnosed with NHL his support never waivered and I'm in awe of his ability to overcome any obstacle with a smile. He makes living life possible and survivable (if that's a word)! I also want to acknowledge Isabella, our daughter, who is a huge inspiration in my life and brings me more joy than ever imaginable. To my family, friends and business colleagues, your support and encouragement have been invaluable through this process (thank you)! I'm also deeply grateful to Jennifer Lo Prete for joining me in this book adventure. What started out to be a simple eBook has now transformed itself into a must-have resource for families everywhere due to Jennifer's many late working nights and complete dedication (she rocks). Thank you to all of our experts and eco mamas for their valuable contributions to our book. Thank you to Lisa Elliot of Elysium for her exquisite design talent. This book looks fabulous because of her! Last but not least, I want to thank Nancy Grossman (Back Channel Press) & Nanette Cardon (IRIS Indexing) for powering through the editing.

From Jennifer: Writing this book with Melissa has been a wonderful journey. Working together through late night emails and conference calls with kids screaming in the background we've developed a friendship that goes beyond our book collaboration. Without my longtime friend Meredith Stowe, I never would have met Melissa—thanks for introducing us. I am thankful for having found our awesome graphic designer Lisa Elliot, and her amazing design talent and a strong sense of business strategy. Nancy Grossman, our editor, was a joy to work with and taught me much about editing and publishing. I would also like to thank all our green expert contributors. This book would not be complete without their help, knowledge and generosity. Thank you to my parents, Steve and Colleen Wright, for their encouragement. And special thanks to my husband, Diego—my contribution to this book would not have been possible without his unconditional love and support.

baby green steps

• • •

It used to be "lions, tigers and bears, oh my!" Today, it's phthalates, parabens and bisphenol A, OH MY! How can any mom or dad ignore the onslaught of media buzz we see on TV and on our computers!? And as a new parent you'll do absolutely anything you can to protect your children from every toxic substance you've ever heard about.

Gone are the days where bath and body products in happy, pink bottles off store shelves were items we could trust. Baby products that once came with illusions of purity, cleanliness and a fresh, alluring scent now make us paranoid. As new parents it used to be natural to think that diapering, bathing, feeding and skincare products that said "clinically proven" or "fresh, clean scent" on the bottle were statements worthy of our trust.

Melissa had given little thought to organic and green baby products until her Isabella was about seven months old. Melissa was not your typical tree-hugging, wheat-grass-eating, Birkenstock-wearing new mom. She was the new mom who trusted that "clinically proven" or "doctor approved" meant safe—only learning later that, sadly, this was not the case. Little did she know that taking a magnifying glass to product labels would become her favorite thing to do in store aisles. However, with all of her research in co-authoring this book, Melissa will be extremely well prepared to go as green as possible with her second baby!

eco mom tip:

Trust your maternal instincts for guidance, and don't be afraid to ask for help.

—*Rosetta,* Mama Rose's Naturals, LLC

Jennifer, on the other hand, was very much in tune with how to choose the safest, eco-friendly products for her family, because living green had been ingrained in her growing up. Even though she knew what products or ingredients to avoid, she still found shopping frustrating. After all, no one's opened a green baby super store yet (now wouldn't *that* be a great store!). And, many "green" products are also quite expensive. Although the premium is often understandable, it can be hard to hand over the cash, especially in a one-income family.

Although we started thinking green at different times in our lives, we both have one very important thing in common—the passion to protect our babies from toxic substances by reading labels cautiously and choosing products wisely.

eco mom tip:
Anything that touches baby's skin, goes in baby's mouth or affects the air quality that surrounds baby should be priority number one when considering organic and non-toxic items.

So, what turned out to be a focus on just protecting our families has now turned into a quest to live a more sustainable lifestyle and understanding how products can affect not only our children, but all children.

Through Itsabelly Baby Concierge, Melissa and Jennifer help families navigate the world of going green. We've found that many expectant families use their pregnancy as a time to make healthier life choices. New babies make us conscious of not only protecting them, but of the world they will inherit.

Jennifer and Melissa realize that going green can be difficult on the wallet though as demand increases, prices will decrease—we hope! The most important thing we have to share with new parents going green with baby is to consider first products that will go in baby's mouth, touch baby's skin or affect what she will smell. When going completely green and organic puts too much of a strain on the wallet, we recommend taking baby steps (no pun intended).

We wrote this book with the hope of making going green easier for parents. We have selected products that our friends, our clients and we love. We understand that going green can mean something different to each and every reader. We have included information to assist you in your

GOING GREEN ON THE CHEAP

You don't have to purchase an $800 crib made from sustainable birch-wood to go green with baby. There are many ways to find green alternatives, and there are plenty of affordable options for organic crib bedding, clothing (start with organic onesies) and baby care products as well.

- Buy organic on certain foods and start with the most pesticide-laden items like dairy and produce (for more tips see Feeding Section—Choosing Safe Food).
- Check your local market and buy organic items that are on sale. Buying in bulk can also add money back into your wallet.
- Go to baby consignment stores to find second-hand baby clothing and gear.
- Check out www.target.com, which carries the Organics by Tadpoles line of creepers, an inexpensive line of organic baby clothing.
- If purchasing a new crib, buy a quality one not made of questionable particleboard and glues, and let it air out for a few months before baby sleeps in it for offgassing.
- Use an eco-friendly diapering system like cloth diapering versus spending a ton of money on disposables.
- Remember, breastfeeding is not only healthier for baby, but another good way to keep money in your pocket.
- Make nutritious meals and save money by preparing and freezing homemade baby food. Find less expensive organic ingredients at local farmers' markets or cooperatives.
- Use concentrated "green" household cleaners so they last a long time.
- Go even cheaper by making home-made solutions of distilled white vinegar and water as substitutes for chemical-laden cleaners. Put baking soda and a damp sponge to work cleaning surfaces.

search for green knowledge. We hope that you use our information and resources as a springboard for your own research to choose what is best for your family. We have included a range of products (where possible) that are as eco-friendly as possible for that category. If a completely green alternative didn't exist, we researched the business practices of each manufacturer. We felt it was equally important to include products that you may find at your local big box store along with products from small businesses that only sell online.

We also want every reader to know that you don't need to have a celebrity-parent bank account like Julia Roberts or Matt Damon to go green. You can go green in the simplest of ways, especially with baby's essentials and your family's needs. Yes, it takes some more research and planning, though we hope our book helps cut down on that. The peace of mind of your family's health is well worth it.

Jennifer and Melissa suggest that new and expectant parents do a "needs assessment," concentrating on the items and areas their baby will be exposed to the most and what areas are important to them. For example, a vegan family may have a very different list than a family concerned with toxic plastics. Additionally, when going organic and spending a pretty penny, make sure what you purchase is "certified" organic if possible. Print out the shopping guides we recommend and check labels carefully to be sure no toxic chemicals are hidden in the ingredients list. When in doubt, contact the manufacturer directly.

green choices: understanding product materials and ingredients

• • •

BECOMING AN ECO MOM
By Katherine Scoleri, Safe Mama, www.safemama.com.

There was a time when being a "green" parent meant you recycled, ate tofu and maybe had a compost pile in the yard. Now phrases like "going green," "greening your baby" and "eco-friendly" are not just a fad, they're fast-growing trends bordering on paradigm shift. Celebrities are stocking up on organic onesies and glass bottles faster than Angelina Jolie accumulates children. Moms today are considering so much more when it comes to bringing a baby into the world. They think about what they wear, what they eat, what they use, what they play with and how those things will affect their children, the environment and the future.

When I became pregnant with my son my head swirled with worries, questions and planning. I was going to be the perfect mother! I was going to buy the perfect clothes and have a pristine, sweetly decorated nursery. I was going to feed him the right food and bathe him with the best shampoo. All that preparation and I still didn't "do it right." A year into my son's childhood I received an unsettling email from a fellow parent about a chemical called bisphenol A in baby bottle plastic. There went all my mothering perfection right out the window. I know, first hand, how frustrating pregnancy and the thought of embarking on parenting is to begin with, let alone doing it with every new revelation that pops up in the news we have to worry about. We worry! It's what mothers and fathers do. The modern parent needs to know terms like polycarbonate, phthalates and bisphenol A (BPA). We all need degrees in chemistry to have kids! However frustrating these topics are, it's important to learn about them so we can choose safer alternatives for ourselves and our children. Whether it's safer plastic, safer sustainable materials, safer skin care . . . at the end of the day, we all want what's best for our families and the planet.

Having a baby, as any mother will tell you, changes your perspective on the world we all live in. We all want what is safe for our kids while paying attention to how we impact the earth. I truly believe that parenting is becoming a powerful voice in the dialogue on instigating needed changes. Taking the steps toward making greener choices not only benefits you and your children, it benefits the earth and the future we hope our kids will flourish in.

We don't all have to move into a mud hut and wear loin cloths. Although simplicity sounds appealing . . . it just isn't going to happen and working towards an unattainable goal of *never* negatively impacting the planet is overwhelming. However—any parent can make better choices and can make gradual steps toward living a life that negatively impacts the planet *less*. By doing so, we are also negatively impacting our children's health *less*. Choosing a safer baby bottle or opting for organic cotton is the way forward. For example, by buying organic cotton, we are supporting organic farming, and with the same small purchase, we are eliminating toxic agricultural chemicals and pesticides from the equation.

I can't say I didn't *try* to do everything the right way, but once I became a mother I gained that magical sixth sense, that sense that makes you acutely aware of how everything affects your children. That sense likewise led me towards a growing awareness of so many other safety and environmental issues. That parenting "sense" makes you question everything for the sake of protecting your children, and in turn, makes you want to protect the earth as well. It's not perfectly easy, thanks to the aisles upon aisles of plastic and synthetic chemicals lining the aisles and aisles of baby supply stores. However, it is doable, and you can start right here with this chapter to navigate through the sea of information.

About Safe Mama
SafeMama.com was created by busy mom, business owner, and author Katherine Scoleri. Finding the amount of time she spent researching safety issues for her two-year-old son completely overwhelming, Katherine had an "a-ha" moment: surely she wasn't the only parent scouring the Internet for information about issues that affect our children. So she

started SafeMama.com as a way to keep it all in one place. Between the onslaught of toy recalls, bisphenol A in baby bottles and other health concerns popping up in the news, SafeMama.com is a site where parents can keep up with the latest, and find what they need to make educated and informed decisions. Katherine Scoleri is the co-owner of busy web design company Moxie Design Studios, the co-author of *The IT Girls Guide to Blogging with Moxie* and creator and editor of www.SafeMama.com.

BAMBOO
Why is bamboo different and why does that matter?
By Cort Bucher and Gwen Gallagher, Baby Bambu, **www.babybambu.com.**

Everywhere you look today, there's a growing awareness of the things we buy, eat and wear, where they come from and what they're made of. People are starting to make the connection between having these things and the impact on the environment and amount of resources required to produce them. Consequently, the concepts of "organic," "eco-friendly" and "sustainability" are becoming more important and a bigger factor in the choices we make.

This is one of the reasons bamboo is such an amazing plant. Bamboo has a multitude of uses as a resource for building products, textiles, food, and medicine. Bamboo as it grows also works as a highly effective air filter, absorbing huge amounts of carbon dioxide while cooling and oxygenating the air. Bamboo is actually categorized as a grass and there are over 1500 species that grow in all different climates—even three species that are native to the US. Bamboo is highly sustainable, as it is one of the fastest growing plants (some species grow up to four feet a day), requires no chemical fertilizers and can be responsibly harvested in about four years. Bamboo grows in a 'stand,' continually sending up new shoots, forming a dense network of roots that help improve soil quality and minimize erosion. Bamboo is also drought tolerant, requiring minimal rainfall to sustain it, unlike conventional cotton which is chemical- and water-intensive to grow. Additionally, one acre of bamboo yields ten times more than cotton. *Bambusa* is one of the common genera used to create the pulp and yarns that go into clothing and textiles. Bamboo has a unique and naturally occurring antimicrobial agent called "bamboo kun," which gives bamboo fibers their inherent antibacterial properties that help fight odors. Chemicals have to be applied to other fabrics to achieve this quality. In addition to these antibacterial characteristics, bamboo fabrics have other unique benefits that make it really special:

- Soft and luxuriously silky, like cashmere—even softer than pima cotton—you have to touch it!
- Natural UV protection
- Thermal and breathable—this means you stay warmer when it's cold and cooler when it's hot
- Absorbs and wicks away moisture—bamboo cloth is highly absorbent, up to four times more so than cotton
- Anti-static
- Strong and durable
- 100% biodegradable, decomposes naturally

How is bamboo fiber manufactured?
Much like the paper-making process, bamboo pulp needs to be broken down and separated until it becomes cellulose, which can then be spun into thread and woven into fabric. There are essentially two methods of manufacturing bamboo into bamboo 'rayon' or thread, mechanical and chemical.

The mechanical process uses natural enzymes to help break down the bamboo walls into mush so it can be combed out and spun into yarn. The resulting fabric is often called "bamboo linen." While this process is eco-friendly, it is also labor intensive and costly, so most manufacturers opt for the chemical method. This is why most bamboo clothing cannot be called "organic." With the chemical method, chemicals are used to break down the cellulose (in a multi-phase chemical process) which is then spun into bamboo thread, and finally, woven into fabric. This process is commonly referred to as "viscose" (for more information on the viscose process, visit Wikipedia at: www.en.wikipedia.org/wiki/Viscose) and is very similar to the way rayon is made from wood and cotton waste products.

However, due to the growing demand for bamboo fiber and the environmental impact of the chemicals used in the processing, manufacturers are working on developing less intensive methods of processing. One such method is the same as that used to produce lycocell (which we know as Tencel in clothing) from wood products. This is a "closed loop" process that uses non-toxic chemicals where 99.5% of the chemicals are captured, recycled and re-used. This is a much more eco-friendly and healthy method.

Currently, China is the only manufacturer of bamboo fiber, leaving no local alternatives to source from. While there are no North American producers at this time, some clothing manufacturers are purchasing the thread and yarns and doing the remaining production, sewing and assembly here in the US.

About Baby Bambu

Baby Bambu was conceived in December 2006 when the company founders decided their futures in technology and pharmaceutical advertising weren't the type of life-path they wanted to continue on. A shared entrepreneurial spirit, a love for textiles, and the desire to build a business that was meaningful and makes a positive contribution is the driving force behind Baby Bambu.

After reading articles about bamboo and all its amazing uses, our first vision was using it in clothing for menopausal women. The next thought was—how great would this be for baby clothing!?! And off we went . . .

We've started from square one, designing the clothing, finding manufacturers to make the clothes who are Oeko-Tex certified, to the marketing and sales to get the word out about the benefits of bamboo. We put a lot of thought into what we offer our customers. We also want to show people that they can make conscious choices about the things they buy without sacrificing quality, style or substance.

Our styles and colors are clean, simple and not too fussy. They are functional, feel good to wear and hold up to the life and launderings of babyhood. We have two main lines of products: "bambu basics" and beautiful hand knits. The "bambu basics" consist of a full layette selection; onesies, pants and socks with additional pieces coming this summer. These are a combination of bamboo and organic cotton blends. Our hand knits are made of 100%, undyed bamboo and we offer over 14 different styles of sweaters, pants, hats and blankets. We also have some of the most delicious crib blankets you've ever felt, and will soon have crib sheet sets available as well—all made from a material that has unique, inherent benefits no other fabric can match.

HEMP
Hemp Baby!
By Adam Eidinger, Hemp Industries Association, **www.votehemp.com**.

When a baby is born in America, it doesn't take long for the child to be exposed to harmful petrochemicals. For example, most hospitals immediately wash a newborn using a petroleum-based detergent "tear-free body wash," just moments after birth. Jump forward a few more moments and the child is wrapped in cotton blankets that most likely contain multiple chemicals that were sprayed on the cotton when it was grown. The pesticides and defoliants sprayed on the cotton are linked to cancer, are persistent in the environment for decades and can be found in most cotton clothing people own, even after numerous washings.

Hemp, long known as a sustainable natural fabric due to its relatively low impact on the environment, is an ideal substitute for conventional cotton to make clothing, bags, shoes, towels, socks, hats, curtains, furniture and much more. Hemp is so versatile the uses are only limited by one's imagination—so it is no surprise hemp baby clothing has become more popular in recent years.

So what makes hemp so great? Most importantly, hemp is not sprayed with pesticides. In fact no pesticide has ever been developed for the crop, as there is no need. Hemp also doesn't require chemicals to process the plant's long fibers which are very durable when spun into fabric.

One misconception about hemp is that it's scratchy and similar to burlap. Parents know that if their kids' clothing is uncomfortable they simply won't wear it. In recent years numerous techniques for softening hemp fabric have been perfected. Blending hemp with other fibers has produced luxurious materials that are being embraced by high fashion, and kids alike.

For example, at New York's Fashion Week in 2008 hemp fabrics were featured by numerous mainstream designers such as Donatella Versace, Behnaz Sarafpour, Ralph Lauren, Donna Karan International, Isabel Toledo and Doo.Ri. Strutting down the runway, models wove their magic with everything from hemp/organic cotton jersey knits to hemp/silk charmeuse.

Hemp fabric in the mainstream fashion world is a crowning achievement for pioneering hemp entrepreneurs who have struggled for the last ten years to literally stitch together a way to make hemp clothing even though raw materials must be imported. US farmers have not been able legally to grow the crop for the last 51 years. Ending the misguided prohibition on hemp farming, which stems from the prohibition of hemp's cousin marijuana, is a top priority of the hemp industry.

"We see 2008 as a breakthrough year for hemp fashion, thanks to more than a decade of work by members of the Hemp Industries Association (HIA)," says Summer Star Haeske, Sales Manager for EnviroTextiles, LLC. "Hemp/silk shiny charmeuse, one of my favorite fabrics, has been the hit for top couture designers," adds Haeske.

EnviroTextiles is joined by many other innovators including Los Angeles-based Hemp Traders, which supplies numerous small and large scale clothing designers with hundreds of varieties of hemp blends.

Hemp baby clothing is now common, and numerous designers have made a niche market of hemp baby and kids clothes in recent years. Some of the leading hemp clothing brands include: Livity, Swirlspace, Ecolution, Two Jupiters, Jung Maven, Satori Hemp, Mountains of the

Moon, Envirotextiles, Hemp Hoodlamb, The Hempest, Sweet Grass, Hemp & Chocolate and Hemp Sisters. Hemp is also being used by shoe companies including Simple, Black Spot and Adidas. Hemp, because of its antibacterial and absorbent properties, is also being used in cloth diapers.

The Hemp Industries Association estimates that the North American retail market for hemp textiles and clothing exceeded $100 million in 2007 and is growing around 10% per year. For the record, if you managed to smoke hemp it wouldn't get you high. The DEA wrongfully considers hemp to be a drug crop under their interpretation of the Controlled Substances Act (CSA), even though drug varieties of *Cannabis* are significantly different from oilseed and fiber varieties (industrial hemp). The industrial varieties are low in THC and high in CBD—just the opposite of cannabis, making them useless as a recreational drug.

About Hemp Industries Association

Adam Eidinger is the communications director for Vote Hemp, a nonprofit organization dedicated to the acceptance of and free market for industrial hemp and to making changes in current law to allow US farmers to grow low-THC industrial hemp. More information about hemp legislation and the crop's many uses can be found at www.VoteHemp.com.

ORGANIC COTTON

Healthier for the Planet, Healthier for your Family
By LaRhea Pepper, Executive Director, Organic Exchange,
www.organicexchange.org.

In our lifetime, the world's population is projected to grow from more than 6 billion people today, to nearly 10 billion people. We will all need clean water and air, healthy food, clothes, shelter, energy, and economic opportunity to meet our basic needs. Much of this will come from our agricultural system, which provides all of our food, the fiber for our clothes, and much of the material used to create shelter.

Unfortunately, modern agriculture is based on an industrial model that requires tremendous quantities of toxic and non-renewable inputs to create the food and fiber commodities we all need. These food and fiber commodities are then processed by a worldwide manufacturing system that uses large quantities of water, energy, toxic chemicals, and non-renewable materials to create consumer products. Most of these products, after limited use by consumers, find their way into the trash.

Each step in the lifecycle of a product, from the growth of the materials to its final disposal, has profound, and usually adverse, consequences on the planet. Humans, plants, animals, and all other living organisms feel the effects of toxic inputs and manufacturing processes. Toxic agricultural chemicals are found in ground water, in the air above our cities, and in our food. These chemicals affect communities and ecosystems around the world.

As you might expect, the production of clothing and household goods for worldwide consumption (including sheets and towels for your baby) requires a lot of fiber. In fact, nearly half of the world's textiles are made from natural fibers. Of these, cotton is the most popular fiber by far.

The Problem with Conventional Cotton
Cotton is the go-to choice for most people in the world—especially for moms and babies. Cotton feels soft against the skin, it breathes well, and it comes in a large variety of weights, colors, and textures, making it one of the most comfortable fabrics available. However, despite cotton's good reputation as a "natural choice," cotton production has a surprisingly large environmental and social footprint.

Conventional cotton is one of the most chemical-intensive crops on the planet, receiving a staggering 55 million pounds of pesticides each year in the US alone. Although cotton uses only 2.4% of the world's agricultural land, many experts estimate that it uses 16% of the world's toxic insecticides, a shockingly disproportionate figure. This dependency on synthetic inputs such as insecticides, herbicides, defoliants, and fertilizers, comes at a hefty price—harmful environmental and human health impacts for the communities that produce this popular fiber and their neighbors downstream.

While the use of technological and chemical inputs has increased the volume of cotton produced during the past ten years, it has also contributed to the decline of public health, environmental quality and in some cases, economic opportunity in farming communities around the world.

Consider this:

- Chemical farming sterilizes the soil and kills most of the microorganisms, bacteria, worms and other living things that create healthy ecosystems.
- More than 90% of the synthetic fertilizers and more than 99% of the pesticides and fungicides used in cotton farming do not end up in the cotton plant where intended. Modern pesticide application is like using a shotgun to kill an ant. Farmers frequently apply far more than is needed, hoping that saturation will do the job.
- According to the World Health Organization, nearly 220,000 pesticide-related deaths and more than 3 million pesticide poisonings are attributed each year to the use of agricultural chemicals. Chemical drift is becoming a significant public health issue in rapidly urbanizing agricultural areas such as California's Central Valley.

Think that's bad? These negative impacts reach farther than just farming communities; cotton products and cotton chemicals are found in many unexpected places. Beef, milk, cheese, potato chips and baby food are not items that people normally associate with cotton. But consider that by weight, only 40% of the cotton boll is fiber. The remaining 60% is cottonseed which, made into cottonseed oil, is a ubiquitous ingredient in many of our favorite foods. Cottonseed oil is found in snack foods like cookies, potato chips, and popcorn, in addition to other common foods like salad dressings. With conventional cottonseed oil, trace amounts of toxic chemicals pass into the world's food chain.

Organic: The Healthy Alternative

Luckily there is a viable and sustainable alternative to conventional production—organic cotton farming. Organic farming is very different than conventional production because it treats the farm as an interdependent system of living organisms—human, plant and animal—whereas conventional production focuses on one thing: yield.

Instead of synthetic fertilizers and pesticides, organic farmers use compost, naturally occurring substances and beneficial insects to boost biodiversity and increase yields. Organic farmers protect the environment and create safe rural economies, based on respect for the land and other people. By refusing to use toxic chemicals, they prevent the widespread contamination of local air and water, as well as contamination of places far downstream. Organic farms are healthy, functioning ecosystems that encourage balanced life of all types.

For some perspective, if only 10% of the world's cotton was grown organically, the reduction in synthetic pesticides and fertilizers could range from .5 to 1.5 billion pounds each year. This represents a 1% to 3% reduction in total global synthetic pesticide and fertilizer use, a significant amount of chemicals that could be removed from our environment with a simple purchasing decision from consumers. In fact, the price increase for organic is not that great when you consider that the price of conventional cotton goods does not include the hidden costs of environmental damage, human illness and widespread damage to global ecosystems. The price of organic is simply a fair price, given that organic farmers take greater responsibility for their actions.

Because the majority of cotton farming in the world occurs in developing countries, the increased financial stability brought by organic cotton is even more valuable for farmers and their communities. The fair price paid for organic fibers helps farming communities by contributing extra resources for infrastructure development and maintenance—schools, health centers, and safe water—which enhance human development. Organic farming also greatly enhances local food security without the risks associated with genetically modified organisms (GMO), and increases food safety through the elimination of pesticide residues.

Organic cotton is truly the healthy choice for consumers and farmer alike. When you buy organic cotton, you support regions where growers and their communities are not exposed to cancer-causing chemicals, neurotoxins, and other substances whose long-term effects are still not fully known. You also support the safety and health of a growing global work force in the entire cotton supply chain, and ensure that consumers are safe from chemical contamination in food containing cotton products. Choose organic cotton and make the world a healthier place for your family and for families around the globe.

About Organic Exchange
Organic Exchange is a nonprofit organization committed to supporting and expanding organic fiber agriculture worldwide—particularly cotton. We bring together farmers, manufacturers, brands, and industries in our mission to grow the organic cotton market. Visit us online to learn more about organic cotton, and how you can make a difference: www.organicexchange.org.

Please visit the following websites for more information:
www.aboutorganiccotton.org
www.organicexchange.org

W O O L
The Wonders of Wool!
By Janice Emanuelsson, RN, BSN, IBCLC, President Danish Woolen Delight, **www.danishwool.com.**

When I decided to start selling woolen nursing pads back when my teens were young, I did it out of my passion for breastfeeding and because I felt woolen nursing pads could help women prevent and resolve breastfeeding problems, while also helping to free the environment from the waste of disposable pads. Since then, I've learned what an amazing textile wool is!

Wool holds many wonderful, yet forgotten properties. Most think of wool as protection against the cold, yet wool's temperature-regulating characteristics provide comfort even in warm temperatures. Because wool breathes, it maintains a comfortable temperature against your skin in cool and warm environments. Wool's ability to absorb moisture adds to the comfort of wearing wool—untreated wool can absorb up to 40% of its own weight without feeling wet! And uniquely, when wool feels wet, it feels warm. It's the perfect textile to wear while working out. Rain *or* shine, it will keep the chills away.

Lanolin, the natural oil in wool, contributes to its unique characteristics. When wool absorbs any kind of moisture, lanolin is activated to cleanse away bacteria and remove odors. No need to wash woolens after each wear—hang them up to air-dry and the lanolin will go to work. Wool which still contains its natural lanolin feels softer as well. When the lanolin is extracted from the wool, it becomes dry and brittle, similar to hair which has been dyed and permed.

Using natural wool as bedding also has its health benefits. Untreated wool with its lanolin intact has been shown to repel dust-mites, a cause of allergies. Wool is naturally flame-retardant, always a concern in infant sleepwear and bedding. And because wool is temperature regulating and breathes, it can help prevent over-bundling, also a concern in infant health. One thin layer provides breathable warmth.

Even those who think they are allergic to wool most often react to the chemicals used to extract the lanolin from the wool, often done so wool can be treated with colorful dyes. When wool is untreated and soft from its natural lanolin, itching and allergic reactions are rare.

The wool used for all of the products our company imports has been certified as organic by the highest European standards—meaning no pesticides have been used on the wool itself nor on the fields where the sheep graze.

Many of those who are concerned about the environment are also concerned about the welfare of animals and how they are treated in the process of providing humans with resources they have to offer us. LANACare of Denmark and Hocosa of Switzerland share this same concern. Our wool comes from sheep that are kept in their natural environment. The wool is shorn by hand and is free from pesticides. Using wool can help us maintain a healthy balance in our own lives and in the world we share.

About Danish Woolen Delight

Danish Woolen Delight, a home-based business located in Vermont, was started by a nurse-midwife/lactation consultant. American-born, yet living and working in Sweden during the 90s, the owner became familiar with LANACare organic wool products, made by a Danish nurse. Impressed with their woolen nursing pads, which provided so many benefits for breastfeeding mothers, she decided to import their products to the US when her family relocated to Vermont.

Recently, Danish Woolen Delight began importing Hocosa Demeter wool long-underwear from Switzerland, as a complement to LANACare's unique products, to satisfy customer requests for high-quality organic wool long-underwear for the entire family.

The philosophy behind each product sold by Danish Woolen Delight is to promote health and well-being among those who use and wear their products. The company is currently run by the original owner and her husband.

W O O D
Why Sustainable Forestry?
By The Rainforest Alliance, **www.rainforest-alliance.org.**

Your choice of furniture can do more than add comfort or aesthetic appeal to your home. It can make a difference to people—and to the planet. By shopping for tables, chairs and cribs made from sustainably harvested wood, you can help to support responsible forestry that conserves the environment and supports the rights and welfare of workers and neighboring communities.

When trees are harvested sustainably, they are carefully selected and cut in such a way that the forest ecosystem remains intact. Wildlife habitat, soils and waterways are protected, workers enjoy decent conditions and their families benefit from respectable housing, education and health-care—all of which is far from standard, particularly in the tropics, where

42 million acres of forest are lost each year.

Through sustainable forestry, trees and other forest products can be used to meet the need for lumber and paper without degrading forest ecosystems, and forestlands can retain their economic value for the long term. Sustainable forestry is important not only to protect plant and animal species, but also the Earth itself. Because forests store large amounts of carbon, cutting them down releases these global-warming gases into the atmosphere. In fact, deforestation is responsible for roughly 20 percent of greenhouse gas emissions worldwide.

In recent years, a growing number of businesses and consumers have made the decision to support sustainable forestry. The "green building" movement—in which only sustainably produced wood is used—has taken root among architects, designers and their clients. Now, many consumers are using the same standard when choosing furniture, as they try to create living spaces that reflect their personal values as well as their tastes. And more and more furniture companies are taking notice— increasingly, they are offering sustainable furniture items to the public.

How can you be sure that responsible practices were used to produce the wood in your furniture? By making sure that it was certified as sustainable to standards set by the Forest Stewardship Council (FSC). The FSC, an international nonprofit founded by a diverse group of forestry businesses and environmental organizations, sets global standards for responsible forestry—standards that protect the rights of workers and people living in and around forested areas, prohibit the use of hazardous chemicals and protect animal habitat.

About The Rainforest Alliance
The Rainforest Alliance, an international conservation organization that works to protect the world's ecosystems and ensure sustainable livelihoods, certifies companies that meet these standards. For more information on purchasing FSC-certified furniture, please visit http://www.rainforestalliance.org/forestry/documents/smartguide_furniture.pdf.

For furniture buyers, "think global, act local" is more than a slogan. By purchasing sustainably produced furniture, you can help reverse the destructive trends that threaten our planet—and keep the Earth safe for future generations.

PLASTIC
Cause for Concern
By Alicia Voorhies, The Soft Landing, **www.thesoftlanding.com**.

Raising a healthy baby in a toxic world can be difficult. We're surrounded by chemicals and each day we become aware of something new to avoid. It's overwhelming for new and seasoned parents alike, so how can we possibly decide what to prioritize for our children?

A good place to start is by learning about two chemical groups recently brought to mainstream discussions by environmental scientists. Bisphenol A and phthalates are considered by environmental scientists to be "endocrine disruptors." Laboratory studies have shown that both chemicals can mimic hormones, setting the foundation for potential health problems, especially in children.

According to the Center for Health, Environment & Justice, babies face greater exposure due to their small size, behaviors and because they are more sensitive as a result of their ongoing development. A baby's normal growth and development may even increase their vulnerability to chemicals.

What is Bisphenol A?
Bisphenol A (BPA) is an industrial chemical used to make polycarbonate plastic. BPA has become one of the most commonly used chemicals, racking up a stunning six billion pounds each year. Over 90% of major US baby bottle manufacturers use BPA. Bisphenol A can also be found in water bottles, the lining inside metal cans (even baby formula cans) and food storage containers. Studies have shown that the unstable BPA bond will allow the chemical to leach into food or beverages in contact with

the plastic during normal, everyday use. BPA may cause adverse health effects, such as: increase in obesity and diabetes, interference with the normal development of unborn babies, stimulation of mammary gland development, which is a risk factor for breast cancer and early onset of puberty.

What are Phthalates?

Phthalates are a class of chemicals that are added to children's plastic toys and teethers to make them more flexible. They are also found in many household and personal care products, and medical supplies. Phthalates have been shown to cause reproductive and neurological damage in animal tests.

Avoiding Toxic Plastic

As a parent you can make small, but important changes to help your baby avoid contact with these chemicals.

- Avoid baby bottles, pacifiers, sippy cups, and breast milk/food containers made of polycarbonate plastic. An easy way to identify these products is to look for clear, hard plastic.
- Avoid teethers and toys containing phthalates.
- Safer plastic choices may be labeled with recycling numbers 1, 2, 4 or 5. Avoid products labeled with numbers 3, 6 and 7 as they are more likely to contain BPA and phthalates.
- Purchase products specifically labeled as BPA- and phthalate-free. Contact the manufacturer if you are unsure.
- Breastfeed and make your own baby food. Many companies line their baby food jars and formula cans with BPA, greatly increasing risk of exposure.
- In order to decrease exposure to unborn babies, pregnant moms should avoid perfumes, makeup, nail polish and other products containing phthalates. You should also be careful to avoid polycarbonate water bottles and food storage containers.

About The Soft Landing

Alicia Voorhies, a former nurse, was shocked two years ago when her sister called to say her son's pediatrician suggested she throw away her polycarbonate baby bottles. Alicia went right into action pouring over research on plastics, fully expecting to prove the doctor wrong.

The more studies she read, however, the more concerned she became about the chemical compounds used in plastics. A growing awareness of toxic plastics became a mission to care for her own children and newborn nephews. And so the search for safer feeding gear began.

Over the last year, a highly motivated team has grown from Alicia's concerned family members. She and her sisters now work together to find BPA-, PVC- and phthalate-free baby products, bringing them together in one place for an easy shopping experience.

Their goal is to provide trustworthy information to help concerned parents make informed choices. Alicia started a blog to share her findings and she also creates quick reference guides to help parents find safer baby feeding products at other stores (www.thesoftlandingbaby.com).

SKINCARE PRODUCTS
Soothers and Smoothers for Mamas and Babies
By Melinda Olson, founder of Earth Mama Angel Baby,®
www.earthmamaangelbaby.com.

In an ideal world, mamas could pick up a bottle of baby lotion or shampoo without having to become a detective to tell exactly what was used to manufacture the product. So many products making "organic" claims have been found to contain toxic ingredients. Eco-conscious mamas need to do some research and find out which preservatives, surfactants, emulsifiers and fragrances their personal care products use. The next step: learn how to spot them on a label.

In this country, many bottles of lotions, diaper creams, body washes and stretch mark potions are sold containing known carcinogens and toxic chemicals. Using databases like Environmental Working Group's Skin Deep (www.cosmeticsdatabase.com) can help you identify companies that do not use harmful chemicals, and find out more about the chemicals themselves.

What to Look For
As a starter list, learn about artificial preservatives and ingredients like grapefruit seed extract that sound natural but can contain hidden formaldehyde or chemical preservatives. Another trick companies use is to name an ingredient like cocoamidylpropyl betaine and in parenthesis name the source before it was chemically altered, such as (coconut-derived). Because it was derived from a coconut originally does not necessarily mean that it is now as safe as a coconut!

Also, the more you know about why a chemical is used, the easier it is to know what to look for. For example, parabens are used as artificial preservatives. All products that contain water have to be preserved in some way, so figure out how the company is preserving the product and then you can tell if it's a healthy choice. Another ingredient class that has gotten a lot of press recently are phthalates, which are usually found along with artificial "fragrance oils." Look for a phthalate-free sticker, and check brands before you shop to see if they include phthalates in any of their products. A reputable company will answer your questions about their ingredients, and list ALL ingredients on their labels and web site.

If having a baby has taken you into label-reading for the first time, don't despair. There is a lot of good information online, and you'll learn quickly what to look for. You'll also find a favorite brand that you trust, and enjoy knowing that the products that you use for all those adorable fingers and toes are safe.

About Earth Mama Angel Baby
The founding Mama of Earth Mama Angel Baby is a nurse and herbalist who saw the need for pregnancy, childbirth and baby products to support the natural process of birthing babies. Just as our foremothers did, Earth Mama Angel Baby honors the ancient knowledge of natural and herbal remedies and plant medicine. The wisdom we rely on has been passed down from great-grandmother to grandmother to mother to daughter,

which we combine with the safety and assurances of contemporary evidence-based research.

Supporting pregnancy, postpartum recovery, breastfeeding, baby care, and even baby loss, naturally with nature's gifts makes sense to us. We don't think of pregnancy as an illness, merely a phenomenal process that has many wonderful and sometimes difficult stages. We trust in the wise women who have historically exalted the glories and eased the common discomforts of pregnancy naturally.

We use the highest-quality, certified-organic or organically grown herbs and oils for our teas, bath herbs, gentle handmade soaps, salves, lotions and massage oils. Our products are 100% toxin-free, cruelty-free, vegan, and free from all artificial preservatives, fragrances and dyes. Our commitment to honor the earth and her valuable resources extends to our packaging as well—we use only eco-friendly recyclable or reused/reusable packaging and packing materials. We strive to provide research, tools and products to empower women with knowledge about the earth's natural resources for nurturing themselves and their angel babies.

green labels: understanding certification and labels

• • •

So, you have decided to go green and started reading product labels. You're probably spending a lot of time staring at an alphabet soup of acronyms along with "certified by" next to its product features. It can be hard to decipher the standards behind these certifiers. And frankly, until there is more awareness about the certifiers it is difficult to be able to evaluate their claims while you're standing at the shelf in your health food store.

We have included a list of common certifiers. Although these are the organizations we came upon most often in our product searches, it is by no means a complete list of *all* eco-certifiers. Most probably, by the time this book comes out, there will be more organizations claiming to certify organic products. Also, we narrowed our focus by concentrating on certifiers of products related to baby gear and food. We would like to thank these organizations for providing us with background information on their certification standards and for use of the logo to help you better identify certified products.

Be aware that currently, there is *no standard* for using words like "organic" and "natural." And keep in mind that different certifiers may have different definitions and standards by which they claim that a product is organic or natural.

As the popularity of organic and natural products grows, third party certifiers will help assure quality by setting manufacturing standards. These standards for certification will help give consumers confidence that they understand the ingredients and background of the product they are purchasing. We hope that these certifiers also do public relations campaigns so that the general public can learn about their standards. We feel this is the only way to weed out the good certifiers from opportunists who are merely riding the green wave.

Consumer Reports Greener Choices EcoLabels Center
Consumer Reports offers a great resource to better understanding organic certifiers and product labels. Consumer Reports evaluates the labels on food, wood, personal care products and household cleaners. You can search the database by product, category or certifier at www.greenerchoices.org.

Demeter® Biodynamic
Certifies: Food
www.demeter-usa.org

Demeter® USA is the non-profit American chapter of Demeter International, the world's only certifier of Biodynamic® farms, processors and products. From farm to market, their rigorous standards ensure compliance to the highest agricultural and environmental practices. Only those companies that meet these standards are permitted to display the Demeter certification mark on their products. As part of an 85-year-old global certification network spanning 45 countries, Demeter USA asks consumers to join their effort to heal the planet by choosing Demeter certified Biodynamic products.

Food Alliance (FA)
Certifies: Food
www.foodalliance.org

Food Alliance is a non-profit organization that certifies farms and ranches, and food packers, processors and distributors for socially and environmentally responsible agricultural and business practices.

The certification standards for farmers and ranchers address safe and fair working conditions; humane treatment of animals; the least toxic approach to pest management; conservation of soil and water resources; protection of wildlife habitat; the addition of no hormones or non-therapeutic antibiotics; no genetic modification of crops or livestock; and the continual improvement of practices.

The certification standards for food packers, processors and distributors address sourcing of Food Alliance certified ingredients; safe and fair working conditions; reduced use of toxic and hazardous materials; conservation of energy and water; reduction and recycling of waste; quality control and food handling safety; no artificial flavors, colors or preservatives; and the continual improvement of practices.

Forest Stewardship Council (FSC)
Certifies: Wood and Paper Products
www.fsc.org

The FSC logo identifies wood and paper products that have come from well-managed forests. As a consumer, the FSC label means that you can trust the wood was harvested from a forest that meets FSC's strict environmental and social standards. FSC certification is supported by the world's leading conservation organizations, including World Wildlife Fund, The Nature Conservancy, Greenpeace, and National Wildlife Federation.

Green Seal
Certifies: Cleaning Products, Skin Care Products and Paper Products, **www.greenseal.org**

Green Seal is a not-for-profit, independent certification and standards development body. Since 1989 they have promoted the manufacture, sales and use of sustainable products and services.

What the Green Seal Means: a Green Seal-Certified mark on a product means that it has gone through a stringent process to prove that it has less impact on the environment and human health. The Green Seal means that the product works as well as others in its class, and that it has been evaluated without bias or conflict of interest. The mark proves without a doubt that the product has passed the test and is a truly green product. You can find links to the thousands of Green Seal-certified products and all of their environmental standards at www.greenseal.org.

Leaping Bunny
Certifies: Skin Care Products and Cleaning Products
www.leapingbunny.org

The Coalition for Consumer Information on Cosmetics' (CCIC) Leaping Bunny Program administers a cruelty-free standard and the internationally recognized Leaping Bunny Logo for companies producing cosmetic, personal care, and household products. The Leaping Bunny Program provides the best assurance that no new animal testing is used in any phase of product development by the company, its laboratories, or suppliers. In 1996, the CCIC was formed from the nation's largest animal protection groups in order to promote one standard and one logo for cruelty-free products. Companies that join the Leaping Bunny Program must obtain assurances from their suppliers and third party manufacturers that, with respect to the specific ingredients and products supplied, no animal testing has been conducted on their behalf after a fixed date. Companies must recommit to the program annually and be willing to submit to an independent audit. Because not all companies choose to license the Leaping Bunny Logo, consumers interested in shopping with compassion should visit www.LeapingBunny.org for the full list of companies that have made this cruelty-free commitment.

Marine Stewardship Council (MSC)
Certifies: Seafood
www.msc.org

Overfishing is a problem that affects us all, threatening fish species, millions of jobs around the world and marine eco-systems. What can consumers do to help? Look out for the MSC's blue eco-label when shopping for fish. It identifies fish that have been caught in a responsible way, and it is only awarded to fisheries that meet the MSC's strict environmental standards.

MSC-certified fisheries ensure that there are enough fish for the future; they keep marine habitats intact and protect endangered species.

Independent experts ensure that the fisheries live up to the MSC criteria. This way consumers can rest assured that products with the MSC eco-label truly come from sustainable fisheries.

The MSC is an independent, non-profit organization founded in 1997 to provide a solution to the problem of overfishing. Together with scientists, fishery experts and conservation groups, the MSC has developed environmental standards to evaluate and reward fisheries. Consumers can identify products from certified fisheries by the blue MSC eco-label.

Worldwide (as of August 2008), more than 1,600 seafood products have earned the MSC's seal of approval, making it easy for consumers to identify fish and seafood from well-managed and sustainable fisheries. Target, Whole Foods, Wal-Mart and many others have introduced fish and seafood products with the MSC's blue logo. Consumers choosing fish with the MSC eco-label reward responsible fishing practices and contribute to a healthy marine environment.

Oeko-Tex 100
Certifies: Textiles
www.oeko-tex.com

The Oeko-Tex label, "Confidence in Textiles" certifies that the product is independently tested for over 100 harmful substances according to the Oeko-Tex Standard 100. Textiles with the Oeko-Tex label do not contain allergenic or carcinogenic dyes, pesticides, chlorinated phenols, heavy metals or formaldehyde, to name just a few. Product usage categorizes how products are tested. Therefore, a baby onesie is evaluated differently than an adult t-shirt, taking into account the fact that a baby's system is more delicate than an adult. More than 8,000 companies in 84 countries worldwide currently use the Oeko-Tex system.

People for the Ethical Treatment of Animals (PETA)
Certifies: Cosmetics, Personal Care and Household Products
www.peta.org and www.caringconsumer.com

cruelty free

PETA's Caring Consumer Project was created to help consumers support companies that have decided to make a compassionate choice. PETA's bunny stamp of approval can only be used by companies that have pledged to PETA in writing that neither they nor their ingredient suppliers test their products, formulations or ingredients on animals.

Hundreds of thousands of animals are experimented on and killed every year in painful tests for cosmetics, personal care products and household cleaning products. Although more than 700 companies have banned all animal tests, some businesses continue with experiments such as force feeding toxins to rabbits. These tests are not required by law, and they often produce inaccurate or misleading results.

PETA's Caring Consumer Project helps responsible shoppers support companies that use modern, animal-free product tests that are faster, cheaper, and more accurate than animal experiments, which were developed in the 1920s. Human cell cultures, tissue studies (*in vitro* tests) and artificial human "skin" and "eyes" mimic the human body's natural responses, and a number of computer virtual organs serve as accurate models of human body parts. For information and to view our entire list of cruelty-free companies, visit www.CaringConsumer.com.

Quality Assurance International (QAI)
Certifies: Food
www.qai-inc.com

When shopping for organic foods, how does one really know if the manufacturer's claims that the product is organic are true? The answer is simple —look for QAI's certification mark.

Before a product can be labeled "organic," a government-approved certifier must inspect the location where the product is grown and handled to make sure the producer or handler is following all the rules necessary to meet USDA organic standards. Since 1989, QAI has been certifying the organic integrity of food products from seed to the store shelf. In fact, two out of three certified organic products on US store shelves have been certified by QAI.

Sustainable Forestry Initiative® (SFI)
Certifies: Wood and Paper Products
www.aboutsfi.org

The SFI program is a forest certification program that integrates the perpetual growth and harvesting of trees with the protection of biodiversity and water quality. As the only North America-wide program, SFI shepherds a collective effort of individuals, organizations and companies committed to sustainable forestry.

The SFI standard is grounded in science, research and regional expertise, and is endorsed by leading conservation groups such as The Conservation Fund. Their members include environmental and conservation organizations, public officials, professional and academic groups, forest products industry companies, loggers and foresters. Look for wood and paper products carrying the SFI logo.

TransFair USA—Fair Trade Certified
Certifies: Food, Herbs and Beverages
www.transfairusa.org

TransFair USA is the only independent, third-party certifier of Fair Trade Certified products in the United States. TransFair USA audits and certifies transactions between US companies offering Fair Trade Certified products and their international suppliers to guarantee that the farmers and workers producing Fair Trade Certified goods were paid fair prices and wages. TransFair USA certifies coffee, tea, herbs, vanilla, cocoa, chocolate, rice, sugar, bananas, flowers and now honey.

USDA Organic
Certifies: Agricultural Products
www.ams.usda.gov/nop

The United States Department of Agriculture runs the National Organic Program (NOP) that develops, implements, and administers national production, handling, and labeling standards for organic agricultural products. NOP also accredits the certifying agents (foreign and domestic) who inspect organic production and handling operations to certify that they meet USDA standards. Organic crops are raised without using most conventional pesticides, petroleum-based fertilizers or sewage sludge-based fertilizers. Animals raised on an organic farm must be fed organic feed, given access to the outdoors, and not be given antibiotics or growth hormones. NOP prohibits genetic engineering, ionizing radiation and sewage sludge in production or handling. NOP labeling standards are based on the percentage of organic ingredients in the product. NOP labels products either "100% Organic" or "Made With Organic Products." To qualify for the "Made With Organic Products" label, a product must contain at least 70% organic ingredients. The USDA Organic seal will not appear on these products. Products with less than 70% organic ingredients can only use the term "organic" to identify specific organic ingredients. The name of the certifying agent must be displayed on the label. If skincare products include organic agricultural ingredients and meet both USDA and NOP standards, the products may be USDA/NOP certified.

apparel

• • •

Ask parents why they choose to go green with baby's clothing and you'll hear, over and over again, two reasons—for their baby's health and to support environmental change. Many parents find it important to choose organic and natural products for those items that come in direct contact with baby's skin. Conventional clothing may be treated with chemicals that are toxic either in the growing or finishing phase of garment production. Choosing organic cotton, bamboo or humanely raised wool clothing can help the environment by reducing harmful farming practices.

Just because a garment is labeled 100% cotton doesn't mean it's safe for baby. Conventional cotton is one of the most pesticide-heavy crops in the world. Those pesticides harm not only the cotton farmers who work with them, but wildlife and water systems as well. Conventional cotton clothing may be treated with toxic additives, such as heavy metal-based dyes, formaldehyde and chlorine bleach. Besides being possibly carcinogenic, these chemicals may cause skin rashes, nausea, muscle pain, dizziness and breathing difficulties in people sensitive to them. According to the Organic Trade Association, less than 1% of cotton is grown organically. As more consumers choose organic cotton, more farmers will switch to growing organic and, hopefully, the price will become more affordable!

We know, you're thinking that organic clothing is too hippy dippy for *your* black t-shirt, denim wearing baby. Well, thank goodness the days of oatmeal-colored organic clothing are over. As green becomes the new black, there are many vibrant, fun and hip eco clothing options. The fast growing, and therefore easily renewable, bamboo plant has found a new use—as a naturally soft and antimicrobial fiber for clothing. And did we mention that it wicks moisture too? Bamboo clothing is perfect for babies!

Wool is another great fiber that works well for our little ones. Are you kidding, you say? Wool is too itchy and hot for sensitive baby skin! We're not kidding. Wool is hypoallergenic and naturally resistant to bacteria. Wool's natural wicking and insulating properties keep baby warm in cold weather and cool in warm weather. Another natural benefit for sleep clothing made of wool: it's naturally fire-retardant.

Please read our Green Choices chapter to find out more about the benefits of organic and natural fibers and how your choice impacts the environment.

GOING GREEN TIPS

By Janice Masoud, President of Under the Nile, **www.underthenile.com**.

Ten years ago, there was virtually no information available to parents about organic cotton. Today it is an entirely different story. The media has picked up on this new trend and consumers are demanding more information. For this reason, parents have increasing access to green information that will help them to make better decisions in regards to their babies: their diapers, the clothing they wear, and the toys that they put into their mouths. This is a trend that shows no signs of leaving.

Making organic cotton choices for your family is easy and has many benefits. First, start with the basic items that are centered around your baby's wardrobe—for example, babybodies (onesies), undershirts, and sleep-related clothing that your baby is wearing all the time. By purchasing organic cotton sheets, this also eliminates extra toxins that your baby is exposed to for long periods of time. Remember that your baby's clothes are in direct contact with their skin. Conventional cotton clothing contains pesticide residues and can be transferred into their body through their skin.

Secondly, choose organic cotton toys for your baby. With all the recalls in today's market you want to make sure that the toys that your baby puts in his or her mouth do not contain any toxins. You should also look for toys that are stuffed with organic cotton and not fluff. Many babies are allergic to the fluff that is in most conventional soft toys on the market today.

Lastly, going green not only helps your family, but has a great impact on the environment. With the purchasing power of ordinary families who make the choice to turn green, thousands of tons of pesticides that are used on the world's cotton fields have been and continue to be eliminated. These simple, conscientious choices have helped immensely in cleaning up the ground water, and have made for a more nurturing and sustainable environment for our world's wildlife.

ITSABELLY'S LAYETTE RECOMMENDATIONS

Remember, you may receive lots of baby clothing gifts. Few people can resist buying tiny newborn-size clothes. So, wait to do any clothes shopping. Jennifer was lucky enough to not have to buy any clothes the first six months or so of Malena's life (her firstborn). Sure, some of these little outfits weren't exactly her taste; she saved them for her "at home" days. Babies grow out of clothes really fast, so there's no need to stock up in the small sizes.

One baby item we love is the sleep sack. Trust us, come midnight you'll prefer having one piece to undo to change baby's diaper. Save all those confusing crotch snaps for the daytime when you've had a few hours' rest. Besides, the First Candle/SIDS Alliance joined the American Academy of Pediatrics, the Consumer Product Safety Commission and the National Institute of Child Health and Human Development to recommend the use of wearable blankets such as sleep sacks over traditional blankets in the crib to reduce the danger of suffocation in the crib.

eco mom tip:

Hand-me-downs are not only smart for all the reasons you know, they keep your kids from wearing the same fashions as every other kid on the block.

—*Liz Gumbinner*, editor, coolmompicks.com

As you organize your baby clothes, make sure you have the following in newborn and small sizes. Some items, such as a sweater are fine to buy in a size small; just roll the sleeves and it will fit baby in no time.

- Four one-piece sleepers or gowns
- Two sleep sacks
- Six side-snap t-shirts (three long sleeve, three short sleeve)
- Four to six onesies
- Four small baby caps
- Six pairs socks/booties
- Two to three soft, comfortable daytime outfits
- Cotton sweater or light jacket
- Cotton mittens

SUMMER BABIES

Your baby will love discovering all the wonders of nature during the summer, and sunshine is a great source of vitamin D. However, sun damage often occurs while we are young and children are more sensitive to sun exposure. The AAP does not recommend using sunblock on infants under one year, unless sun exposure is unavoidable and clothing cannot be used to cover the infant. Your best bet is to cover up with clothing and a brimmed hat, stay in the shade and limit sun exposure during peak hours.

BRIMMED HAT

FlapHappy Hats: FlapHappy's popular baseball-style hat with flaps that cover the ears and neck is now available in 100% organic cotton. FlapHappy also makes a wide range of other hat styles from crusher to floppy hats. We hope they offer these in organic cotton soon! Price: $12, www.flaphappy.com.

Nuno Organic Sun Hat: An organic cotton baseball-style hat with a protective covering for the ears and neck. We love that this hat ties under the chin—perfect for those babies who insist on pulling off their sun hat. Price: $28, www.nunoorganic.com.

WINTER BABIES

Even during winter, babies enjoy their daily walks. While it can be difficult to get baby bundled and out the door in cold weather, the fresh air
does everyone good.

Parents wishing to avoid petroleum-based products should be aware that
insulation used in winter coats, jackets and buntings may be polyester-
based. We found these natural alternatives to keep baby warm and dry
all winter long. We even found some coats for mama so you can keep
baby held close in your baby carrier (a whole lot easier than maneuvering
a stroller in inclement weather).

SNOWSUIT OR HEAVY BUNTING

Sherpa Baby Bunting: An adorable, certified organic cotton sherpa
bunting by Kate Quinn Organics. This comfy bunting comes in four beautiful color combinations. Your baby will be snuggly warm with fitted feet,
reversible hand mitts, side kimono snaps and furry trim. The bunting is
completely lined with a fine knit. Price: $62, www.katequinnorganics.com.

SnuggleWool Organic Bunting: A soft merino wool baby bunting to keep
your baby cozy and comfortable. The bunting is fully lined with wool
fleece and an outer layer of organic cotton flannel fabric. The bunting
features a Velcro® closure and center split for the stroller safety strap.
Please note that this bunting is not intended for use in a car seat. The

Snugglewool bunting fits newborn babies up to six months. Price: $84, www.snugglewool.com.

Hanna Andersson, REI, L.L. Bean, Lands' End, Patagonia: While these baby snowsuit manufacturers don't yet make an organic or natural-based insulation snowsuit (we hope they do soon!), as companies they support organic products and corporate social responsibility. Patagonia offers Synchilla fleece that is made from recycled soda bottles. Prices vary: www.hannaandersson.com, www.rei.com, www.llbean.com, www.landsend.com, www.patagonia.com.

HEAVY STROLLER BLANKET
Keep baby warm during your daily walk with these natural alternatives.

SnuggleWool Organic Merino Wool Blankets: These soft merino wool blankets, backed with organic cotton flannel, are offered in a number of sizes. We like the smaller blankets for swaddling and the larger ones for lap and floor blankets. They even offer a SnuggleWool Blankie, for your baby's lovey. Prices: $68.50 to $136, www.snugglewool.com.

Danish Woolen Delight: These Oeko-Tek certified wool blankets come in grey and natural white colors and a baby, toddler and even adult size. These incredibly soft and cuddly blankets can be trimmed with or without a lace edge. Price: $87.99 to $115, www.danishwool.com.

WARM KNIT HAT
Most body warmth is lost through the head, so it is important to keep baby warm with a natural knit hat. A natural fiber hat also provides moisture wicking so that baby does not become too hot.

Lapsaky: We love Lapsaky's beanie hat and a cute pilot hat offered in organic cotton, organic thermal knit and eco-wool. The pilot hat is popular because it covers baby's ears and ties under the chin. Lapsaky also makes great eco-wool and organic cotton mittens and scarves. Price: $8 to $20, www.lapsaky.com.

Etsy: An online collective of hip crafters. Type in "organic knit hat baby" in the etsy search engine and marvel at all the cute, handmade options to support artisans in their craft. Prices vary, www.etsy.com.

MAMA COAT

What a great invention! Actually, probably not a new invention since moms have been wearing their babies for ages and have needed protection from the weather. A mama coat allows mommy to wear a coat while wearing her baby in a carrier. These coats are also convenient to wear during pregnancy. And don't be turned off by the "mama" in the name. Daddies can also wear some of these jackets.

KinderCoat: Suse's Kinder offers several mama coats for warmth while wearing your baby during winter weather. The original KinderCoat is a waterproof shell with a removable fleece liner; baby can be worn on the front and back. It even comes with an instructional DVD. They also make a rain jacket and a fleece vest. KinderCoats come in sizes S, M, L, XL, XXL. The larger sizing works well for men. Prices range from $50 to $139, www.suseskinder.com.

MamaPoncho: A great versatile babywearing poncho made from 100% eco-friendly and non-itching virgin Oeko-Tex certified wool. This poncho has a warm pouch for the baby with two openings, one for the baby's head and one for the mother's head. It can be worn over baby slings and most brands of baby carriers in front and back carry positions. You can even wear this poncho during pregnancy by leaving the baby's head opening closed—once baby is born, simply un-stitch the baby's opening. Available in three different styles and four colors. A little expensive, but it may be well worth the investment if you live in a cold climate and enjoy babywearing. Price: $219, www.mamaponcho.ch.

MamaJacket: This practical and classically styled babywearing coat can be used during pregnancy, babywearing and even without baby. It is made from ecologically grown wool and is lined in viscose. The MamaJacket can be used with slings and other baby carriers for front and back babywearing. It comes in sizes XS, S, M, L and XL. Price: $247, www.tragemantel.ch.

- **Baby Bambu:** A line of baby clothing and accessories made from soft bamboo fiber and organic cotton, www.babybambu.com.
- **Babystar:** Design-savvy clothes for tots that are 100% cotton and formaldehyde-free and soon to be released soy and organic knits and organic denim items. Babystar believes in responsibility, sustainability and creating safe products for children, www.babystar.com.
- **Buchic Bamboo Clothing:** Wonderfully soft bamboo fiber knit layette essentials, adult clothing and blankets based in Oregon, www.buchic.com.
- **Disana:** For twenty years Disana has been making wool and cotton baby items for feeding, sleeping and bathing. Disana offers a wonderful wool sleep sack, www.disana.de.
- **Green Babies:** Since 1993, Lynda Fassa has been creating comfortable and cute organic clothing for babies and children, www.greenbabies.com.
- **Hanna Andersson:** Vibrant and bold organic pajamas, sleepers, clothing and thick knitted baby hats. You may even find a Hanna store at your local mall, www.hannaandersson.com.
- **Kate Quinn Organics:** Classic, clean designs made from soft fabrics with gorgeous colors, www.katequinnorganics.com.
- **Pure Beginnings:** Organic cotton knit sleep gowns, sleepers and onesies in a range of soothing colors, www.purebeginnings.com.
- **Sage Creek Naturals:** Organic layette sets and bedding in sweet pastel colors and prints, www.sagecreeknaturals.com.
- **Sckoon:** A large selection of 100% fair-trade and certified organic cotton clothing, diapers, menstrual pads, toys and even pet items. Sckoon offers a variety of clothing collections in hip colorful prints and designs. All Sckoon products are un-dyed, unbleached or dyed with low-impact, environmentally friendly dyes, www.sckoon.com.
- **Under The Nile:** A complete 100% organic line of all the baby necessities, from clothing, towels and accessories to adorable toys, www.underthenile.com.

travel & transportation

• • •

Finding 100% organic car seats and strollers is virtually impossible because their construction require some metal and a bit of plastic. So that your choices can have the least eco-impact, we have selected manufacturers that use green manufacturing practices and those that practice social corporate responsibility. This list isn't exhaustive, just a sampling of manufacturers who are going above and beyond current practice. We hope that more manufacturers will follow the lead of companies like Orbit and adopt greener manufacturing processes.

CAR SEATS

We are going to ruffle some green feathers here and say that when choosing a car seat, going green should not be your first priority. Safety should be priority number one. As more consumers value green products, we hope that manufacturers will meet the demand—just look at the innovation and greenness behind Orbit.

Please remember that car seats are one baby gear category where recycling is not encouraged. You're probably thinking of how much money and carbon you can save by using your sister-in-law's old car seat. But we advise against it. And many car seat experts agree. With a second-hand seat you may not know its crash history—what is moderate to you may be minor to the previous owner. A secondhand car seat may be missing important parts, instructions or model/make number. Even if the car seat was your previous child's seat, car seats don't last forever. After all, they are mainly made of plastic, and that can wear down or crack. The NHTSA and some baby gear books recommend against using a car seat that is over six years old. However, we advocate a more conservative approach (after all, it is safety we are talking about here!). Call manufacturers and get specific recommendations for their car seats' expected life span.

You must select the car seat that meets the requirements for your child's age, offers the safety features you require and fits both your car and your child well. We provide some general guidelines for car seats as recommended by the American Academy of Pediatrics (AAP), car seat experts and the National Highway and Traffic Safety Administration (NHTSA). All car seats sold in the United States must meet strict federal safety standards. Unfortunately, not all car seats work well in all cars or fit different shapes of children. In order to work properly, the car seat must fit in your car properly and secure your child properly. The best way to know if your car seat fits properly is to talk with your local professional car seat installer (see our resources to find a free installer). They can give you tips on what seats work well with your car and they can install the seat once you purchase it. NHTSA has started to publish "Ease of Use" ratings. However, they do not test all car seats.

Since September 2002, all cars sold in the United States must feature a Lower Anchors and Tethers for Children (LATCH) system. Rather than using a seatbelt to secure the car seat, you attach secure hooks onto anchor bars that are permanently installed to your car. LATCH makes installing your car seat easier—gone are the days of threading seat belts through car seats. Since 1999, all convertible car seats must be sold with a tether strap. These straps hook onto an anchor bolt that is permanently installed to your car. In a crash, the tether strap helps restrain the top of the car seat from moving forward. Only tether your car seat to the tether strap hook. Other hooks in your car, such as for cargo nets, are not permanently installed to your car and could become loose.

We strongly suggest you also research the topic, as it is one of the most important purchases you will make. We recommend reading *Baby Bargains*, *Consumer Reports* and *The Baby Gizmo Guide*. These books give specific recommendations on a wider range of car seats and a good run-down of qualities to look for when buying a seat. Our list is not as comprehensive because we have chosen to focus on car seat manufacturers who are making eco-friendly choices. We did this in part so that parents who wanted to choose more eco-friendly car seats would be aware of these company's products. The other reason we did this was to praise those manufacturers for making eco-friendly choices in the hopes that others will follow their lead.

You often see parents carrying and setting their infant car seat on top of grocery carts or restaurant high chairs. May we suggest a sling instead? An infant car seat is terribly heavy to carry and it can be unstable to place on items like grocery carts.

Infant car seats can only be used rear-facing. Typically, you can use an infant car seat with or without a base that is installed in the car. We loved using a base with our car seat. When baby was asleep, it was easy to lift the seat out of the base and bring baby into the house without disruption. Infant car seats can generally be used for infants up to 20 lbs and 26" in height. The maximum weight and height limit varies depending upon manufacturer. The average baby can usually use an infant car seat for about six months.

Convertible car seats can be used rear-facing and then turned around to use forward-facing when baby meets forward-facing requirements. Many car safety experts recommend keeping baby rear-facing for as long as possible. The AAP states, "Infants should ride in rear-facing car safety seats until they have reached both 20 lbs AND one year of age." The AAP recommends "keeping children rear-facing to the highest weight or height allowed by their car safety seat's manufacturer." You should also never place a rear-facing car safety seat in front of an air bag. Jennifer kept her son rear-facing until he was about 18 months old. Convertible car seats' maximum weight limit is typically 40 lbs and 40" tall. We have noticed many manufacturers introducing new convertible car seat models with even higher weight and height limits. We believe this is a result of parents' desire and safety experts' recommendations to keep children rear-facing longer. Another benefit of a convertible car seat with a higher weight and height limit is that you can keep a child in a five-point harness longer before moving on to a booster seat.

Car Seat Crash Replacement and Secondhand Guidelines
- The National Highway Traffic and Safety Administration is a great resource for car seat safety information. The NHTSA provides clear guidelines so that you know what to do with your car seat if you have been in a fender bender. Please visit www.nhtsa.org and www.nhtsa.dot.gov/people/injury/childps/newtips/pages/Tip5.htm for more information
- The NHTSA recommends that child safety seats be replaced following a moderate or severe crash to ensure a high level of crash protection from car seats.
- The NHTSA recommends that child safety seats do not automatically need to be replaced following a minor crash. Minor crashes are those that meet ALL of the following criteria:
    - The vehicle could be driven away from the crash site;
    - The vehicle door nearest the safety seat was undamaged;
    - There were no injuries to any of the vehicle occupants;
    - The air bags (if present) did not deploy; AND
    - There is no visible damage to the safety seat.

NHTSA provides a helpful checklist to evaluating a secondhand car seat. If ALL statements can be checked, then the second-hand child safety seat may be okay to use.
- The seat has never been involved in a moderate to severe crash.
- The seat has labels stating date of manufacture and model number. (This is needed to find out if there is a recall or if the seat is too old).
- The seat has no recalls. (Contact the manufacturer; some problems can be fixed).
- The seat is less than 6 years old. (Normal wear and tear may cause the seat to not work as well).
- The seat has all its parts. (Some parts can be ordered from the manufacturer).
- The seat has its instruction book. (This can be ordered from the manufacturer).

NHTSA Child Passenger Safety Guidelines

When you're an expectant mother, it's important to always wear your seat belt to protect you and your unborn child. Wear the lap belt across your hips and below your belly with the shoulder belt across your chest (between your breasts). Once your baby is born, follow these important safety steps from www.nhtsa.gov.

- **Rear-Facing Car Seat:** For the best possible protection keep infants in the back seat, in rear-facing child safety seats, as long as possible up to the height or weight limit of the particular seat. At a minimum, keep infants rear-facing until age 1 and at least 20 lbs. (You may need to switch from an infant seat, the type that you can carry, to a rear-facing convertible seat, the toddler type, if they reach 20 lbs before their first birthday. This will allow your child to stay rear facing until they are one year old – and hopefully longer because convertible seats usually have higher rear facing weight limits.)

- **Forward-Facing Car Seat:** When children outgrow their rear-facing seats (at a minimum age of 1 and at least 20 lbs, although you can wait until they reach the rear facing limits of your car seat to allow them to rear face longer), they may ride in forward-facing child safety seats, in the back seat, until they reach the upper weight or height limit of the particular seat (usually around age 4 and 40 pounds—seat limits may vary).
- **Booster Seat:** Once children outgrow their forward-facing seats (usually around age 4 and 40 lbs), they should ride in booster seats, in the back seat, until the vehicle seat belts fit properly. Seat belts fit properly when the lap belt lays across the upper thighs and the shoulder belt fits across the chest (usually at age 8 or when they are 4'9" tall).

ITSABELLY'S CAR SEAT RECOMMENDATIONS

Britax Car Seats: A pioneer in child passenger safety for more than three decades. Britax is popular and trusted for their innovations that enhance the safety and improve the ease of installation and use of their products. Britax makes a wide line of seats with different features and prices. Britax rear-facing infant seats fit babies from 4 to 22 lbs and 30" or less. Britax convertible car seats are for children who weigh up to 35 lbs in the rear-facing mode and up to 65 lbs in front-facing mode. Forward-facing only seats can be used with children up to 80 lbs. Britax also makes booster seats for children 38" to 60" and up to 100 lbs. Melissa and Jennifer chose Britax seats because the higher weight limits mean that your child can be in a five-point harness longer. Britax has a Chemical and Heavy Metals (CHM) Standard in which all approved component suppliers must demonstrate compliance by substantially reducing or eliminating certain chemicals and heavy metals from their components and surface coatings and finishes. Britax products are free from phthalates and PVC as of January 1st of 2008. By the end of 2008, Britax products will be free from BPA as well. We applaud this industry leader for creating healthier products. Price: $134.99 to $299.99, www.britaxusa.com.

Cosco Scenera Convertible Car Seat: Dorel Juvenile Group USA will soon offer the Cosco Scenera convertible car seat packaged in a travel and storage bag rather than the huge cardboard box car seats normally come in. This effort to conserve natural paper resources will save an estimated 2,700+ trees per year. We hope they begin taking other eco-friendly measures on other products (and that other manufacturers follow their lead). This car seat is rear-facing for babies up to 35 lbs and forward-facing until your child reaches 40 lbs. It offers a five-point harness system, adjustable shoulder strap and buckle locations, two-position recline and up-front harness adjuster. This seat isn't as plush as we'd like, but the low price makes it worth considering. $43 to $70, www.coscojuvenile.com.

Loll Car Seat Cover: Well, it isn't a car seat, but it can green a conventional car seat. Nest makes a fun and colorful car seat cover that is meant to replace your original cover. The bonus: this cover is formaldehyde-free, and comes in three colors—pink, blue and green. Of course, we love the green dots! This cover should fit every major car seat. Price: $76, www.nestplease.com.

Orbit Baby: Definitely a leader in offering greener car seats and stroller options. The Orbit Infant System is modular and expandable and includes an Infant Car Seat, Stroller Base and Car Seat Base. Expandable options include a Bassinet, Toddler Stroller Seat, Toddler Car Seat, and Rocker, all sold separately. The Infant car seat is designed to accommodate babies from 5 to 22 lbs or 29". The Toddler car seat goes from 15 to 50 lbs (15 to 35 lbs rear-facing, 20 to 50 lbs forward-facing) or 49". As a company, Orbit is extremely eco-friendly, reducing carbon emissions and striving to be carbon neutral. Orbit recycles and donates a portion of their profits to The Nature Conservancy, and Orbit's partner factory is environmentally conscious as well. Further, Orbit is committed to being the first baby gear company to rid their supply chain of PVC, chrome-plating and oil-based packaging inks. We are happy to report that Orbit is also launching a stroller recycling program. Price: $50 to $900, www.orbitbaby.com.

STROLLERS

Like car seats, strollers are another baby item that is impossible to make organic. But that doesn't mean you need to increase your carbon footprint if you want to take baby for a stroll to the park.

Check into a stroller system that allows you to use the stroller from infancy through preschool-age. Some stroller systems have a bad rap for giving out long before your child is a toddler. Luckily, we have a whole new niche of design-savvy higher-end expandable and versatile strollers to suggest. Yes, they may cost more, but probably not much more than if you bought two or three strollers through a child's lifetime. We believe it is better to buy one stroller that will last until preschool and be ready to hand down to a new baby.

When you are evaluating a stroller, consider how you will use the stroller. Yes, it may be tempting to buy the latest must-have stroller—there are some cool ones out there! Take a few strollers for a spin before buying. Test your friends' strollers. Strollers have different handle lengths, types of wheels and take up different amounts of space. You want to buy a stroller that is comfortable for you *and* baby. Consider how you will use the stroller. Do you live in an urban environment where you will be taking baby to the market in the stroller? Or will the stroller be in the trunk and used only occasionally? How often will you be using the stroller? How does stroller use fit in with your babywearing plans? Will you be using the stroller for exercise on bumpy roads or for leisurely, smooth strolls?

eco mom tip:

Some local waste disposal agencies and recyclers may be able to recycle the metal and plastic used in your stroller if it cannot be used secondhand.

Another great way to lessen your eco-impact is to recycle/reuse your stroller. If your stroller is in good condition, save it for your next child, pass it onto a friend, sell it on consignment or donate it to a local family-oriented charity. Be sure to read our Green R's chapter for tips on locating a donation site near you.

Baby Planet: Baby Planet offers the Solo Sport lightweight stroller, the Solo Deluxe lightweight stroller, the Unity Sport twin stroller, the Max Universal car seat carrier stroller, the Max Traveler three-wheel stroller and Max Pro three-wheel travel system. Melissa liked the sturdy wheels of the Max Traveler, which provided a smooth ride on uneven pavement. The only minor issue was that it comes apart in two large pieces to collapse for travel. We love the Endangered Species Stroller Line in which a donation is made to the Wildlife Conservation Society for each stroller sold. Another reason we love Baby Planet is that they offer a free stroller donation and recycling program. If your stroller is still in good condition, Baby Planet will coordinate its donation, even if it isn't a Baby Planet stroller. If your stroller is not suitable for donation, Baby Planet will coordinate the recycling of your old Baby Planet stroller. Baby Planet strollers can be used with children from newborn/one month old up to 65 lbs (exact limits vary by stroller). Prices: $169 to $400, www.baby-planet.com

Orbit Baby: We love the interchangeability, innovation and thoughtfulness of the entire Orbit line. The Infant System includes an infant car seat that docks into the stroller base. There is also a Bassinet Cradle and Toddler Stroller Seat that locks into the stroller base. Orbit has also added the Green Edition Orbit Bassinet Cradle. The Green Edition is made of 100% organic cotton interior, durable natural wool exterior and PVC- and phthalate-free materials. The stroller has 360-degree rotation allowing your baby to be rear-, forward-, or even sideways-facing! The stroller also features adjustable handles, aerospace-grade aluminum tubing, compact folding, front suspension and rear pneumatic tires. Depending on components, the stroller can be used from birth to toddlerhood. Orbit is extremely eco-friendly, reducing carbon emissions and striving to be carbon neutral. Orbit recycles and donates a portion of their profits to The Nature Conservancy, and Orbit's partner factory is environmentally conscious as well. Further, Orbit is committed to being the first baby gear company to rid their supply chain of PVC, chrome-plating and oil-based packaging inks. Orbit products can easily be disassembled so that individual pieces can be recycled. And, we are happy to report that Orbit is also launching a stroller recycling program. Price: $180 to $900, www.orbitbaby.com.

Stokke Xplory: We love that the baby seat height lets you see baby without having to look too far down. This stroller features two-way seating, an adjustable footrest to grow with your child and a two-wheel mode to carry up the stairs. This stroller can even function as a high chair while dining out. All Xplory plastics parts are marked for future recycling, re-use and handling. Stokke, manufacturer of the Xplory, practices environmentally friendly practices. Xplory can be used from birth up to 45 lbs. Price: $900, www.stokkeusa.com.

Quinny: Manufactured by Dorel Juvenile Products, which is reducing packaging on some car seat models. We offer this brand to support a company that is making eco-friendly manufacturing choices. Quinny makes two different models suited to meet consumers' unique needs. The Buzz is good for urban use because it unfolds easily, has a rear- and forward-facing seat and adjustable handle. And for those cold northern city months, you can buy a matching foot muff separately. The Buzz includes a canopy, shopping basket, bug net and rain shield. Both the Buzz and the Zapp work with Maxi-Cosi infant car seats. The Zapp is geared for quick use with the smallest fold in the world—this stroller is perfect for traveling families wanting to bring a stroller. The Zapp includes a canopy, rain shield and travel bag. Both the Buzz and Zapp have a highly maneuverable, lockable front swivel wheel. The Dreami bassinet may be attached to the Buzz to use for newborns up to 15 lbs. The Dreami can also function as a freestanding bassinet. Price: $239 to $550, www.quinny.com.

DIAPER BAG

Do a search for organic diaper bags and you won't find much these days. However, this past spring, we were excited that Stella McCartney's new line for LeSportSac included an eco-friendly "mum" tote (doesn't that sound nicer than diaper bag?). We suspect that there will be more eco-friendly diaper bags on the market soon. If none of these options interest you, create your own diaper bag with a large tote that you already own. All you need to add is some waterproof pouches (check our diapering section for wet bag recommendations). Also, we noticed that many second time moms skip the bulky diaper bag, realizing that they don't need to bring every baby toiletry with them. However, you know good ole Murphy's Law. The day you don't bring a change of baby clothes is the day you'll need to them the most.

LeSportSac: Designed by Stella McCartney, this line is made from recycled eco-polyester. The "mum tote" features a changing pad, removable pocket and insulated pockets for baby bottle or sippy cup. All the pieces in this eco-friendly line work together to extend the product's lifespan. For example, when you aren't using the tote for a diaper bag, slip in a coordinating lap top sleeve for travel. Price: $350, www.lesportsac.com.

Re-Run: Created by Fleurville, Re-Run is a line of messenger and stroller diaper bags made from recycled plastic water bottles. Each Re-Run Messenger bag keeps ten 600ml plastic water bottles out of a landfill. An adjustable shoulder strap enables you to wear it as a shoulder bag, messenger bag or hang it over the stroller handle. The Re-Run is fully-loaded with a changing pad, see-thru Fleurville wipe case, carabineer, three elastic topped pockets, interior pockets, two external pockets with magnetic closure, earbud pass-thru badge and internal fleece-lined sunglass pocket. The main flap of the bag is silk-screened with a botanical print. The bag is Teflon and PVC free. Price: $75, www.fleurville.com.

New Native Organic Diaper Bag: Made of lightweight, durable cotton in a wide variety of color options and accents that coordinate with New Native organic baby slings. The bag features six large pockets—two outside and four inside, a zipper top closure and cell phone pocket on the outside. The New Native diaper bag is made in the USA. Price: $46, www.newnativeinc.com.

ITSABELLY'S DIAPER BAG ESSENTIALS

- Water-resistant changing pad
- Waterproof pouch/bag for storing soiled clothing or cloth diapers
- Diapers—usually 1 for every hour
- Wipes
- Change of baby clothes
- A small toy or book to entertain baby
- Diaper cream
- Baby hat
- Mama's essentials—wallet, lip gloss and cell phone
- Insulated bottle holder if using a bottle or sippy cup

babywearing

• • •

Babywearing has been practiced in various ways by many cultures down through the ages. Jennifer only used her Snap N' Go Stroller a handful of times, opting for the convenience of her handmade cloth ring sling instead. Melissa found that the versatility of her Moby Wrap and ease of use was faster than using a stroller when she was on the go. Babies worn close to their caregiver reap many benefits, typically crying less than their non-carried counterparts, spending more time in an ideal learning state, feeling a stronger sense of trust and security, thus becoming more independent at an earlier age. Just the opposite of what everyone tells you can happen! Babywearing isn't just for mom. There are dad-appealing carriers, too. We have even heard of people convincing daycare providers to babywear.

BABYWEARING IS GREEN
By E. Naomi Sandoval, Owner, SoBeBabies.com, Inc.

Babywearing is "green" in so many different ways.

Organic: As more attractive organic fabrics become available, more baby carrier manufacturers are starting to offer organic baby carriers. Current choices are still limited, but expect this to improve and do your part by buying organic apparel whenever possible. No matter what baby carrier you buy, be certain to wash it before regular use.

Simplifying: Organic or not, baby wearing is such a simple, streamlined way to go—it simply makes life easier. Having baby strapped on frees your hands and allows you to accomplish things that are otherwise impossible. Carrying a huge box while pushing a stroller—impossible. Pop baby on your back and casually waive off offers of help—empowering! Remember to lift with your legs and enjoy the workout!

Fitness: Carrying a baby around ergonomically encourages correct alignment, easily achieved with today's baby carriers. Going about your daily activities with a happy baby strapped on means you will burn more calories and get fitter. And don't forget all those good endorphins that come with exercise! So pop your baby on for a walk and enjoy.

Closeness with Baby: Good for baby and good for parent both! It has become the norm to put babies down but imagine, if you will, a time of grass and trees and predators lurking nearby. Babies rarely spent much time out of nurturing arms. Babies are meant to be held. The long term effects of closeness cannot be underestimated. Nurturing touch has been sadly lacking in recent generations. Help heal future generations and hold on to your precious little one while you can—these early years are fleeting. Did I say years? That brings me to my last point,

Babywearing is for toddlers too! My little ones have wanted to be carried for more than just a few months! Rather than throw my back out of alignment and lose my hands again by always doing the awkward hip shuffle, I chose to pop them into baby carriers even at four years of age! Today's baby carriers are designed to easily accommodate older little ones, who still enjoy the view from on high. And there is nothing like the calmness that comes with a need for closeness that is so easily met by spending a few minutes on mom or dad's back.

FIVE BENEFITS OF BABYWEARING
By Dr. William Sears

Dr. Williams Sears and his wife Martha have introduced many families to babywearing through their series of pregnancy and baby books, the informative Sears practice website at www.askdrsears.com and their advocacy of Attachment Parenting.

Sling babies cry less. Parents in my practice commonly report, "As long as I wear her, she's content!" Parents of fussy babies who try babywearing relate that their babies seem to forget to fuss. This is more than just my

own impression. In 1986, a team of pediatricians in Montreal reported finding that
infants who received supplemental carrying cried and fussed 43 percent less than
the noncarried group.

eco mom tip:

Check babywearing forums
and Yahoo groups for baby
carrier co-ops and swaps
to get a great deal
on a carrier.

Sling babies learn more. Sling babies spend
more time in the state of quiet alertness. This
is the behavioral state in which an infant is most
content and best able to interact with his environment. It may be called the optimal state of learning for a baby.

Sling babies are more organized. Think of a baby's gestation as lasting
eighteen months—nine months inside the womb and at least nine more
months outside. Babywearing extends the womb experience. Mom's
familiar rhythm, imprinted on baby's mind in the womb, now reappears
in the "outside womb" and calms baby. Regular parental rhythms have a
balancing effect on the infant's irregular rhythms.

Sling babies get "humanized" earlier. Baby is intimately involved in the
caregiver's world. Baby sees what mother or father sees, hears what they
hear, and in some ways feels what they feel. Baby becomes aware of, and
learns from, all the subtle facial expressions, body language, voice inflec-
tions and tones, breathing patterns, and emotions of the caregiver.

Sling babies are smarter. Environmental experiences stimulate nerves to
branch out and connect with other nerves, which helps the brain grow
and develop. Babywearing helps the infant's developing brain make the
right connections. Because baby is intimately involved in the mother and
father's world, she is exposed to, and participates in, the environmental
stimuli that mother selects and is protected from those stimuli that
bombard or overload her developing nervous system.

SAFE BABYWEARING
By E. Naomi Sandoval, Owner, SoBeBabies.com, Inc.

In general, a baby carrier should mimic the position(s) in which your baby has told you she's comfortable. Generally these include:
- Newborns: Front Carries (cradle, tummy to tummy, burp position, Buddha facing in or out)
- Starting four to six months: Hip Carry
- Starting six to eight months or later: Back carries (but some people or babies are not ready for this so be patient as it gets easier)

Many of today's well-designed baby carriers allow you to do more than one of these positions well even as your baby grows! Also, remember you are allowed to own more than one baby carrier just as you are allowed to own more than one pair of shoes! You don't go hiking in stilettos nor crash a wedding in hiking boots! Have the right tool for the job.

When learning babywearing, there are many things to be aware of.
- Start with a happy baby. Tend to baby's needs first. If she is hungry, feed her! If she is crying, calm her.
- Start with a happy you and quit if you need to! If you are frustrated or stressed, baby will pick up on it. You'll get there.
- Understand how all the adjustments work and try the carrier on with a stuffed animal or weighted doll, getting it adjusted properly. This is especially important if you are adopting; take the time to practice now!
- If you are pregnant have your spouse or a non-pregnant friend model your baby carrier while you play with the adjustments.
- Attend a babywearing meeting and soak it all up; nothing beats seeing the art of babywearing in person.
- Watch videos. Youtube.com has many excellent submissions! See the resource section below for more ideas.
- Be patient! Don't give up in a week or even a month.

Now you are ready to try wearing your baby.
- For front carries, make sure you are standing.
- Use a mirror to help you see what you are doing. (Tip: When out and

about, check out your reflection in your car or store windows to verify correct positioning. This is not cheating!)

- Put your baby in and don't take a long time with the adjustments while standing still; rather, begin moving. Walk, rock, bounce, dance, sway, or stride aggressively while fine-tuning the fit, all the while keeping one hand on baby until the carrier is safely adjusted. This may feel awkward but you'll get used to it. The younger the baby, the more you may need to move. As baby gets older and/or used to being worn, you won't need to move as much unless she's very fussy. Note that when your toddler is becoming overwhelmed or is overwhelming to you, she may be very tired. Putting her in a baby carrier will often calm her right down. This is amazing if you are running errands or in Grandma's house full of fragile objects.

Special Newborn-Specific Considerations
M'Liss Stelzer, R.N. and babywearing expert, reminds us to always be cognizant of proper breathing positioning with a newborn up to four months.

- One finger must fit under baby's chin! Baby can't breathe properly if she is chin to chest!
- No fabric on baby's face. This means no baby carriers that envelop baby completely.
- Baby's face should not be against your body; baby must have airspace for breathing.

Signs of difficulty breathing include: Rapid or labored breathing, grunting, sighing with every breath and restlessness. Check your newborn often.

Considerations When Choosing a Safe Baby Carrier
- Ergonomic for baby—Baby should be supported from under the knees to well up the back and her tush should be lower than her knees.
- Ergonomic for parent—For anything other than quick carries, I recommend two-shouldered baby carriers. These are the workhorses of babywearing.
- Can you nurse in it? Even if you do not intend to nurse, most well

designed baby carriers allow you to wear the baby in different positions so you can tailor to your child's current needs and mood.

Considerations When Choosing a Pouch, Sling or Hip Carrier
- Alignment: When wearing any baby carrier, your spine should be straight. If you do find yourself out of alignment, correct your positioning.
- Switch sides regularly. It is important to work both sides of your body equally.
- Comfort: Any strap that rides up your neck indicates a poor baby carrier.
- Distribution of weight: The best hip carrier on the market today, the Scootababy, is the only one available with a structured waistband and a shoulder made of a wide band of fabric that caps your shoulder.

Test your baby carrier for safety! Think about the fact that the stress on a baby carrier could equal much more than the actual weight of your baby if you were to, for example, trip while babywearing. The seams on a safe baby carrier should not rip or pop when you tug on them. Proper baby carriers are tested to well over the recommended weights, which are actually comfort guidelines; most people find that over 40 to 45 lbs is just too heavy. But if you had to, you could actually put an adult in most of today's soft structured baby carriers or mei tais!

Learning Back Carries
- If possible, have someone spot you. If practicing alone, kneel on the floor or a big bed until you are proficient.
- Bend at the waist and get your back parallel to the floor like a table.
- Always keep one hand on the baby.
- Watch your reflection.
- Keep baby's head high and body aligned and centered on your back.
- If baby arches or fusses, try again later.
- Do not stand up straight until baby is properly positioned deeply in the baby carrier; verify that baby is covered from under knees and well up his back.
- Refer to manufacturer's instructions for specifics on your baby carrier.
- Use online forums such as www.thebabywearer.com for support.

DIY Baby Carrier Safety Tips

- If making a sling, please use safe rings. Due to recent recalls with other brands, I only feel comfortable recommending www.slingrings.com. Don't mess around with craft rings or imitations!
- Find an online forum to be certain about proper fabric weight and methods of attaching straps.
- When in doubt, use a long piece of cloth, otherwise known as a wrap. Learn everything you need about wraps, including how to make your own, at www.wearyourbaby.com.

E. Naomi's Favorite Resources

- **The BabyWearer:** Everything plus the kitchen sink when it comes to babywearing! Visit www.thebabywearer.com.
- **Wear Your Baby:** How to make and use wraps. Loads of videos and photos, www.wearyourbaby.com.
- **Safe BabyWearing Blog:** www.babyslingsafety.blogspot.com.
- **Sling Rings:** The *only* source for safe sling rings, www.slingrings.com.
- *Mothering* **Magazine BabyWearing Issue Reprint:** Comprehensive babywearing articles by M'Liss Stelzer and featuring photos of yours truly! www.mothering.com/shop/ index.php?target=products&product_id=29888
- **You Tube:** Search "babywearing how-to videos", www.youtube.com.

· · ·

Babywearing is convenient. You can discretely breastfeed with most baby carriers. Many grocery shoppers would be surprised to know that those cute babies in a carrier are nursing as mom shops. Because you have your hands free, you can get something done around the house or running errands. Babies love to be held—can you blame them? Babywearing allows you to meet baby's needs while doing other things. Oh, and for those people who say you will spoil babies by holding them too much, quote Dr. Sears, who believes that "during the first several months of life, a baby's wants are a baby's needs." He continues on to say that "a child whose needs are met predictably and dependably does not have to whine and cry and worry about getting his parents to do what he needs."

Babywearing is beneficial. Babywearing is especially helpful with your second child. Jennifer doesn't know what she'd have done without a sling when her second child was born. She could put him in the sling and still help her busy preschooler with projects. Babywearing provides great skin-to-skin contact, often advised for babies who are slow to gain weight. Being close to mom encourages baby to eat more frequently. Babywearing may reduce crying and colic. A 1986 study of 99 mother-infant pairs (reported in *Pediatrics*) showed that carrying babies at least three hours a day reduces crying and fussing 43% during the day and 51% at night. Babywearing enhances baby's learning. Carried babies participate in their wearer's world rather than seeing it happen from a stroller, swing or exersaucer. This enhances their visual and auditory alertness and results in increased "quiet alertness" times. Because they participate in more experiences and conversations, cognitive development and speech development are promoted. Most importantly, babywearing promotes a bond between baby and wearer. It is emotional *and* scientific. Mama's "mothering hormones" are stimulated by frequency of feeding and touching with baby.

We have divided our product recommendations by baby carrier type. By no way does this mean that we want you to go out and buy each different style of baby carrier. Some babywearing mamas acquire quite a stash of different baby carriers. You don't need a sling, soft structured *and* pouch carrier. Each baby carrier style serves a purpose and has its pros and cons. We suggest that you first find the most practical carrier based on your needs and budget. Later, you can start to experiment. Branch out and see what you like. In this chapter, you will find some tips to select the right baby carrier for you.

It is important to find a carrier that is right for you and your level of activity. There are many types of baby carriers. These include adjustable slings with rings (which come padded or unpadded), pouch slings that are not adjustable, Asian-style carriers, and wraps that simply tie on. Both

Melissa and Jennifer had their favorites (Moby carrier and ring sling respectively), but they loved babywearing so much that they had several different styles for different occasions. Ask any babywearing die-hard; there are so many fun baby carriers to choose from that babywearing can be addictive. We had baby carriers for hiking and even a fancy silk sling for dressing up (which quickly became the sling du jour). In addition to a wide variety of carrier types, there are many different carrying positions with each carrier. Baby carriers allow you the versatility to choose the best carrier for your activity paired with baby's favorite position for that activity. A baby about to drift off to sleep may enjoy a cradle hold in a ring sling, while a soft-structured or wrap carrier may be best for an alert baby during a walk.

In our recommendations, we have tried to offer a popular organic (and sometimes non-organic) option for each baby carrier category. Even if a carrier isn't organic, babywearing is a pretty green activity. Lots of your baby carrier shopping will be done online, although many baby boutiques are starting to carry a variety of baby carriers. We recommend reading product reviews at The BabyWearer (www.thebabywearer.com), a popular online babywearing community. Be sure to check out all our babywearing resources and store recommendations in our Green Resource Directory.

Itsabelly's Baby Carrier Evaluation Tips
When evaluating baby carriers keep these points in mind:
- Baby's age and size: What works best for a sleepy newborn may not be a favorite for a squirmy toddler.
- If you have any health or back problems that may affect babywearing.
- How will you use your baby carrier? Some carriers are better for walking, getting housework done or dressing up. They've even designed carriers for use in water!
- How adjustable would you like your carrier? Will multiple wearers use the same carrier and need to make adjustments for comfortable wearing?
- Consider your personality. There are carriers to suit every style, from outdoorsy and sporty to classy and refined.
- What is the climate like where you live? Different carriers may work

better in cold or hot weather.

- Do you have twins? You can still wear your babies; however, certain carriers may work better than others.
- What is your budget? While some prices seem high, consider how often you will be using the carrier.

The BabyWearer has a thorough carrier comparison chart to help you find the right carrier for you. www.thebabywearer.com/articles/WhatTo/ ComparisonofCarriers.htm.

These tips are adapted from *The BabyWearer*'s "What type of babycarrier is right for me?" at www.thebabywearer.com/index.php?page=whattype.

ITSABELLY'S BABY CARRIER RECOMMENDATIONS

ASIAN BABY CARRIER (ABC)

Based on the style of carriers long used in Asian countries. We like ABCs because they are a simple two shoulder carrier—basically a square of fabric with straps at each corner. The two lower straps tie around the wearer's waist. The two top straps go over the wearer's shoulders and tie. Because the weight is distributed over both shoulders it is good for heavier babies and toddlers. On the other hand, ABCs can be trickier for beginners to use with newborns. An ABC can easily be shared between wearers because there are typically no buckles to adjust—just the ties.

BabyHawk: These ABC-style carriers are popular with design-savvy parents. They have carriers that any indie music-loving daddy would be happy to sport. With their easy online shopping tool, you can custom design your own BabyHawk. First, you choose the body and straps color, then the fabric panel. The straps and body are made from heavy-duty cotton twill in several colors—even organic cotton. There are over 50 fabric choices including Amy Butler prints, batiks, punk, geometrics, floral and oriental. The fabrics are all pre-washed and dried to prevent shrinkage. The top straps and baby headrest are padded for a comfortable ride.

The regular BabyHawk has a headrest of approximately 16.5" x 21.5". The ToddlerHawk is a bit taller than the BabyHawk with measurements of 16.5" x 23.5". The BabyHawk fits most newborns until their toddler years. The ToddlerHawk is for children at least 18 months or older. You can use either until 40 lbs. These carriers fit up to a women's size 22/24 or men's XXL. The straps, which are 3-3/4" wide and slightly padded, are 70" to 72" long (you can order XL straps if needed). You may also add a toy loop and a pocket (seamlessly hidden behind the colorful fabric panel). You can even choose two different panel fabrics for a reversible carrier! Price: $80 to $105, www.babyhawk.com.

EllaRoo Deluxe Mei Tai: A versatile and sturdy ABC baby carrier that can be used for front and back positions. The deluxe version has a folding headrest with invisible magnetic snaps and optional waist buckles sold separately. The fabric is 100% certified organic cotton. The padding is made from recycled polyester made from soda bottles. You can use this carrier from birth to 35 lbs. Price: $89, www.ellaroo.com.

SOFT STRUCTURED BABY CARRIER

Probably the most commonly seen baby carriers, you can easily find plenty of models from mainstream suppliers in any baby super store. We focus on carriers made by smaller companies that pay great attention to detail and ergonomic improvements. Soft structured carriers do not have metal frames; however, they are more rigid than other cloth baby carriers. They are usually made with heavier twill fabric, with padding and adjustable buckles. Switching the carrier between wearers is not as easy as other carriers because it does require adjustment of buckles, though most buckles are fairly simple to adjust. Some soft structured carriers come in different sizes. If there is a significant size difference between wearers, it may be necessary to buy a carrier for each wearer.

Beco Baby Carrier: Designed by a 'babywearing' parent, active sailor and rock climber Gabby Caperon. Beco combines ergonomics, balanced weight distribution and stylish design. Each carrier is handmade in California in a fair trade production facility. You can use the Beco for newborns to 55 lbs in front, hip and back carry positions. Amazing fabric options and continuous product development and improvement make the Beco a popular choice among babywearing parents. The padding is made from recycled soda bottles. The Beco features a removable hood and easy-to-use dual adjustable buckles on the body and waist belt. The padded waist belt conceals a storage sleeve. We love the built-in infant insert that allows baby to sit a bit higher than other carriers. Price: $139 to $145, www.becobabycarrier.com.

ERGObaby Organic: A popular and comfortable soft-structured baby carrier that can be used from newborn to toddler for front and back carries. To wear with a newborn, an infant insert (sold separately) must be purchased. The ERGObaby Organic carrier, infant inserts and accessories are certified 100% organic cotton. Oeko-Tex Standard 100 certifies the dyes. ERGObaby Organic backpack and front pouch are available in two different colors combinations: chocolate with caramel lining, and forest green with moss lining. Infant inserts are available in caramel and moss. The ERGObaby carrier features a sleeping hood for baby, adjustable shoulder and chest straps. The ERGObaby carrier fits a wearer height from 5 ft to 6.5 ft. The carrier has been tested for weight up to 90 lbs, though ERGObaby recommends the carrier be used with babies up to 40 lbs. Price: $112, www.ergobabycarriers.com.

POUCH BABY CARRIER

We love pouch carriers for infants and smaller babies in a cradle carry. We found that once our babies were passed the "sleeping all the time" stage, they preferred to be a bit more upright. You can achieve an upright carry with a pouch, but we were more successful with other carriers for that type of carry. A pouch is a very basic and simple carrier—just a sleek loop of fabric that you wear over one shoulder as you would a "Miss America" sash. There are adjustable and fitted pouches. Often pouches come in different sizes based upon the wearer's size. If there is a significant size difference between wearers, it can be difficult to share pouches. Most vendors provide detailed sizing information on their websites. Because pouches are so simple without bulky padding or buckles, they are great for traveling. Many pouches have reversible fabric, making the pouch quite a fashion accessory.

Hotslings: This popular and fashionable brand has a wide range of hot fabric choices. Hotslings even makes a hemp/organic cotton/Lycra blend stretch twill in natural or blue. There are nine different Hotsling sizes, making a precise fit totally achievable. You should be able to find a HotSling to fit women from petite to size 3X. Hotslings are made in USA under fair labor conditions. Price: $48 to $60, www.hotslings.com.

Peanut Shell: Goo Ga makes this pouch with sleek leg padding for baby's comfort, a hook for attaching toys, and a small pocket. All products are formaldehyde-free. They offer a wide range of fabric choices, including micro-fleece, cotton sateen or stylish cotton reversible pouches, even an organic cotton jersey pouch. Jennifer loved her micro-fleece Peanut Shell for her winter baby. You can use your Peanut Shell from birth to 36 lbs. The Peanut Shell is a fitted pouch with small, medium and large sizes for women ranging from XS to XXXL. Their website has detailed sizing information. Price: $48 to $72, www.goo-ga.com.

New Native: This fitted pouch carrier comes in silk, organic cotton and regular cotton with lots of variety for each fabric in colors and trims. As a company, New Native is dedicated to social responsibility and a clean environment. The carriers are not pre-shrunk. New Native has an informative sizing guide to download from their website. They can make up to size 5XL carriers. You may need to special order the larger sizes. You can use your New Native from birth to 35 lbs. An additional infant insert made from organic cotton is sold separately. The carrier also includes an instructional DVD. Price: $54 to $118, www.newnativeinc.com.

Kangaroo Korner: These adjustable cotton pouches, with four rows of snaps, are designed to both grow with baby and accommodate the wearer's changing size. Kangaroo Korner makes pouches of fleece, cotton and even mesh and Solarveil® for waterside activities. Their huge selection of fabrics are rated with the degree of stretch. You can use a Kangaroo Korner pouch for babies under 25 lbs. All Kangaroo Korner brand products are manufactured in Minnesota and under non-sweatshop conditions. Price: $69, www.kangarookorner.com.

HIP BABY CARRIER

A hip carrier usually has a strap that goes over your shoulder and a waist belt. Most hip carriers incorporate buckles on the shoulder strap and waist belt for adjustability. You want to make sure that the shoulder strap is comfortable and distributes weight evenly across your back and waist. You are ready for a hip carrier when your baby has good head control and you start carrying him on your hip (usually no earlier than five months).

EllaRoo Mei Hip: This popular carrier has a unique and comfortable shoulder strap that spreads the fabric across your shoulder. The carrier can be reversed for right or left holding position. Simply slide the carrier onto your back and you have an easy-to-use back carrier. Once baby has good head control, you can use the Mei Hip until baby weighs 35 lbs. The fabric used in the production of this carrier is 100% certified organic cotton; the lining is recycled polyester batting made from soda bottles. Price: $89, www.ellaroo.com.

Scootababy: Another hip carrier highly rated for its ease of use and adjustability, Scootababy's supportive fleece shoulder can be worn on either shoulder, and you can conveniently adjust the custom buckles with one hand. Other comfortable-enhancing features include a padded waist belt and structured seat for baby. The Scootababy can also be used for back carries. The Scootababy fits babies from five months and up to 40 lbs. Scootababy's are manufactured in the USA. Price: $107, www.scootababy.com.

RING SLING BABY CARRIER

A very common baby carrier. A ring sling is a piece of fabric that goes over one shoulder and around the opposite hip/waist, like a pouch carrier. This carrier gets its name for the two sling rings that give the sling adjustability. The sling tail loops through the two rings. This allows the wearer to adjust the bottom and top "rail" (a.k.a. lengthwise sides) by pulling on the end of the tail. In some slings, the rings may be replaced by a buckle or clip. Ring slings can be padded or unpadded. We prefer unpadded for less bulk, though some mothers like the padding for extra comfort. Slings are popular with nursing moms because you can drape the tail over the nursing babe—perfect for nursing on the go. Jennifer made several of her own ring slings to match different outfits. Her favorite was her black silk Oopa Baby sling. We're sure your mouth just dropped in disbelief—using silk fabric to carry a baby! Unbelievably, the silk was not slippery; it held the baby well and always looked beautiful. It does take some time to learn how to properly wear and adjust a sling. There are lots of good online resources (see our directory) and friendly mamas to help you learn how to quickly become a pro.

Oopa Baby: Jennifer was lucky enough to attend Attachment Parenting meetings with the founder of Oopa Baby, where she witnessed Amy's dedication to babywearing and her talent for design. Oopa Baby slings are stunning. Oopa Baby is best known for their 100% shantung or dupioni silk, with a colorful silk charmeuse lining on the bottom tail. Oopa Baby has a distinctively long tail that adds dramatic flair to the sling. Oopa Baby also makes slings from 100% cotton pique, feather-weight 100% cotton chambray and cashmere. Price: $79 to $349, www.oopababy.com.

Sakura Bloom: Sakura Bloom makes three models of silk slings and four models of linen slings. The linen line range from basic solid color linen slings, to slings with a tail stripe to fine Belgian linen. Most of the silk lines are made with dupioni silk. You can choose from solid color slings, reversible slings or bold striped tails and linings. Top-of-the-line is the Luxe sling, and believe us, it is luxurious—and it should be, with prices ranging from $540 to $1120! So, the price is totally outrageous, but gee, is this beautiful! For $540, you get Luxe slings handcrafted from eco-friendly wild tussah silk woven with hand-dyed silk threads. Wild tussah is made from the cocoons of wild silk moths after the moth emerges. The more expensive Luxe sling is handcrafted from a rare Laotian silk with natural plant dyes. The sling comes with a detailed booklet with instructions, tips and photos. Machine washable. Price: $88 to $1120, www.sakurabloom.com.

ZoloWear: Wonderful ring sling options in a wide variety of stretch cotton sateens, silk brocades and Solarveil®. ZoloWear makes a limited edition Sustainable Sling. At the time of printing, they were made from 100% certified organic cotton or a mixture of hemp, certified organic cotton and a touch of Lycra. ZoloWear ring slings feature a secure, zippered pocket that can store a diaper, wipes or mama items. These slings even come with a free instructional DVD to teach you the various carrying positions. ZoloWear also makes pouch carriers. The sling is best used with babies and toddlers under 40 lbs. The carriers are made in the USA. Price: $69 to $125, www.zolowear.com.

WRAP BABY CARRIER

The most simple baby carrier structure and yet, perhaps the most versatile. It is just a piece of cloth—no buckles, no snaps, no fasteners. We are always amazed at the interesting and creative baby carrying positions that adept babywearing moms can achieve with a wrap. Usually the fabric is 3.5 to 6 yds x 18" to 36" wide so that it can wrap around the wearer's body. You typically wrap the fabric over both shoulders and create a pocket to hold baby. Some carriers, such as the Moby, may be slightly tapered on the ends for ease of tying. Wraps are usually made out of woven or knit fabric. The versatility of wraps allows you to wear baby facing in, facing out, on your back or hip. There is a learning curve to using a wrap properly, but once you get the hang of it, you will be hooked and proud to display your baby carrying prowess.

Didymos: A European favorite since 1972! Didymos fabric is specially woven for baby carriers that you can use from birth until toddler. There are 55 colors/patterns of Didymos fabric, all from pure organic cotton grown in Egypt, Turkey and Peru and made in Germany or Austria. The Didymos baby sling is offered in seven different sizes. The type of carrying position (i.e. cradle, hip carry, rucksack, cross carry) you plan to use determines the fabric length. Price: $124 to $145, www.didymos.de.

Moby Organic Wrap: One of Melissa's favorites, this sling allowed her to be hands free around the house and on walks to the park. She especially liked that she could wear it different ways and that it accommodated baby's growth. The Moby wraps your entire back and both shoulders with a wide width of 100% soft ECO-certified organic cotton fabric to carry the baby. You can wear your baby facing you, facing out, sideways or on your back. The Moby wrap can be used from preemie to 35 lbs. Machine washable. Includes full color instruction booklet. Price: $70, www.mobywrap.com.

nursery furniture

• • •

Your new family will spend a lot of time in baby's room. Whether it's a decked-out nursery or a co-sleeper in your room, you moms will be rocking your babies, changing diapers, playing, reading and putting them to sleep in their room. By adding green touches to their room, you can make a positive impact on their toxin exposure and air quality. Going green does involve lots of choices. You can choose cribs and furniture made out of sustainable wood, a formaldehyde-free dresser and low VOC, or volatile organic compound, paint. According to Green Home Guide, "VOCs are carbon compounds that evaporate at room temperature and react in sunlight to help from ground-level ozone, an integral component of photochemical smog. Formaldehyde, a VOC commonly found in paint, is a probable carcinogen. The EPA has found that indoor concentrations of VOCs are regularly up to ten times as high as outdoor concentrations, and can climb up to a thousand times as high as outdoor concentrations when you are applying paint."

We understand that baby's sleeping arrangements often mean an evolving location (at least they were in our houses). We have included recommendations for several different sleeping spaces so you can choose the combination that best suits your family.

Shopping and planning baby's nursery is a fun process. Don't wait until the last minute to buy baby furniture—large furniture items may need to be special-ordered from the baby store. You'll want to order at least two months before baby's arrival. Additionally, it's important to check that you have all the pieces and parts once you're ready to assemble your crib. Melissa's husband Randy found out after opening the box that they were missing a bolt; fortunately, they'd allowed enough cushion time for the manufacturer to send them a replacement so he could assemble the crib appropriately. Any solid wood furniture should be made from sustainable sources. Conventional paints and finishes may contain chemicals that can give off toxic gas fumes. When a teething baby chews on his or her crib (and believe us, they will) these toxins may also enter baby's delicate system. If you choose a laminated or pressed wood, chip or particle board, make sure that it is formaldehyde-free and low VOC.

Consignment stores are a great source for nursery furniture that you can keep as is or refinish to your style. Or see if your local unfinished wood furniture store stocks any pieces from sustainable sources; you may find a great bargain on a piece that you can personalize with low VOC paint or simply enhance the wood's natural beauty with a water-based sealer.

Itsabelly's Tips To Create A Safe Nursery
- Read Green Choices chapter to better understand sustainable wood.
- Read our tips on painting and low VOC or no VOC paint.
- If you are pregnant, doctors usually advise that you should not paint.
- If you live in a house built earlier than 1978, you need to test for lead, especially before renovating. Lead can be inhaled or ingested and results in brain damage. To find an EPA-certified lab to test for lead, call 1-800-424-LEAD or www.epa.gov/lead.
- Test furniture, toys and other baby items for lead with do-it-yourself LeadCheck swabs. We advise doing this on any secondhand furniture. It is so easy to do, you'll find yourself testing everything! You can buy them at your local hardware store, www.leadcheck.com.
- Do not place crib, changing table or dresser near windows. Baby can roll out of the window or grab drapery cords.
- Keep drapery cords out of baby's reach.
- Make sure furniture cannot be tipped over by a climbing toddler. Use babyproofing or earthquake proofing hardware to attach furniture to the walls.
- Check for Juvenile Products Manufacturers Association (JPMA) certification. Products credited with the JPMA logo meet safety requirements. Products must be submitted for testing for possible certification, www.jpma.org.
- Fill out your product registration cards. Mail them or submit online to be notified of recalls. Check the Consumer Product Safety Commission for product recalls. Don't forget to sign-up for email notification of recalls, www.cpsc.gov.

ITSABELLY'S ECO PAINT TIPS

- Use a low to zero-volatile organic compound (VOC) paint to cover the walls. Low to zero-VOC paint means that you won't have the toxic chemicals that, according to the EPA, cause respiratory, skin and eye irritation; headaches; nausea; muscle weakness; and more serious ailments and diseases. Common examples of items that emit VOCs into the atmosphere include gasoline, mineral spirits, alcohol, nail polish and paint.
- Great news! More companies are offering safer paint options, with plenty of color selections. The price per gallon is slightly higher, but for a few extra dollars and a little touch of paint, baby's nursery can have that important shade of "green" you're looking for when designing baby's favorite sleeping space.
- Major paint manufacturers such as Sherwin-Williams, Benjamin Moore and Kelly-Moore now offer low VOC paint.
- Check out these small suppliers for low- to zero-VOC paint options: Serena and Lily Organic Paint, www.serenaandlily.com; Hawthorne Organics Paint, www.hawthorneorganics.net; Real Milk Paint, www.realmilkpaint.com; Yolo Paints, www.yolocolorhouse.com; AFM Safecoat Paints, www.afmsafecoat.com; Devoe Wonder Pure, www.devoepaint.com; Cloverdale EcoLogic, www.cloverdalepaint.com.

CRIB

Cribs are one place where your baby will spend time unsupervised, one of the many reasons safety is the most important feature of a crib. All cribs manufactured after 1991 and sold in the United States must meet government safety regulations. We recommend using a new crib as the best way to insure its safety. Secondhand cribs may be missing hardware, parts, and instructions. Worse yet, a secondhand crib may not meet current safety standards or may have been recalled. And speaking of recalls, don't forget to submit your product registration card and sign-up for CPSC recall notification.

When crib shopping bring the CPSC crib safety checklist below. Be sure to check for durable construction and solid mattress support. Consider that as babies grows, their strength and ability to climb grows too. Consider what would happen if a piece broke on the crib—would it compromise baby's safety?

Most crib recalls pertain to mattress support failure. If the mattress support fails a baby can become trapped between the mattress and the crib. Even though there are safety standards, cribs on the market still get recalled for safety flaws. Be diligent about checking the safety of your crib. Make sure you assemble the crib correctly. Call the manufacturer if you have assembly questions. Check monthly for loose screws, bolts and compromised mattress or wall support. Yes, it means crawling around to peek underneath, but the time will be well spent. And please, never place a crib near a window where baby can reach drapery cords or climb out the window. You'd be surprised how many babies learn to climb out of their cribs!

We chose cribs that are made with socially responsible and sustainable practices in mind. As for style, choose a crib that can work in various nursery designs so that you can save the crib for your next child. This is especially true if you buy a convertible crib. Your opinionated preschooler sleeping in a big-girl bed may not like the cutesy baby theme.

Crib Safety Tips
The Consumer Product Safety Commission offers these requirements for evaluating that you are using a safe crib at www.cpsc.gov/CPSCPUB/PUBS/5030.pdf. There should be:
- A firm, tight-fitting mattress so baby can't get trapped between the mattress and the crib.
- No missing, loose, broken or improperly installed screws, brackets or other hardware on the crib or mattress support.
- No more than 2-3/8" (about the width of a soda can) between the crib slats so that a baby's body can't fit through the slats; no missing or

cracked slats.
- No corner posts over 1/16" high so a baby's clothing can't catch.
- No cutouts in the headboard or footboard so a baby's head can't get trapped.

The organization Keeping Babies Safe grew out of the successful Danny Foundation, which focused on crib safety after the tragic death of Danny Lineweaver. Parents have the Danny Foundation to thank for the huge strides made in safe crib requirements. As you use your crib, please follow these tips to make sure you are not endangering your baby.
- Never add a mattress, pillow, comforter or padding to a portable, non-full-size crib. Use only mattress/pad provided by the manufacturer. Infants can suffocate in gaps between an extra mattress and the meshing of a portable crib.
- Never put infants to sleep on fluffy, plush products such as sheepskins, quilts, comforters, and pillows. These products may cause infants to re-breathe exhaled air and suffocate.
- Never fasten a pacifier (or any other item) around a baby's neck. Never tie cords, ribbons, or yarn to a pacifier, even if you do not plan to place it around a child's neck.
- Never hang any stringed object, such as a toy on a string, or a diaper/laundry bag on any part of the crib, or nearby where a child could become caught in it and strangle.
- Never leave a child in the crib with the side rail lowered.
- Never allow your child to crawl underneath a crib. Sharp edges under the mattress support could puncture and cause severe lacerations.
- To help prevent the chance of Sudden Infant Death Syndrome (SIDS) always put infants to sleep on their backs.
- Always keep drapes, ribbons, blind cords, and decorative wall hangings out of your child's reach. It is recommended that *no* corded window blinds be in a child's room; preferably, none should be used in the house at all. The crib should be at least 3 ft from any window.

A Natural Home: An Ohio-based, family-run company that works with Amish communities to make two eco-friendly crib models. Both models are made from American oak or ash and are finished with natural tung oil with no synthetics added. The basic model is a simply designed crib. The Americana offers a bit more design detail. The mattress spring is locally forged iron. Price: $450 to $500, www.anaturalhome.com.

Ikea: Well-known for their socially responsible manufacturing, sourcing and business practices, Ikea offers cribs made of wood from not-intact natural forests and renewable resources, such as wool. Check out the Gulliver, Hensvik, Hermelin, Leksvik and Sniglar models. Prices range from $99 to $150, www.ikea.com.

NurseryWorks: This modern furniture company offers three different crib models. All cribs offer three-point adjustable mattress height and convert into a toddler bed. The Aerial crib by Lawson-Fenning features an adjustable side rail, an under-the-crib drawer option and a variety of end, slat and rail color and design options. The Aerial crib measures 41"H x 62"W x 30"D. The Loom crib by Truck Product Architecture features a fixed side rail, and a slat color choice. The Loom crib measures 39.5"H x 53.5"W x 31"D. The Studio crib by Truck Product Architecture features a fixed side rail, changing table hideaway cabinet, changing pad and color choices for slats, drawer and frame. The Studio crib measures 42.25"H x 65"W x 76"W (with changing table/desk open x 32"D). Toddler conversion kit is sold separately ($165 to $250 depending on model). As a company, Nurseryworks uses renewable materials, Grade EO MDF (the safest grade available), formaldehyde-free dyes and low-VOC finishes, lacquers, and glues. Price: $590 to $1780, www.nurseryworks.net.

Oeuf Convertible Crib: The Oeuf crib is inspired by European aesthetics and Shaker simplicity and is also environmentally friendly. The crib has a three-position mattress support and converts into a toddler bed. A diaper changing station (sold separately) can fit securely to the top of the crib. The crib base is available in walnut or birch stain. The crib walls are MDF from recycled wood fibers, covered with a non-toxic white lacquered finish. It measures 54.25"L x 30.25"W x 36"H. Conversion kits sold separately. As a company, Oeuf is an FSC certification holder, practices 100% recycling of wood wastes into briquettes that provide 100% self-reliant heating and has a packaging recycling program through Green Points. Price: $890, www.oeufnyc.com.

Sleepi: Winner of numerous awards, Sleepi is made from durable and sustainable-harvest European beech wood. Sleepi converts from bassinet to crib to toddler bed and can be used until about 5 years of age. It features four mattress heights, locking caster wheels, canopy rod (canopy sold separately). Bassinet dimensions: 32"L x 25"W x 33.5"H. Crib/toddler bed dimensions: 50"L x 29"W x 33.5"H. Price: $749 to $1,150, www.stokkeusa.com.

CRIB MATTRESS

If you buy a crib, you will need to buy a mattress for it. Crib mattresses typically use materials such as vinyl/PVC, phthalates and polyurethane foam that over time release toxic chemicals. Mattresses are also treated with chemicals, such as ones from the polybrominated diphenyl ethers (PBDE) group, to make the mattress fire-retardant, water- and stain-resistant. The three main types are referred to as penta, octa and deca.

Healthy Child states that recent studies and evidence show that PBDEs can enter human tissue and interfere with the thyroid hormone. Studies, such as one done by the Environmental Working Group, have shown that PBDEs build up in breast milk and can harm learning development. In August 2003, the State of California outlawed the sale of penta- and octa-PBDE and products containing them, effective January 1, 2008. In April 2007, the legislature of the state of Washington passed a bill banning the use of PBDEs. In May 2007, the legislature of the state of Maine passed a bill phasing out the use of DecaBDE. The EU has banned all three PBDEs.

Federal regulations (FR1633 effective July 1, 2007) require that mattresses must be fire-retardant. But don't fret; it is possible to buy a PBDE-free mattress that satisfies the flammability mattress laws. Check that the mattress meets the CSPC and California's mattress fire safety regulations and ask what they use to comply with the law. Wool's natural properties may help in passing flammability standards. Borate can be used to treat a cotton mattress to make it fire-retardant. Although borate is less toxic than conventional fire retardants, some still feel it is also questionable. White Lotus cites the safety of borate powder on the website listed in Research Fire Retardants below.

RESEARCH FIRE RETARDANTS

Here are some good sources for researching fire retardants.

- Environment California Research and Policy Center: *Body of Evidence, New Science In The Debate Over Toxic Flame Retardants And Our Health,* www.environmentcalifornia.org/center/improving-environmental-health/body-of-evidence; *Growing Threats, Toxic Flame Retardants And Children's Health,* www.environmentcalifornia.org/center/improving-environmental-health/growing-threats2
- Environmental Working Group: *PBDEs in Breast Milk,* www.ewg.org/reports/mothersmilk; Independent Studies List: www.ewg.org/node/8417
- Healthy Child Healthy World, HealthyChild.Org: PBDE information, www.healthychild.org/resources/chemical/polybrominated_diphenyl_ethers/; Safe Bed information, www.healthychild.org/resources/checklist/make_a_safe_bed/; A study on this subject, www.healthychild.org/resources/body_of_evidence_february_2004/
- Naturepedic: *Five Problems with Crib Mattresses,* www.naturepedic.com/research/fiveproblems.php
- White Lotus Borate Powder FAQ, www.whitelotus.net/Page-32.html

A Natural Home: This Ohio-based, family-run company offers several Amish-made organic crib mattress options. The most affordable is their $230 organic crib mattress, aptly named the "Simply Affordable Organic Mattress." This mattress does not have top quilting, to keep the costs low. Both the quilted and non-quilted mattress consist of a tempered steel innerspring unit and layers of organic cotton batting, topped with organic cotton fabric. Both innerspring mattresses have 150-coil-count, 12.5 gauge wire coils and an 8 gauge side border wire. A Natural Home offers two sizes of 100% natural rubber latex mattresses: a 4.5" travel mattress and a 6" mattress. Their latex mattresses have a 5" core and are fully wrapped on all sides with a 1/4" thick layer of organic cotton quilted to a pure gown-wool cover. They also offer custom-made mattresses. Innerspring mattresses typically measure 28"W x 52"L x 6"H; however since they are handmade, measurements could vary slightly. Price: $230 to $350, www.organicbabymattress.com.

No-Compromise™ Organic Cotton: Naturepedic fills their organic mattress with organic cotton filling that is unbleached and undyed, making it a good option for those with allergy sensitivities to latex and wool. The mattress features a waterproof organic cotton cover (100% polyethylene-clear food-grade waterproof coating), firm support from 252 coils and non-toxic FlameBreaker™ fire barrier system. The FlameBreaker™ fire protection system is based on the fire retardant properties of baking soda and silica bonded to cellulose fiber. It measures 27.75"W x 52"L x 6"H. Naturepedic offers a 20-year prorated limited warranty on this mattress. Price: $359, www.naturepedic.com.

Pure Beginnings: An affordable 180-coil-count innerspring mattress layered with hand-tufted organic cotton pads and covered with quilted organic cotton and Pure Grow Wool™. The top-finishing layer is the soft organic cotton. It measures 28"W x 52"L x 6"H. These mattresses are handmade to order and take 4 to 5 weeks for delivery. Price: $254.99, www.purebeginnings.com.

The Coco Mat Organic Crib Mattress: This crib mattress is free of synthetic chemicals and materials and is naturally fire-retardant. Its core of natural latex is 100% non-allergenic. Coir (coconut fibers) made from the only certified organic coir plantation in the world provides a supportive and breathable fibrous layer. Lamb's wool surrounds the coir treated in natural extracts to make it dust/mite-free. The entire mattress is covered in a removable and machine washable unbleached cotton herringbone cover. It measures 28"W x 52"L x 2"H. Made in England. Price: $375.00, www.naturalmatusa.com.

White Lotus: A crib mattress with a firm sleeping surface and no exposure to chemicals and harmful off-gassing. It measures 28"W x 54"L x 3.5"H. The mattress is made slightly larger than the standard crib size frame so that there is no space between mattress and frame. They offer all cotton; non-borate cotton and wool; organic cotton and wool; and organic cotton, wool and latex versions. As this mattress is all cotton, you should use a wool puddle pad to cover the mattress. Made in the USA. Price: $340 to $620, www.whitelotus.net.

CO-SLEEPER / FAMILY BED PRODUCTS

In 2005, the AAP recommended that breastfeeding mothers should sleep within close proximity to their baby, using safety precautions, to promote a healthy and safe breastfeeding relationship. Co-sleepers are a great solution for baby to be nearby but in a safe sleeping space. Jennifer used an Arm's Reach Co-Sleeper. She loved the close snuggle time for 3 AM feedings and felt reassured that baby was in a safe sleeping space when he returned to the co-sleeper.

Arm's Reach Co-Sleeper: This popular manufacturer offers certified organic co-sleeping products (mattresses and linens). These products are handcrafted using certified organic cotton, premium Eco-Wool, 100% natural rubber, and untreated Baltic birch. Made in the USA. The sheets and bumper are 240-thread-count certified organic cotton sateen in ivory. The bumper trim is certified organic cotton in gingham check. Arm's Reach recently released a new line of co-sleeper sizes: the Original, the Universal, the Mini, the Mini Convertible™, the Mini Metro, the Clear-Vue™, the Sleigh Bed, the Little Palace™ and the Cocoon. Price: $25 to $369, www.armsreach.com.

Baby Bunk: An all-wood co-sleeper that is available for purchase or monthly rentals. Organic mattresses and bedding are available. The Baby Bunk comes in solid maple, with a non-toxic, child-safe lacquer finish, clear water-based lacquer or white primer finish that you can then paint yourself. When baby has outgrown the Baby Bunk it can convert into a child's bench (conversion kit sold separately). The Baby Bunk can support up to 35 lbs. It measures 12"H x 15.75"D x 36.25"W with 12.5" to 20" adjustable legs. Mattresses and accessories are priced separately. Rentals cost $40 per month. Price: $245 to $295, www.babybunk.com.

Humanity Family Bed: Endorsed by *Mothering* magazine online expert panel member Sarah J. Buckley M.D. This family bed sleeper features a 5-ft long body pillow so that roll-offs don't happen when bed sharing and an extra thick absorbent pad made from 100% organic cotton flannel. It is non-toxic, hypoallergenic and does not off-gas. This pillow can be detached and used as a body pillow during pregnancy. It is sized to fit children from birth to toddler. The Humanity Family Bed can also be used to keep children from rolling off their own big kid bed. It measures 36"W x 58"L. Price: $199. www.familysleeper.com.

TresTria Pillow: A versatile pillow that can be used as a pregnancy pillow, family bed pillow, nursing-in-bed pillow and reading pillow. The pillow is made with certified (Eco Umwelt Institut) 100% natural latex, which means no petroleum products are used. The pillow is covered with a 100% organic cotton sateen cover certified by Control Union Certifications and Fair Trade Labeling Organization. TresTria pillow measures 36"L x 11"W x 5.5"H. Price: $129.95, www.betterforbabies.com.

CRADLE / BASSINET

A cradle or bassinet is another nice option if you would like baby sleeping close to you yet not sharing a bed together. A cradle or bassinet can be moved close to your bed so you can attend to your baby during the night. Cradles and bassinets also offer a great option of mobility—you can simply move baby's sleeping space to wherever you are in the house to keep baby close.

Cariboo Bassinets: Cariboo offers three different bassinet models: the Classic, Gentle Motions™ and the Folding Bassinet. The Folding Bassinet comes in an Earth model with 100% unbleached, all natural cotton bassinet bag, fitted sheet and an eco-dyed veil. Sleeping pads are organic wool (Classic model) or PBDE foam (Folding model). All bassinet boards are formaldehyde free. We love the Cariboo Bassinets because they are stylish, simple and space efficient. A changing station can also be purchased to attach onto the bassinet. Price: $290 to $450, www.cariboo.us.

MOSES BASKET

A natural Moses basket makes a wonderful and comforting sleep space for your newborn. Moses baskets are easy to carry from room to room— but please don't carry the basket while baby is inside. Because they are lightweight, Moses baskets travel well when visiting friends and family. They also come in handy for naptime when you would like baby near, but are in other parts of the house.

Lillébaby EuroTote: This versatile cradle carrier marries stylish Scandinavian design with American functionality and safety. Although it is not made with organic cotton and it is filled with polyester, we like this product for its versatility. The EuroTote can convert from an ergonomic cradle carrier to a bunting bag to a toddler stroller bag. Its uses don't stop there —it can also be used as travel bedding or a play blanket. We love the idea of using the EuroTote along with a convertible car seat. When baby needs to be taken out of the car, simply lift out the EuroTote and carry a lighter bundle than the bulky car seat. We also love the idea that baby can have a cozy and familiar surrounding in both car seat and stroller. We'd love it more if they started using eco-friendly materials. Price: $120, www.lillebabyusa.com.

eco mom tip:

We prefer to use products that serve a multi-purpose. Our EuroTote works as a carrier, Moses basket, travel bedding, blanket, and stroller muff.

—*Brenda Berg,*
Scandinavian Child

Little Merry Fellows: Zoe B. Organic introduced us to this beautiful basket made from corn husks. The set includes a bumper, and a receiving blanket in 100%

organic cotton flannel. The mattress can be filled with hypoallergenic filling, organic cotton or wool. The basket measures 28"L x 14"W x 9"D. They also make a Moses Basket Rocker that can be placed beneath and secured to the Moses basket. The rocker measures 30"L x 14"W x 24"H. Price: $80 to 180, www.littlemerryfellows.com.

Moses Basket & Organic Pad: A hand-woven palm Moses basket with a thick organic cotton pad and attached handles. Price: $70, www.purebeginnings.com.

DRESSER / CHANGING TABLE / ARMOIRE

A dresser may be a good and necessary choice if you don't have large closet space or you prefer to fold clothing in drawers. You will probably get a lot of baby clothes in sizes ranging from newborn to 12 months that you will need to store.

Reduce consumption and choose a well-made dresser that will last throughout childhood or can be passed down to younger siblings. We also recommend using a combination dresser/changing table. It will save you space and money. Some dressers from baby furniture brands offer an integrated changing table option. The recommendations below include dressers and combination pieces.

You can also find changing tables and pads that can be added onto the top of any dresser. Melissa used a regular dresser and converted the top into a changing table area by utilizing a secure changing table attachment. Isabella will also be able to use the dresser as part of her bedroom decor when she's older. If you add your own changing table, please don't place a changing pad on top of the dresser. Invest in a piece that is designed to be used on dressers, such as the Oeuf Changing Station recommended in the Changing Table section below. And don't forget to use the safety strap that comes with the changing pad. Babies can roll earlier than you know.

Do not place your dresser near a window. If you are using it as a changing table also, baby can roll off the table and out the window (screens are not sturdy and this has happened before). And, babies can reach drapery cords and can strangle themselves. When your baby enters the climbing stage, dresser drawers become a tempting jungle gym (so don't forget to install anti-tip babyproofing hardware to the wall). Include checking the hardware, structure and support of your dresser to your monthly nursery safety check.

It isn't necessary to choose a dresser made from a baby manufacturer. You can find a great dresser at secondhand shops or your local unfinished wood store (check for a sustainable wood). Remember to read our tips for creating a safe nursery if you choose a DIY dresser and changing table.

A Natural Home: These solid wood fair-trade dressers and armoires are assembled on Amish farms and made from sustainably harvested wood from their own forest. The Moxy dresser and armoire are made from ash and walnut, and measures 72"H x 40"W x 20"D with four hidden drawers. The Moxy dresser has three 18"-deep drawers and measures 46"W x 42"H x 20"D. The Spencer dresser and armoire can be made in ash, oak, maple, cherry or walnut, and has plenty of storage with four hidden drawers and two drawers at the bottom. It measures 70"H x 20"D x 46"W. The Spencer dresser has three large drawers and two smaller drawers. It measures 48"H x20"D x 44"W. Zen Baby Coordinating changing table stations can be added to the tops of the dressers. Prices $1230 to 3200, www.anaturalhome.com.

Ikea: Well-known for their socially responsible manufacturing, sourcing and business practices, Ikea offers several different options for children's dressers. Check out the Hemnes, Leksvik and Mammut dressers. Price: $120 to $130, www.ikea.com.

NurseryWorks: The Two Wide Changing Table by Lawson-Fenning is available in cabinets and drawers or all drawers. Featuring a removable tray that fits a standard changing pad and shelf inside cabinet, the Two Wide is available in color options for the doors and platform. The Two Wide's door pattern can also be customized. The Two Wide measures 34"H x 44"W x 19"D (changing tray adds 3"H). As a company, Nurseryworks uses renewable materials, Grade EO MDF (the safest grade available), formaldehyde-free dyes and low-VOC finishes, lacquers and glues. Price: $1200, www.nurseryworks.net.

Oeuf Dresser: The Oeuf makes two models of dressers inspired by European aesthetics and Shaker simplicity. The Classic dresser features three stylish drawers. The Classic dresser can be all white or white drawers accented with either walnut or birch stain. The Classic dresser measures 36"W x 32.5"H x 19.75"D. The Sparrow with two drawers and an open shelf space, measures 34.5"W x 19.125"D x 34"H and comes in a white or grey finish. Both dressers are made from Baltic birch plywood, with an environmentally friendly MDF and non-toxic lacquer finish. A changing station can be purchased separately that sits on top of the Classic dresser. A changing pad can be added onto the top of the Sparrow dresser. We love that these dressers can work in rooms beyond the nursery. As a company, Oeuf is an FSC holder, practices 100% recycling of wood wastes into briquettes that provide 100% self-reliant heating and has a packaging recycling program through Green Points. Price: $230 to $895, www.oeufnyc.com.

CHANGING TABLE

You do not need a separate piece of furniture for your changing table, unless, of course you would like one. You'll be changing a lot of diapers (around 5,000 to 8,000 until potty time!), so a proper changing table may be more comfortable. Many dressers have a compatible changing table component that can be added to the top of the dresser and removed when you no longer need to change diapers (yes, that day will come). You will find those listed above in the dresser section. Below are those tables without dresser functionality.

According to *Consumer Reports*, "changing tables are associated with

2,000 to 3,000 injuries per year, and many of these involve changing tables that have just three side rails." It isn't uncommon to hear a mom say that seeing baby roll off the changing table was baby's first accident. Make sure that your changing table is stable, has preferably four guard-rails and a safety strap. Do not place your changing table near a window, for two reasons. One, baby can roll off the table and out the window (screens are not sturdy and this has happened before). Two, baby can reach drapery cords and can strangle themselves. The smart gals over at *Baby Gizmo* recommend placing your changing table in a corner so that the two walls provide stability and close off possible baby "escape routes." Include checking the hardware, structure and support of your changing table in your monthly nursery safety check.

A Natural Home: This Amish manufacturer produces two different changing table options. The European Oak and Zen Simple are more basic changing tables with open shelving below the changing table top, and coordinate nicely with their other collections. The European Oak model measures 37"H x 20"D x 33.5"W. The Zen Simple changing table measures 30"H x 20"D x 33"W. These solid wood, fair trade changing tables are assembled on Amish farms and made from sustainably harvested wood from their own forest. Price: $450 to $550, www.anaturalhome.com.

Cariboo Changing Tables: Cariboo offers the Folding, the Classic and the Bassinet changing table, which coordinate beautifully with their bassinets. These solid wood tables are made in New Zealand of sustainable Radiata wood, with a choice of four beautiful finishes. When baby outgrows diapers, it can be reused as a table or stand. The Bassinet model attaches onto the Cariboo bassinet. Price: $260 to $360, www.cariboo.us.

DIY CHANGING TABLE TRANSFORMATION

When you are done with your changing table, turn it into a hip bar with directions from *Better Homes and Gardens*! www.bhg.com/decorating/makeovers/furniture-makeovers/furniture-makeovers/?page=2

Ikea Changing Tables: Well-known for their socially responsible manufacturing, sourcing and business practices Ikea offers several different options for changing tables. Check out the Leksvik, Sniglar, Hemnes and Trofast changing tables. Price: $35 to $150, www.ikea.com.

Nurseryworks: The Loom by Truck Product Architecture features a top tray that accommodates diapers and other supplies, removable side rails and top compartments and a two door cabinet. This changing table offers more storage than traditional changing tables, yet not as much as a dresser combination. It can also fit a diaper hamper and includes a canvas bag. The Loom frame comes in three-color finishes and measures 36"H x 44.5"W x 19.5"D. As a company, Nurseryworks uses renewable materials, Grade EO MDF (the safest grade available), formaldehyde-free dyes and low-VOC finishes, lacquers and glues. Price: $875, www.nurseryworks.net.

Oeuf Changing Station: A simple and space-saving changing station that can attach securely on top of the Oeuf crib, as well as on most other standard size cribs and the Oeuf dresser. The station is available in birch or walnut. As a company, Oeuf is an FSC holder, practices 100% recycling of wood wastes into briquettes that provide 100% self-reliant heating and has a packaging recycling program through Green Points. Price: $230 to $245, www.oeufnyc.com.

GLIDER / ROCKER

You will spend a lot of time rocking your little eco-baby. Invest in a piece that looks good in other rooms besides the nursery. You can enjoy a change of scenery while you rock or use it as a piece of living room furniture later—it's hard to part with a piece of furniture where you spent so much time bonding with your baby. Your little ones will always want mama's lap when they are feeling down and a few minutes rocking can quickly calm any toddler tantrum. Jennifer rocked and nursed her babies in the same rocking chair her mom used with her and her brother, and recently passed the rocker down to her brother in hopes he may soon have his own baby to rock. Melissa used an all-wooden, light weight rocker to breastfeed and rock Isabella. Since their nursery space was small the option of using a less bulky rocker was important.

We offer some contemporary rockers. If you prefer a more classic style, check out wooden rockers made from sustainably-harvested wood.

A Natural Home: Natural Home's line of organic rockers includes the Organic Cupcake Rocker, Mod Mommy Rocker and Organic Swivel Rocker. These rockers are handmade by the Amish in Ohio. The Organic Cupcake Rocker has a hemp fabric base with organic cotton piping. The Cupcake chair measures about 37"W x 36"H x 36"D. Both chairs have a sustainable maple frame, organic cotton batting, organic wool batting and an all natural Dunlop latex. You can choose hemp or organic cotton fabrics for the Organic Swivel Rocker. The Organic Swivel chair, offered in either hemp brown or white, measures 32"D x 34"H x 37" to 38"W. This fair-trade chair is assembled on Amish farms and is made from sustainably harvested wood from their own forest. Price: $2000 to $2200, www.anaturalhome.com.

Danko Design Equilibrium Rocker: A modern take on an arts and craft style wooden rocking chair. Made with colorful webbing (your choice of colors), recycled from surplus automotive seat belt material that is easy to clean and fade resistant. The wood is FSC-certified European beech. Adhesives and finishes are waterborne. Price: $446, www.peterdanko.com.

DucDuc Rockers: The Collins and Eddy from DucDuc are a modern alternative to the nursery rocker. The Collins rocker has an art deco style, while the Eddy is mid-century modern. Both are made from 100% sustainable hardwood with non-VOC lacquer finish. The Eddy comes in three wood finishes: white, natural or espresso stain, while the Collins is only available in white lacquer. Both chairs come in wide range of colors—even Marimekko and Knoll prints and colors! You may even supply your own fabric for upholstery. Price: $1295 to $1350, www.ducducnyc.com.

bedding

• • •

So have we told you that newborns sleep a lot? About 16 hours a day! During the first three months, we wondered if this was really true. Looking back, it's clear that our babies were definitely sleeping more than we were —it just wasn't in the predictable sleep patterns that we adults prefer.

Selecting organic and natural bedding is a simple and easy step to creating your "green" nursery. But, like everything else, it takes research.

Conventional cotton is one of the most pesticide-heavy crops in the world. According to *Green Living*, it "accounts for up to 25% of the insecticides used worldwide, and seven of the top 15 pesticides used on cotton are classified as at least possible human carcinogens." Run-off from cotton farms may poison nearby waterways. Conventional cotton fabric is usually bleached with chlorine, dyed and treated with possibly toxic chemicals.

Organic bedding is getting easier and easier to find in stores and online. It seems that every bedding manufacturer is releasing an organic or natural bedding option. Similar to organic cotton apparel fun, colorful fabrics have replaced the earthy oatmeal-colored organic cotton. We continue to be impressed with bamboo as a fabric. Its natural wicking and antibacterial properties make it a great bedding option. Please read our Green Choices chapter to better understand your choices in organic and natural bedding material.

Itsabelly's Bedding Basics
Here are our suggestions so you're prepared for the (hopefully) odd occasion when baby's diaper leaks.
• Two to Three Fitted Crib Sheets
• Four to Six Swaddle or Receiving Blankets
• Two Mattress Pads (see our recommendations)
Remember: no bulky bedding or bumpers in baby's crib.

SAFE SLEEPING TIPS

To prevent deaths from soft bedding, the US Consumer Product Safety Commission (CPSC) recommend the following:

- Place baby on his/her back on a firm, tight-fitting mattress in a crib that meets current safety standards.
- Remove pillows, quilts, comforters, sheepskins, stuffed toys and other soft products from the crib.
- Consider using a sleeper as an alternative to blankets, with no other covering.
- If using a blanket, put your baby with its feet at the foot of the crib. Tuck a thin blanket around the crib mattress, only as far as the baby's chest.
- Make sure your baby's head remains uncovered during sleep.
- Do not place baby on a waterbed, sofa, soft mattress, pillow or other soft surface to sleep.

ORGANIC BEDDING AND BLANKETS

BabyStar: Formaldehyde-free cotton blankets, fitted sheet, bumper and flat skirt in prints to match modern nursery décor. We look forward to Babystar's new soy and organic knit bedding line. Price: $34 to $380, www.babystar.com.

Buchic Bamboo: Soft and warm blankets and sheets made from bamboo fabric in four to six colors. Price: $20 to $26, www.buchic.com.

Danish Woolen Delight: These soft blankets come in natural white and grey in both newborn and toddler sizes, and are available with a natural white lace edge. Price: $87 to $114, www.danishwool.com.

Giggle: Offers organic fitted sheets and swaddle blankets in blue, pink or ivory. They also offer a section of modern crib sets. Price: $34 to $395, www.giggle.com.

NunoOrganic: Wool fleece and knit wool, organic cotton and silk blankets. Price: $59 to $119, www.nunoorganic.com.

Pure Beginnings: A 100% organic fitted sheet that fits Moses baskets with dimensions of 31"H x 12"W x 9"D. It is available in a natural color. They also offer an organic crib set, cotton fitted and flat crib sheets. Price: $21.99 to $359, www.purebeginnings.com.

Robbie Adrian Luxury Organics: Certified organic cotton velour or cotton fleece blankets trimmed with natural silk. Blankets come with a ruffled, straight or piped edge trim. Price: $44 to $130, www.robbieadrian.com.

Sage Creek Naturals: Organic jersey cotton sheets in pink or blue, swaddling blankets in a variety of prints and colors. They also make mid-weight woven cotton blankets. Price: $42 to $99, www.sagecreeknaturals.com.

The Green Robin: A wonderful selection of organic cotton bedding sets, blankets, quilts and crib skirts. Price: $28 to $78, www.thegreenrobin.com.

MATTRESS PAD

Wool makes a wonderful natural alternative for waterproof crib mattress protection. Wool will help keep baby warm during the winter and provide cool air circulation during the summer. Wool is naturally water repellent and antibacterial. It can even absorb up to 40% of its own weight in moisture before feeling wet—what could be more perfect for the eco-baby bed? You'll want to keep your mattress pad around for when your toddler is learning to use the potty and sleeping in a big kid bed.

Danish Woolen Delight: The wool used in these mattress pads is Oeko-Tex certified. A removable coverlet in organic flannel cotton or knitted wool is available. The mattress pads come in sizes 16"W x 36"L and 26"W x 36"L. The 26" x 36" pad has ties to secure pad to crib or co-sleeper mattress. Price: $129 to $169, www.danishwool.com.

SnuggleWool Mattress Pad: These mattress pads come in sizes for a bassinet, various co-sleeper sizes, crib and twin beds. Price: $35 to $135, www.snugglewool.com.

White Lotus Puddle Pads: Mattress pads for beds from crib to king and even a great travel size Puddle Pad for diaper changing on the go. Price $29 to $115, www.whitelotus.net.

eco mom tip:

Wool mattress pads are a great option to adding a natural barrier if you have a traditional mattress.

diapering

• • •

Many eco-minded moms feel that diapering is one of the areas where going green can truly make a difference. Considering that you may change 5,000 to 8,000 diapers before your little one learns to use the potty, it's easy to understand why. Fortunately, it is no longer a choice between pinning cloth diapers and plastic-feeling disposables. Innovation in diapering is really taking off—today you have a number of environmentally friendly and convenient options. Frustrated parents have started businesses creating diapers so evolved that Granny would hardly recognize them. Dare we say, this is a great time to change diapers?

We bet that by now, you've realized that "going green" involves making tough decisions, and figuring out what diaper to use is no different. Even recent life-cycle analysis studies have come up with results that are not so clear-cut. Geared to determine the better, more environmentally friendly diapering method, these studies have demonstrated a balance between production and waste of disposables, and the energy and water usage of dealing with cloth diapers.

Conventional disposable diapers are typically made with a waterproof outer layer, with inner layers of bleached wood pulp and super absorbent sodium polyacrylate. It takes oil, trees, water and energy to create disposable diapers. According to the Union of Concerned Scientists, Americans throw away 18 billion disposable diapers a year. Those diapers *may* take from 200 to 500 years to decompose—since they've only been around since 1948, we really don't know how long they will actually take to decay. There's also worry about all the solid fecal matter contained in diapers that has been wrapped up and tossed into the garbage over the years. Most parents using disposables miss that manufacturer's instruction that says to shake solid waste into the toilet. What happens if that fecal matter gets into groundwater systems? On top of that, chlorine bleaching of the wood pulp used to stuff the diaper releases dioxin, an extremely toxic and carcinogenic substance. Evidence also exists that the components used in disposable diapers may cause health problems such as asthma and reduced sperm count in boys.

Cloth diapers, on the other hand, come with their own range of pros and cons. Pesticides and chemicals are involved in the growing and finishing of conventional cotton used in many non-organic cloth diapers. If the cotton is bleached with chlorine, dioxin is also a concern. However, with cloth diapers, human waste is going where it belongs, into the sewer system. Cloth diapers are reused throughout baby's diapering days, and often reused during for diapering days of a second child, as well, and can then go on to yet another life as household rags. Cloth diapers, though, must be washed, in hot water with laundry detergent, which consumes water and energy resources. Diaper services may bleach diapers with chlorine and thus release dioxin. Some cloth diaper products may actually be made from petroleum products. Organic cotton, bamboo, hemp or ecologically grown wool offer probably the most environmentally friendly diapering options, from a production and waste standpoint.

According to *Consumer Reports,* "you can expect to spend $1,500 to $2,000 or more on disposables by the time your baby is out of them." According the Real Diaper Association, diaper service is "roughly the same cost as disposables, depending on what types of covers are purchased and what types of wipes are used. If one adds in the cost of disposable wipes for either diapering system, the costs increase." However, if you launder your diapers at home, the cost of cloth diapers, including energy usage and the diapers themselves, can range from $430 to $1942. The low end is for prefolds and covers; the high end is for all-in-one diapers. Most parents do a combination, so the cost probably lies somewhere in between. The BIG difference, though, is that cloth diapers can be reused for your next child or resold. Jennifer was able to use her cloth diaper stash for two children and sell the covers to a friend. Jennifer saved the prefolds to use as household rags.

When babies wear disposables, they tend to be changed less often because their diapers feel dry even though they may be soiled. When a baby wears cloth, you (and baby) know immediately when baby is wet. The AAP states, "regardless of which type of diaper you use, diaper rash occurs less often and is less severe when you change diapers often." Many parents report that babies who wear cloth tend to learn to use the potty earlier because they sense when they are wet. In 1999, The *New York Times* reported that 92% of children in 1957 were toilet-trained by 18 months of age. Go into any grocery store today and you will find diapers to fit babies weighing more than 41 lbs (typical for a 5-year-old)!

Because diaper decision-making is so involved, it can be a stressful part of planning for baby's arrival. We want parents to know that your diaper choice doesn't have to be set in stone. Once baby is here you can reevaluate your family's needs. We recommend starting small, seeing what you like and how it works for your family. In working with parents, we have found that many parents choose to work with a combination of diapering systems.

Diaper Choices Research

Here are some good resources for doing your own research on the diaper debate.

- **Born To Love:** www.borntolove.com.
- *Consumer Reports:* www.consumerreports.org.
- **Co-op America:** www.coopamerica.org.
- **Diaper Pin:** www.diaperpin.com.
- **Diaper Decisions:** A good cost comparison chart, www.diaperdecisions.com.
- **Eco-Cycle:** www.ecocycle.org.
- **Elimination Communication:** www.diaperfreebaby.org.
- **Healthy Child Healthy World:** www.healthychild.org.
- **Mother Jones:** www.motherjones.com.
- **National Association of Diaper Services:** www.diapernet.org.
- **Real Diaper Association:** www.realdiaperassociation.org.
- **Sustainability Institute:** www.sustainer.org.
- **University of Minnesota Waste Education:** www.extension.umn.edu /distribution/housingandclothing/DK5911.html.

WHAT IS ELIMINATION COMMUNICATION?
By Diaper Free Baby, **www.diaperfreebaby.org.**

Just as parents learn to read their baby's signs for sleep and hunger, they can also learn to read their baby's signs for needing to eliminate. In fact, most parents already know what some of these signs are, such as the straining facial expression or the telltale grunting and bearing down that precede a soiled diaper. Practicing Elimination Communication (EC) is just a matter of responding a little differently to these signals from your baby. Taking your baby to the potty can be easy and rewarding!

Getting Started
- Prepare yourself and your baby—explain to your baby what you are doing and why.
- Relax, and focus on the goal of communicating with your baby.
- Talk to your baby so that your baby hears the words associated with going to the bathroom.
- Make note of any elimination signs, such as grunting or grimacing.
- Offer "pottytunities"—a "pottytunity" is an opportunity to use the potty. Simply hold your baby over a toilet, potty or other receptacle of your choice and make a cue sound such as "psss psss." Great times to offer "pottytunities" are when your baby first wakes up and at diaper changes, or anytime you notice an elimination sign from your baby. Our website, www.diaperfreebaby.org, shows pictures of various potty positions.
- Change diapers frequently—your baby should know he will be changed as quickly as possible when his elimination is in a diaper or other clothing.
- Practice EC responsibly—use common sense; make sure to give the proper physical support for the baby's age and ability. Also, please be considerate and dispose of eliminations in an appropriate place.
- Get information and support—while EC is the traditional way of caring for babies' elimination needs in most of the world and has been throughout history, it is really a "lost art" in our culture today. Getting support through DiaperFreeBaby groups and using other EC resources can make the EC journey easier.

You may be hesitant to begin EC because you think that it will require a full-time commitment. While many families do practice EC full-time, it can also be done part-time or even occasionally while still reaping many benefits. It is not uncommon for families to find themselves practicing EC differently depending on the needs of their families at any particular time. The beauty of EC lies in its flexibility.

Practicing EC has major benefits for the Earth and for baby

Benefits for the Earth . . .
- Reduces the use of disposable diapers, a major contributor to landfills
- Reduces the use of water and detergents used to wash cloth diapers
- Reduces the use of disposable wipes used to clean baby's bottom
- Does not support the manufacture of dioxins and other toxic chemicals used in the productions of diapers and diapering products
- Reduces use of plastic bags used to individually wrap dirty disposable diapers

Benefits for baby . . .
- Reduces irritation of baby's skin by keeping urine and excrement off baby's body
- Keeps unnecessary chemicals off baby's skin
- Supports positive views about bodily functions
- Builds self-esteem and reduces frustration through increased communication
- Reduces "unexplained" fussiness
- Supports breastfeeding
- Keeps baby more comfortable than disposables or a wet cloth diaper
- Protects baby from germs in public restrooms

For more information visit: www.diaperfreebaby.org and www.cleanearthhappybaby.org.

DISPOSABLE DIAPERS

Fortunately, there are some disposable options that are better choices for baby and the environment. Although not a perfect solution, they are steps in the right direction. The disposables we recommend address both convenience and health concerns. Disposables can be used in conjunction with hybrid or cloth diapering. We recognize that there are some times when cloth diapering can be difficult. Jennifer used cloth diapers; however when she traveled to places where storing cloth diapers would be problematic, she used Tushies or Seventh Generation disposables. Melissa did a combination of half gDiapers and Seventh Generation disposables, and loved the cute gDiapers covers. For her second baby, she will happily be changing cloth diapers.

How Many Disposable Diapers?
Newborns need to be changed frequently, about 12 times per day. Although many disposable diapers may not feel wet, if baby has soiled the diaper, the diaper should be changed. Newborns also grow quickly, so avoid the temptation to stock up on a lot of diapers in a small size to avoid waste. To start, just buy one to two packs of the smallest size and a pack of the next size. You'll have enough diapers to last the first few days home and will be prepared if you have a large baby. After baby is born, you will know baby's size and your preferred brand when you need to buy more.

Seventh Generation: These chlorine-free diapers are hypoallergenic and made without latex, fragrance, or TBT (tributyltin). These diapers, which use absorbent gel (sodium polyacrylate) to keep baby dry, come in sizes to fit babies from newborn to 35+ lbs. Seventh Generation is constantly expanding their distribution, so you may be able to find their diapers at your local grocery store, in addition to health and specialty baby stores. Price: $10.99 to $13.99, www.seventhgeneration.com.

Tushies: A disposable diaper that is free from gel, latex, perfume, dye, TBT, GMO and chlorine. The diapers are made in the USA and use wood pulp from sustainable, family-owned forests. Tushies makes diapers to fit babies from six lbs to toddlers of 27+ lbs. Price: $11.99 to $12.99, www.tushies.com.

HYBRID DIAPERS

These innovative, new-to-the-diapering-scene diapers offer parents the best of both worlds. With a hybrid diaper you'll get the reusability of cloth and the convenience of disposables. Baby wears a cloth cover that you can wash and reuse. The absorbent part of the diaper is flushable. Hybrids are a great option because you can reuse the cover, and the waste goes where it belongs—down the toilet. Currently, in the USA, only one manufacturer makes hybrid diapers, gDiapers. In the UK, the popular MotherCare store introduced a hybrid diaper called the Smart Nappy System. Judging from the popularity of hybrids, we bet other brands will soon be introduced in the USA.

How Many Hybrid Diapers?

For a newborn, we recommend having 6–8 covers and one package of size small refills (40-count). You'll have enough to get started and see if you like using hybrid diapers.

gDiapers: These diapers consist of a washable, cotton outer pant and a plastic-free flushable refill. The covers/pants are made of a breathable material. The liner is flushable, disposable and can even be composted. The snap-in liners are made of breathable polyurethane-coated nylon. The absorbent flushable is made with viscose rayon and a natural polymer that comes from trees, elemental chlorine-free tree-farmed fluff pulp and super-absorbent polyacrylate. They break down in 50–150 days. gPants come in nine cool colors, from grasshopper green to goodnight blue. Price: $26.99 (starter kit), $16.99 (cover) and $14.49 (liner refills), www.gdiapers.com.

CLOTH DIAPERS

When you think of cloth diapers, you probably think of flat pieces of cloth, rubber pants and sticky pins. You will be amazed at how much cloth diapering has changed when you start researching cloth diapers. You can buy cloth diapers that are as easy to use as disposables. You don't need pins, and you don't need to dunk and swirl poopy diapers in the toilet. Cloth diapering is much easier than you think. In fact, with all the innovative diapering options in fun fabrics, it can almost *be* fun—well, at least selecting the diapers can be. You can find cloth-diapering options in conventional and organic cotton, hemp and bamboo. Hemp and bamboo make interesting diapering options. Both are naturally antibacterial, durable and soft, and both grow well for the environment. Bamboo requires no herbicides or pesticides and renews easily. Hemp resists pests, requires less fertilizer than cotton and grows easily.

How Many Cloth Diapers?
We worked up this little cheat sheet to make selecting your cloth diapering system easier. How many cloth diapers you buy depends on baby's age and how often you want to do laundry. Of course, these numbers are just a guideline that you can adjust once you know baby's habits. You will usually change a younger baby about 10 to 12 times a day. These numbers are for newborns and doing laundry every three to four days. Our recommendations are conservative; we don't want you facing a diaper crisis on laundry day. Whatever diapering system you choose, we recommend only buying enough for the first few weeks to see if you like it before making a large investment.

• **Diapers:** You will need about 36 to 48 cloth diapers for doing wash every three to four days. You can divide this quantity with a mixture of AIO (all-in-one), fitted, contours and prefolds. We like having at least four to six AIO, pocket, fitted or contour diapers for outings. We love using pocket diapers for nighttime diapers. If you are using nothing but AIOs, you can usually buy a few less as they tend to be more absorbent than prefolds. For pocket diapers you'll also need diaper doublers/ inserts. For fitted and contours, you'll also need diaper covers and three to four Snappis or pins.

- **Covers:** If using wool you'll need 3 covers. If using other materials, 8 covers. Include covers for nighttime use.

- **Diaper Doublers:** If using pocket diapers, 36 to 48. Many pocket diapers come with free inserts. If using other diapers, 12 to 24 doublers/ inserts. These aren't necessary, but they can add extra absorbance if needed.

Because of the investment of AIO, fitted and contour diapers, we recommend purchasing a small number of several different brands to see what works best for you. Many cloth diapering stores offer starter and sampler kits.

How To Wash Cloth Diapers
By Amy S. Nogar, Owner Zany Zebra Designs, LLC, **www.zany-zebra.com.**
If you use cloth diapers on your baby, eventually you'll have to wash them, but don't worry, you *can* have fresh, clean diapers with a minimum of effort! Washing cloth diapers requires a little more care than washing clothing, but it's easy once you find a routine and a detergent that works for you.

The Basics
These are the bare-bones basics; follow these to start creating a washing routine that you'll love.
- Remove as much solid matter as possible if your child is not exclusively breastfed.
- Wash every two or three days to avoid smells and excessive staining.
- Start with a cold rinse.
- Wash in hot water.
- Use the highest water level your machine allows.
- Use one-quarter to one-half the amount of detergent recommended

by the manufacturer.
- Rinse in the warmest water possible.
- Do an extra final rinse.
- Dry on warm or hot in the dryer* or hang outside for extra freshness and to sun-bleach stains.
- NEVER use bleach or fabric softeners, including softener sheets.

* *We've heard that microfiber will stay absorbent longer if line-dried or dried on low, but we don't use microfiber so we can't say from personal experience.*

Variations

This is where you personalize your routine; try one variation for a while and if that one doesn't work, try something else.
- Add baking soda to the initial cold rinse to fight stains and odors.
- Use one-half to one cup of white vinegar in the final rinse to soften your diapers and remove odors.
- If you have hard water, add water softener to the wash cycle.
- Try adding one-half cup lemon juice to the wash cycle to help remove stains.
- Use Bac-Out to help eliminate odors and stains.
- Try a couple of drops of Tea Tree Oil in the final rinse to eliminate odors.
- If you can't hang your diapers outside, use a sunny window instead.

Tips and Tricks

Finally, some tips and tricks from the trenches to help you wash your cloth diapers with ease!
- Wash all new diapers before use.
- Don't wash more than two dozen diapers at a time.
- Avoid zinc oxide diaper creams as they will stain your diapers.
- Fasten hook/loop closures before laundering to avoid the dreaded "diaper chain."
- Use flushable diaper liners to make it easier to get rid of solid matter.
- Don't allow dyed diapers to lie around wet or the dye may transfer to other diapers.
- Fasten diapers and covers inside out so the insides get clean and to

protect any applique or embroidery.

- Avoid laundry "soaps" as they may leave a residue on your diapers.
- Avoid detergents with brighteners or enzymes as these will break down your diapers and may cause a rash.
- Take a "sniff test" after washing. If your diapers smell like detergent do another hot rinse or two.
- Use a fabric softener ball to dispense vinegar in your rinse cycle if you don't do an additional rinse.
- Apply lemon juice to stains before sunning to help get rid of stains, then rewash those diapers before use.
- If your diapers are "crunchy" after drying outside, toss them in the dryer on the fluff cycle for 10 to 15 minutes to soften them up.
- Running an extra spin cycle will help your diapers—or any laundry— dry faster.

Choosing a Cloth Diaper Detergent

Believe it or not, cheap detergents can actually be better for your cloth diapers than expensive ones—cheaper detergents are less likely to include problem-causing additives than expensive ones. For a list of popular laundry detergents and their ingredients, visit www.zany-zebra.com/diaper-detergent-chart.shtml.

Most detergents are designed to leave some residue behind: fabric softeners, scents, brighteners, stain guards, and the like are all intended to remain on the fabric after laundering. While this may be beneficial to clothing, it's not good for cloth diapers! Here's a list of the most common detergent ingredients and their function:

- **Surfactant**, short for "surface-active agent," is the main ingredient of any detergent. It improves the wetting ability of water, loosens and removes dirt, helps suspends dirt in the water, and prevents dirt from being redeposited on the clean laundry.
- **Builders** are the second major component in detergents and are basically water softeners. They enhance surfactants' action by deactivating calcium and magnesium and by producing alkaline solutions to aid in cleaning. Most builders are phosphate-based, except in phosphate-free detergents.

- **Fillers and Processing Aids** like sodium sulfate or borax are used to absorb water and help powdered detergent flow. Removing most of the filler yields "concentrated" or "ultra" detergents. Alcohols are added to liquid detergents to keep everything in solution and to lower the freezing point.
- **Bleaches** are the third main ingredient in detergents. North American detergents usually contain chlorine-based bleaches that work at lower temperatures. Most detergents for colors contain no bleach.
- **Corrosion Inhibitors** like sodium silicate, also known as water glass or liquid glass, is generally added to detergents to help reduce corrosion inside the washing machine.
- **Anti-Foaming Agents** are chemicals added to reduce the amount of foam produced, especially when detergents are present in waste-water.
- **Color and Fragrances** are added to improve the appearance of detergents and to make the clean clothes smell nice.

Many detergents also incorporate other additives to perform a specific function or meet a particular need. Some of these additives are listed below:

- **Brighteners** are in any detergent that says it "brightens colors." Brighteners absorb UV light and re-emit white light, thus brightening the fabric. The blue tone caused by the brightener hides yellow and brown tones, making the fabric appear whiter and cleaner. Some brighteners can cause allergic reactions. Most major brands of detergent contain brighteners, including many "free and clear" types.
- **Enzymes** help break down organic stains like oil, blood, grass, and the like. Unfortunately they may become reactivated when they get wet and cause painful rashes on some babies. Enzymes seem to react differently with different children so they don't necessarily need to be avoided; just be aware that some babies, particularly younger ones, may be too sensitive to wear cloth diapers washed in detergents that contain enzymes.
- **Stain guards** aren't always named separately in a detergent's list of ingredients, but the detergent will probably indicate that it repels stains or guards fabric. These substances coat fabric fibers to prevent stains. Unfortunately this coating not only repels stains, it also repels wetness, making your cloth diapers less absorbent.

- **Fabric Softeners** are used to prevent static cling and make fabric softer. They coat the surface of the fibers with a thin layer of chemicals designed to make the fibers feel smoother, prevent buildup of static electricity, increase resistance to stains, and reduce wrinkles. Unfortunately this coating also decreases the water absorbency of fabric, which isn't good for cloth diapers. Dryer sheets will cause the same problems. Be sure to watch out for fabric softeners hidden in detergents.

Laundry soaps like Ivory Snow and Dreft have been advertised for years as being better for baby than regular detergents. Free and clear detergents also claim to be gentler than regular detergents, but these claims are not necessarily true, nor do they mean that these formulas are good for cloth diapers.

- **Laundry Soap** is not the same as laundry detergent. In hard water soap will leave a waxy residue, or scum, which will be hard to rinse out and will eventually give your laundry a grayish tint. Soap also leaves a film on your laundry similar to what you would find in a shower stall that uses hard water. Even in areas with soft water, soap will produce a gradual build-up of minerals that will remain in your diapers or other laundry. As if this isn't bad enough already, soap's cleaning ability diminishes over time as it is stored. Only fresh soap provides maximum cleaning power.
- **Free and Clear Detergents** have received mixed reviews in the cloth diapering community. Some families can use them without a hitch while other families suffer with build-up. Keep in mind that free and clear detergents are often intended for consumers with allergies and often include fungicide and/or bactericide ingredients to eliminate some of the fungal or bacterial causes of allergies. These are the ingredients that may cause build-up, especially on microfleece or suedecloth.
- **Natural Detergents** are popular with many families because they don't contain phosphates, animal-derived ingredients, and are formulated to be gentle on the environment. However, many natural detergents contain orange oil, citrus or grapeseed extract, and other plant-based oils which may cause build-up and problems with your cloth diapers over time. Fortunately build-up caused by plant-based oils isn't as difficult to remove as build-up caused by other additives, so you may decide the

risk is worth it to use a natural detergent.

The use of bleach is a controversial subject in the cloth diapering world. Supporters and critics of bleach use are at polar opposites and often engage in heated debates regarding the pros and cons of bleach. We offer this information so you can form your own opinion regarding bleach.

- **Chlorine Bleach** weakens fibers, and causes fabric to break down faster. Since cloth diapers are washed twice a week or more, they need gentler treatment than chlorine bleach provides. That said, many families believe that there is a time and a place for chlorine bleach. Sometimes cloth diapers retain odors no matter what you do. If you're about to tear your hair out or toss your cloth diapers, that's the time to consider using chlorine bleach. Try a scant quarter-cup (or a small "glug") the wash cycle, then do one to two extra rinses to make sure all the bleach has been rinsed out. Regular use of chlorine bleach is not recommended, but as a last resort, it may be a lifesaver!
- **Oxygen Bleach** is a good alternative to chlorine bleach. The liquid version of oxygen bleach is hydrogen peroxide, which has been used to remove stains for years. It's safe for fabric, gentle on sensitive skin, and won't harm the environment. It even helps kill viruses and bacteria! Try adding a couple scoops of oxygen bleach to your hot wash, stopping the cycle and letting your diapers soak for four to six hours. Finish the cycle, run an extra rinse, and your diapers will be like new!

ITSABELLY'S CLOTH DIAPER RECOMMENDATIONS

PREFOLD / FLAT CLOTH

These are the same diapers that Grandma used. Prefolds (aka Diaper Service Quality [DSQ] or Chinese Prefolds), have a thick center panel. Flat diapers are a large one-layer piece of cloth that must be folded many times to fit baby. Prefolds save you the folding routine. Nowadays, there is no need to use pins with prefolds, unless of course you want to use pins. We think it's a little crazy, but we've met some mamas who love the retro look of prefolds and pins. A great invention called the Snappi fastens diapers like pins, but without the sharp points. Depending on the cover you choose, you may not even need to fasten the prefold—just fold it in threes and place in the cover. When you first receive your prefolds they are very flat and stiff. After washing, the prefold will "quilt" and become soft, cushion-like and absorbent. Washing removes the nat-ural oils of the fiber to make them absorbent. You can buy cotton, organic cotton and hemp, and we have even seen bamboo prefolds starting to appear on the market (we can't wait to test them and let you know what we think!). Depending on the fabric and size, prefolds can cost anywhere from $1 to $9 per diaper, mak-ing prefolds the most economical cloth diapering system.

BabyKicks Hemparoo®: A hemp-based, absorbent prefold diaper that is 55% hemp and 45% cotton fleece. Hemparoos come in sizes from new-born to large toddler. Price: $6.59 to $9.56, www.babykicks.com.

Green Mountain Cloth-Eez: One of the most popular sources for high quality, heavyweight 100% cotton twill diapers. The white prefolds are bleached using hydrogen peroxide, not chlorine, and are dioxin- and acid-free. Green Mountain also sells unbleached Indian prefolds. Since unbleached prefolds have not been de-gummed, they need to be washed in hot water to remove the natural cotton oils more than bleached pre-folds. Green Mountain prefolds are offered in nine sizes ranging from preemie to toddler. Price: $14 to $36 per dozen, www.greenmountaindiapers.com.

Pro Services: Many diaper services use these durable 100% cotton twill prefold diapers. Pro Services prefolds are available in five sizes from preemie to toddler. Price: $18.50 to $24.50 per dozen, www.prodiaper.net.

Under The Nile: These prefolds are 100% Egyptian organic cotton made with milton knit and a three-layer terry liner. Price: $34 for 4, www.underthenile.com.

FITTED CLOTH DIAPERS

Similar in appearance to disposable diapers, fitted cloth diapers have a contour shape and gathered edges around the legs designed to control leaks. Fitted diapers are closed with Velcro, APLIX® or snaps. We have found fitted diapers with several snaps make getting the right fit—well, a snap. If you want waterproof protection, you will have to use a diaper cover with fitted cloth diapers. While at home, Jennifer often used fitted diapers without covers. Since she knew immediately when baby was wet, she was able to change the diaper and swears this helped with early potty usage. Averaging $4 to $20 per diaper, fitted cloth diapers are more expensive than pre-folds.

Bamboozles: A super-soft fitted diaper made of four layers of bamboo fabric in a choice of five vibrant colors. Bamboozles won the Mother and Baby award for Best Reusable Nappy. Bamboo absorbs 60% more than cotton and is naturally antibacterial. This diaper has easy-to-adjust snap closures and a sewn-in adjustable doubler for extra absorbency. Made by TotsBots in Scotland and Oeko-Tex certified. The diaper comes in two sizes that range from preemie to toddler. It takes ten washes for the Bamboozle to reach full absorbency. Price: $19, www.totsbots.com.

Crickett's Diapers: Highly rated in user reviews on the Diaper Pin, Crickett's fitted diapers are made of a hemp/cotton fleece blend. Blending hemp with cotton results in a cloth that is more durable and absorbent. And of course, the fleece is soft. The diaper front can be folded down to protect the umbilical cord on newborns. These fitted diapers have adjustable snaps, and elastic in the legs and back. A snap-in doubler is included for extra absorbency at night or for longer outings. The newborn size should fit babies eight to 20 lbs, and the toddlers for over 20 lbs. Price: $12.98 to $13.98, www.crickettsdiapers.com.

Kissaluvs Fitted Diaper: A textured fabric and stretchy elastic at the legs and back openings help to control leaks. You may choose unbleached cotton fleece or knit terry. Each diaper features many lifetime-guaranteed snaps to adjust to different size babies. The Kissaluvs fitted diaper comes in size 0 (newborn, 5 to 15 lbs), size 1 (medium, 10 to 25 lbs) and size 2 (large, 20 to 40 lbs). The Size O for newborns has a popular snap-down notch to protect the sensitive umbilical cord. Kissaluvs often offers limited edition versions with unique colors and trims. Price: $11.50 to $12.50, www.kissaluvs.com.

Under the Nile Organic Fitted Diapers: A 100% organic Egyptian cotton terry knit fitted and adjustable Velcro diaper. It comes in newborn, small, medium and large sizes. Price: $12 to $13, www.underthenile.com.

CONTOUR / SHAPED DIAPERS

Similar in shape to fitted cloth diapers but without a closure or elastic around the legs. Contour diapers are more convenient to use than prefolds because they don't require any folding. As with prefolds, you may use a Snappi or pins to close the diaper. For waterproof protection, you must use a diaper cover with contour cloth diapers. At an average of $6 to $15 per diaper, contours are more expensive than prefolds, although usually less expensive than fitted diapers.

Imse Vimse: These 100% organic cotton contour diapers come in two different versions: flannelette and terry. Both versions feature elastic in the legs for leak protection, making them a little closer to fitted diapers. This contour diaper is one-size for use from birth until potty training. The long wings may or may not be pinned. The flannelette version has been approved for the Swedish Environmental License as being quick-drying and energy-conserving. Imse Vimse also offers a newborn size that works well for preemies and with newborn covers. Price: $8.55 to $14.95, www.imsevimse.us.

Kissaluvs Contour Diaper: An economical alternative to fitted diapers, and just as easy to use. This diaper is made of textured cotton fabric and includes a sewn-in soaker/doubler to help control leaks. The long wings make it easy to get a snug fit when used with a Snappi or pins. The Kissaluv contour diaper comes in size NB/small (5 to 20 lbs) and size M/L (15 to 30 lbs). Price: $6 to $7, www.kissaluvs.com.

DIAPER COVERS

A diaper cover is needed for waterproof protection when using prefolds, fitted or contour diapers. Wool or PUL (polyurethane laminate) tend to be the most popular materials for creating a waterproof barrier between the diaper and baby's clothing. Diaper covers can be closed with Velcro, APLIX or snaps.

Originally destined for the medical industry, PUL has become a cloth-diapering staple because of its durable, flexible and waterproof qualities, though we must point out that PUL does use synthetic materials. If you wish to avoid petroleum products, you should steer clear of PUL.

Wool provides a natural water-resistant barrier and is the best alternative to PUL-based covers. Untreated wool is soft, and naturally antibacterial. Untreated wool can absorb up to 40% of its own weight in moisture before it feels wet. Because of its breathability, wool helps maintain a comfortable temperature for baby's tush. In warm temperatures, wool will keep baby cool and in cold temperatures, wool will keep baby warm. And—this will sound crazy, but you only need to wash wool when the lanolin needs to be replenished, about once a week. The lanolin neutral-izes the urine odor, so when the cover starts to smell you will know it's time to re-lanolize your wool covers. Just remember to never puts your wool covers in the dryer. Jennifer learned that lesson the hard way!

Aristocrats: A pull-on wool diaper cover, also known as a soaker, which is made from stretchy, double-layered knit. It is designed for extra absorbency and protection. Jennifer loved the old-fashioned look of her baby in an Aristocrat! Aristocrats come in sizes small (7 to 20 lbs), large (20 to 35 lbs), extra large (35 to 50 lbs) and child. Price: $27.50 to $41, www.aristocratsbabyproducts.com.

Bumkins: A leader in cloth diapering since 1989. Their diaper covers are vinyl-, BPA-, PVC- and phthalate-free. Bumkins diaper covers are well known for their back air vent to keep the diaper area cool and their front inside flap to hold the diaper in place. Extra leg gussets provide leak pro-tection. Bumkins covers come in white and a wide variety of fun designs.

Bumkins sizes are newborn (6 to 10 lbs), small (9 to 16 lbs), medium (15 to 23 lbs), large (22 to 28 lbs) and x-large (27 to 35 lbs). Bumkins are made in the USA. Price: $14.95 to $16.95, www.bumkins.com.

Bummis: Another leader in cloth diapering, their bestseller is the Super Whisper Wrap. It features APLIX adjustable closures, soft elastic leg opening bindings with super-resistant water-proof laminate between two layers of soft polyester knit. The Super Whisper is also available as a pull-on pant. Bummis just released Super Brite, which is similar to the Super Whisper line with the addition of gusseted legs. The Original Covers and Pants are made from lightweight and waterproof nylon with soft and stretchy Lycra bindings around tummy and legs. The Cotton Cover and Pant are similar to the Bummis Original except the exterior is a layer of cotton. The Super Whisper, Cotton and Super Brite are available in a wide range of fun colors and prints. Bumkins covers come in sizes newborn, small, medium, large and x-large, ranging from 4 lbs to 35+ lbs. Price: $6 to $12.95, www.bummis.com.

Danish Woolen Delight: Felted wool diaper in a regular and nighttime version. The regular version is recommended for day use. The nighttime cover has three layers of felted wool and is recommended for heavy or, obviously, night use. The medium, large and x-large sizes have adjustable waists for a perfect fit. The covers come in sizes x-small (less than 7 lbs), small (7 to 13 lbs), medium (12 to 20 lbs), large (20 to 30 lbs) and x-large (+30 lbs). Price: $41.99 to $58.99, www.danishwool.com.

Imse Vimse: Imse Vimse offers diaper covers in several different models. The Organic Cotton model is a wrap-style cover made of a layer of organic cotton fabric on the outside and polyester PUL on the inside with Velcro closures. The Organic Cotton Velour Cover is also a wrap cover with Velcro closures. The outside is organic cotton velour with polyester PUL on the inside. The Wool Cover is a wrap style cover that allows maximum air circulation while protecting against leaks. The cover is made of merino wool with Velcro closures. The Soft Cover uses polyester knit laminated with PUL and Velcro closures. The Organic Cotton and Organic Cotton Velour covers come in preemie, newborn, small, medium, large, x-large and super large to cover babies from 4.4 lbs to 28+ lbs. The Wool and Soft Covers come in sizes newborn through super large for babies 6.5 lbs to 28+ lbs. Price: $11.95 to $26.95, www.imsevimse.us.

Little Beetle: The Merino Wool Jersey Diaper Cover that features APLIX closures and elastic at the legs. The Merino Wool Cover is available in a natural or five other bright colors. These covers work well with trim diapers. The cover comes in size one (birth to six months) and size two (15 to 25 lbs, low rise), size 2-1/2 (20 to 30+ lbs) and toddler. Made in the USA. Price: $29.95 to $36.95, www.betterforbabies.com.

ProRaps: Used by many diaper services, these diaper covers are extremely durable and economical. The Basic ProRap is 100% vinyl-backed polyester with double barrier leg gussets and hook-and-loop closures. The ProRap Classic is a very popular model, made of polyester knit with a leak-proof urethane barrier and double barrier leg gussets. The Classic comes with Velcro or snap closures. Prorap is well known for the umbilical cord notches in their preemie and newborn size covers. Both models come in sizes preemie (2 to 6 lbs), newborn (6 to 10 lbs), small (9 to 14 lbs), medium (13 to 25 lbs), large (24 to 35 lbs) and x-large (34 to 45 lbs). Price: $8.50, www.prodiaper.net.

ALL IN ONES

An all-in-one (AIO) diaper is a diaper and cover together as one piece. Because the cover is sewn onto the diaper, AIOs do not require a separate cover. As you research cloth diapers, you will also run across the term "AI2." This is an all-in-two, which means the soaker part of the diaper is not completely integrated into the diaper. This is the most absorbent part of the diaper. It can be partially sewn, snapped or placed into the diaper. Because this is the thickest part of the diaper and it is separate from the diaper, AI2s may have a more efficient drying time.

AIOs offer the easiest method of cloth diapering, although also the most expensive. However, using AIOs full-time may still be more affordable than disposable diapers. You will have sticker shock at the initial investment, but if you run the numbers and consider that you can reuse or resell your AIO stash, you may find it economically feasible. Whatever your cloth diapering system, it is great to have some AIOs on hand for quick changes, outings or for babysitters. P.S.—we've heard that dads have fewer complaints about changing baby's diaper when using an All-In-One.

bumGenius: Created by Cotton Babies and loved for the patent-pending stretchy tabs combined with hook-and-loop fasteners that give a trim fit. bumGenius AIOs come in five pretty pastel colors. Winner of the iParenting Media Award, the diaper is made with soft knit waterproof PUL and a Cotton Babies microfiber soaker. The Organic One Size AIO diaper has a soft knit waterproof PUL outer layer and certified organic cotton inner layers. The regular AIO comes in extra-small (6 to 12 lbs), small (8 to 16 lbs), medium (15 to 22 lbs) and large (22 to 30 lbs). The Organic AIO fits most babies weighing between 7 and 35 lbs. bumGenius products are made in the USA. Price: $15.95, www.bumgenius.com.

BumWare: A work-at-home mom makes a traditional AIO, AI2 and an Extreme AIO that is quick drying. These diapers are amazingly trim and the hidden leg elastic keeps leaks contained! The AIO have a sewn-in soaker and the AI2 have a snap-in soaker. You can even order custom embroidery designs. Both versions have hook-and-loop fasteners, two inner layers of cotton flannel, a four-layer flannel soaker and PUL outer fabric in a wide range of colors. Each diaper comes with a four-layer flannel contour doubler. The Extreme AIO has the same features as the regular AIO, except for the fabric. A suedecloth inner layer and a super-absorbent microfiber sewn-in soaker make drying faster. For all versions of doublers, you may choose hemp, fleece-topped flannel or fleece-topped hemp. BumWare diapers are made in the USA. Price: $17 to $20, www.bum-ware.com.

Mother-ease AIO: Manufacturing cotton diapers since 1991, this AIO features side venting and adjustable snap enclosures. The inner fabric is knit cotton terry. The outer waterproof fabric is 100% polyester knit PUL. All

Mother-ease products are made in Ontario, Canada, using 100% green power. This AIO comes in sizes small (10 to 20 lbs), medium (20 to 35 lbs) and large (35 to 45 lbs). Mother-ease also makes a popular one-size diaper. Price: $15.95 to $17.95, www.mother-ease.com.

SposoEasy: A 100% cotton AIO without any polyester fleece inside. There are a total of six layers inside the diaper: four layers of 100% cotton terry and two layers of 100% cotton flannel. The outer layer is PUL. The SposoEasy come in x-small (5 to 9 lbs), small (10 to 20 lbs), medium (21 to 30 lbs) and large (28 to 50 lbs). Blue Penguin makes their diapers in the USA. Price: $17.50, www.bluepenguin.biz.

POCKET DIAPERS

These diapers are similar in shape and design to disposables and AIO. The back top edge of the diaper is left open for you to stuff the soaker into the diaper. The soaker is usually sandwiched between an outer layer of knit PUL and an inner layer of microfleece. Jennifer liked using pocket diapers at night because she could control the amount of absorbency needed. Some pocket diaper manufacturers include a soaker insert. You may wish to buy additional soakers for heavy wetters. Pocket diapers are similar in price to AIOs.

bumGenius: A great one-size cloth diapers that fits babies from 7 to 35 lbs. Patent-pending stretch-to-fit tabs and the three snaps down the front allow the diaper to adjust to your growing baby. These diapers have a unique fold-down insert stopper that keeps the insert in place in the diaper, not in your baby's onesie. The regular one-size diaper is made with a soft waterproof PUL knit fabric and a stay-dry inner lining. Each diaper includes a Cotton Babies microfiber insert. If you are using this diaper on a small newborn (under 10 lbs), bumGenius recommends purchasing microfiber diaper doublers or Hemp Babies Little Weeds to use until your baby is a little bit bigger. Price: $17.95 to $24.95, www.bumgenius.com.

FuzziBunz: An extremely popular cloth diaper. Jennifer is still using the Fuzzi Bunz she purchased five years ago! The outer layer is soft knit PUL in an assortment of colors. The inner layer is soft polyester microfleece that wicks away moisture. These diapers also have stretchy elastic around the legs, leg casing mini gussets and adjustable snaps to give a good fit and control leaks. Made in the USA Fuzzi Bunz come with a polyester/polymide microterry cloth insert. Sizes: x-small (4 to 12 lbs), small (7 to 18 lbs), medium (15 to 30 lbs), large (25 to 45+ lbs), petite toddler (20 to 30 lbs) and x-large (45+ lbs). Price: $16.95 to $17.95, www.fuzzibunz.com.

DIAPER DOUBLERS / INSERTS

If you are using pocket diapers, diaper doublers make trim and convenient stuffers. When you need extra absorbency in other cloth diapers, you can simply add a doubler. Jennifer even used diaper doublers alone with snugfitting wraps when a prefold was too bulky.

Hemp Babies: Little Weeds and Diaper Doublers are made with two layers of hemp fleece composed of 55% hemp and 45% certified organic cotton. This insert is serged with natural thread and seamed for easy folding. Little Weeds are available in both a small and a large size, Price: $3 to $7.95, www.cottonbabies.com.

Imse Vimse: Diaper doublers for extra absorbency available in 100% organic cotton terry cloth and 100% organic flannelette cotton liners. Price: $9.65 to $12.65 per pack (varies between 2 to 5 per pack), www.imsevimse.us.

JoeyBunz: Made by BabyKicks and originally designed to work with Fuzzi Bunz, these hemp doublers work well as inserts with any pocket diaper. Made with six layers of absorbent hemp/cotton jersey that is only 1/8" thick. Price: $5.27 to $5.73, www.babykicks.com.

Zany Zebra: This work-at-home-mom (WAHM) makes diaper doublers in an endless variety of hard-working, absorbent fabrics. And to add a little fun to diaper changes, Amy adds a line of fun decorative stitching around the edge. You may find hearts, stars, or positive thoughts like love, grow, play, and soar to make you smile. These diaper doublers are approximately 4" x 12" and are made of two trim layers of hemp/cotton terry or three layers of bamboo French terry or organic cotton. You doubler can be "naked" or topped with microfleece, suedecloth, velour, sherpa, organic cotton and organic velour. Price: $4.50 to $6.50, www.zany-zebra.com.

DIAPER LINERS

A thin material that is placed under baby's tush on the diaper. Liners make solid diaper clean up easier because they are flushable and bio-degradable. They do not add absorbency. Products sold as liners that add absorbency are found in our diaper doubler section. You can also find cloth liners made from silk or microfleece.

Hemp Babies: Raw silk contains antibacterial properties and a natural protein that aids in preventing and healing diaper rash without creams, lotions, or potions. Price: $2.60, www.cottonbabies.com.

Imse Vimse: They offer reusable and flushable options. Imse Vimse makes a polyester stay dry liner. Flushable liner options in baby and toddler sizes. The baby size comes in packs of 100 or 200. The toddler size comes in a pack of 100. Price: $6.50 to $11.60, www.imsevimse.us.

Kushies: These liners are flushable and biodegradable and look like a roll of toilet paper, with 100 perforated sheets per roll. Price: $6.50, www.kushies.com.

Mother-ease: These Stay-Dry Liners are reusable and made with microfleece. Price: $12.50 for a six-pack, www.mother-ease.com.

DIAPER PAIL / WET BAG

We love wet bags. Their uses go far beyond storing stinky diapers. Jennifer found using a wet bag much easier than using a diaper pail. You simply throw in your soiled diapers (after shaking off any solids in the toilet) and zip the bag. When it's laundry time, unzip the bag and push the diapers out into the washing machine. Wet bags are typically lined with PUL so they are waterproof, with a layer of cotton on the outside. You can find wet bags that are made by work-at-home moms and can be customized with your choice of fabric.

Bumkins: These wet bags are stain and odor resistant with a drawstring toggle closure. The bag measures 12" x 16.5" and features a 10" deep mesh pocket. Made of Bumkins' proprietary waterproof fabric that is PVC-, phthalate- and vinyl-free. Made in the USA. Price: $16.95, www.bumkins.com.

eco mom tip:

Keep several wet bags in different sizes on hand. They are great for storing wet clothing on the go, wet swimsuits after lessons and even baby wipes.

—*Janine Anderson,* Willow Glen, CA

Happy Tushies Wet Bag: A custom-made wet bag to hold baby's dirty cloth diapers. You can choose the fabric for the outside of the bag. This wet bag is zippered and the inside is lined with waterproof fabric. The regular size is approximately 11.5" x 12" and the large is approximately 13" x 13.5". Happy Tushies also makes other bags from make-up and wipe size to diaper pail liners. The Wonderbag is an innovative wet bag that allows you store wet and dry items separately. Price: $11 to $25, www.happytushies.com.

BABY WIPES

If you wish to avoid petroleum products, you will be interested to know that many conventional baby wipes may be a blend of cotton and polyester. Many traditional baby wipes are bleached with chlorine, which is hazardous for the environment and creates a carcinogenic dioxin byproduct. Many also contain synthetic ingredients, such as fragrance and parabens, preservatives that may irritate baby's skin and may be potentially toxic to baby. Please see our Green Choices chapter to find out specifics about harmful skin care ingredients. When Jennifer's pediatrician recommended rinsing traditional wipes before use, she searched for wipe alternatives. Fortunately, they exist in "greener" cloth, disposable and flushable wipes. We recommend buying about three to four dozen wipes to start.

bumGenius: The 100% Egyptian cotton flannel wipes are unbleached and sold 12 per package. Bamboo terry wipes are available in four colors: natural, twilight, grasshopper and butternut. Bamboo wipes are sold 8 per package. Price: $11.95 to $12.95, www.bumgenius.com.

Imse Vimse: Reusable cloth wipes in 100% organic cotton flannelette or terry cotton. Price: $4 to $10.20, www.imsevimse.us.

Seventh Generation: These disposable wipes are moistened with natural aloe vera, vitamin E, and water. These wipes are not bleached with chlorine and do not contain alcohol or synthetic ingredients. Wipes are available in an 80-count refillable tub, an 80-count refill pack and a 40-count travel pack. Seventh Generation encourages reuse of their tub, stating that each refill pack uses 90% less packaging than their hard plastic tub container. Price: $2.99 to $5.49, www.seventhgeneration.com.

Small Wonder Wipes: Highly rated by parents, Small Wonder makes a large selection of cloth wipes in fun colors, prints and fabrics. Small Wonder wipes come in two sizes: regular (8" x 8") and travel size (4.5" x 8"). Fabric choices are flannel, flannel with velour, flannel with sherpa, velour with sherpa or velour. Price: $3 to $7.50, www.smallwonderswipes.com.

Tushies: Disposable wipes that are hypoallergenic and alcohol-free. Tushies makes an unscented and lightly scented version. Both are made with aloe vera and vitamin E. Both versions are free of parabens, GMOs, propylene glycol and glutens. Tushies wipes are available in an 80-count tub and 80-count refill pack. Price: $4.29, www.tushies.com.

Tender Care: Also made by Tushies, these are the only natural-formula flushable wipes, making them great for travel. Tender Care wipes are hypoallergenic and made with aloe vera and vitamin E. They are free of alcohol, parabens, GMOs, propylene glycol and glutens. Tender Care wipes are available in a resealable 50-count travel pack. Price: $3.49, www.tushies.com.

Under The Nile: Cloth baby wipes with soft knit on one side and woven terry on the other side. These wipes are made with 100% organic Egyptian cotton. Price: $10 for six-pack, www.underthenile.com.

WIPE SOLUTIONS

If you are using cloth wipes, you can make or buy wipe solution for more effective cleansing. For most diaper changes, warm water and a soft cloth wipe is sufficient. Wipe solutions can offer natural antibacterial, soothing and aromatherapy properties. Wipe solutions can be sprayed onto a cloth wipe or directly onto baby's tush. You can also prepare a stack of wet cloth wipes with a dousing of wipe solution and store in a wet bag.

How to Make Cloth Wipe Solutions

By Amy S. Nogar, Owner Zany Zebra Designs, LLC, www.zany-zebra.com. It's so easy to make cloth wipe solution, and you'll save so much money making your own, we bet you'll never buy wipes solution again. Not only do these solutions work great for diaper changes, they're fantastic for cleaning sticky hands and messy faces too!

Most cloth wipe solutions contain certain common ingredients, each of which has an important role to play in cleansing your child's skin. The type and amounts of these ingredients is what gives each solution its own distinct "personality."

- Oil keeps the skin soft and helps the baby wipe glide smoothly across the skin.
- Soap cleanses the skin by removing all traces of urine and feces.
- Essential oil (EO) is often added for antibacterial and/or aromatherapy purposes.
- Water helps cleanse the skin and dilutes the other ingredients to the proper strength.

How to Mix Cloth Wipe Solutions

To mix a wipe solution, begin by pouring the proper amount of water into a container. Beginning with water helps keep bubbles to a minimum. Then add the oil, soap and EO if used. Measure the oil first—it will coat your measuring spoon so the soap slips right off. Often it's easier to mix your cloth wipe solution in a bottle with a cover, and then pour it into a storage container.

Storing and Applying Cloth Wipe Solutions

There are many ways to store and apply cloth wipe solutions; try a few of the following ideas to find the one that works best for you. Some families use one system at home and another when they're out and about.

- Use a spray bottle to spritz your cloth wipes, or spray directly on baby's bottom. (For baby's comfort we prefer spraying the cloth wipes.)
- Use a bottle with a pull-up spout, like a bottled-water container, to dribble solution onto the cloth wipes.
- Place the solution into a commercial baby wipes container and dip cloth wipes into the solution, or pour solution over the wipes.
- A commercial baby wipes container can be placed in a wipes warmer to provide cozy warm wipes for baby.
- Solution that is stored for a long time may become musty, so check your solution often and plan to make smaller batches more frequently instead of large batches less often. If you pre-wet your wipes, be sure to check them daily because they may grow mildew if they sit too long.

Cloth Wipe Solution Recipes

Here are three recipes to get you started. For more recipes, check out www.zany-zebra.com/wipe-solution-recipes.shtml.

- **Basic Wipe Solution:** *This basic recipe can be personalized by changing the type of soap or oil.* Mix together 3 cups water, 1/4 cup baby oil and 1/4 cup baby wash.
- **Apricot Solution:** *The apricot oil smells absolutely heavenly—what a pampering treat!* Mix together 3 cups water, 1 tablespoon apricot oil and 1 tablespoon unscented baby wash.
- **Lavender Solution:** *Lavender is known for its calming properties, Try this one before nap or bedtime.* Mix together 3 cups water, 1 tablespoon regular baby oil, 1 tablespoon lavender scented baby wash and 2–3 drops lavender essential oil.

ITSABELLY'S BABY WIPE SOLUTION RECOMMENDATIONS

Baby Bits: An antibacterial and fragrant wipes solution. Baby Bits are small squares of soap that you drop into wipe warmer or spray bottle with warm water to dissolve. Baby Bits are made out of mild glycerin soap with oil infused with plantain, chickweed herbs, tea tree oil and lavender essential oil. One box (three ounces) makes approximately 50 cups of wipes solution, and it can be made one cup at a time. Price: $9.95, www.soaps-bydenise.com.

bumGenius Bum Cleaner: A proprietary formula made with natural and organic ingredients including cucumber extract and aloe leaf juice, it contains no essential oils, making this a good choice for sensitive or irritated skin. This spray has a light, 100% natural vanilla scent (*Vanilla planifolia*). It is paraben-free, phthalate-free and is not tested on animals. Price: $9.95, www.bumgenius.com.

Kissaluvs Lotion Potion: A diaper lotion spray and concentrate to use as a wipe solution with cloth wipes. Kissaluv's Lotion Potion is made with witch hazel, jojoba oil infused with chamomile, lavender essential oil and tea tree essential oil. Other suggested uses include as a diaper pail spray, a face and aftershave spray and a soothing bug and insect bite spray. Kissaluv's Lotion Potion is available as a 4-oz spray or a 4-oz bottle of concentrate. Price: $7.95 to $14.95, www.kissaluvs.com.

Sunshine Spray: This 4-oz spray is made with rose, lavender, chamomile, orange blossom and witch hazel floral waters, and is alcohol-free. Mama Rose's Natural's makes this aromatherapeutic, antiseptic, anti-bacterial, and anti-inflammatory spray. Price: $12, www.mamarosesnaturals.com.

DIAPER CHANGING PAD

Most mainstream changing pads may contain vinyl, polyurethane foam, or stain-resistant coatings that may be toxic to baby's health and the environment. You can also use the mattress pads we recommend in the Nursery Furniture section—just fold them.

A Natural Home Changing Table Pad: Machine washable quilted organic cotton changing table pad. This pad also works with Natural Home's Simply Affordable and Zen changing tables. Price: $80, www.anaturalhome.com.

Organic Caboose: A merino wool changing pad that measures 31" x 54". The EcoFleece Changing Pad measures 17" x 28". EcoFleece is made from Polartec's EcoSpun® fleece using 89% recycled soda pop and PETE containers. EcoSpun fleece delivers a soft, luxurious, color-fast product without depleting the Earth's natural resources, without herbicides or pesticides and without extensive energy use. It is a viable end-use for PETE containers. Made in the USA. Price: $7.99 to $27.99, www.organiccaboose.com.

Holy Lamb Organics: An eco-wool-filled pad with sturdy organic cotton canvas that is designed to fit a standard changing table. The pad measures 17.5"W x 34"L x 2"D. Other accessories include wool or flannel covers to use with the changing pad. Price: $50 to $125, www.holylamborganics.com.

Happy Tushies: A custom-design changing pad that works well for travel. You can choose a fun print fabric for the top of the pad. You can even send Happy Tushies your own fabric! The pad has sewn binding around the edge and a layer of waterproof PUL inside with a quilted cotton pad bottom. Very nice place to change a tushie and fits well in any diaper bag. Available in regular or large sizes. Price: $14.50, www.happytushies.com.

DIAPER CHANGING PAD COVER

What baby wouldn't love to be changed on the softness of an organic cotton or wool changing pad cover? We recommend buying two covers.

Giggle: A changing pad cover made from 22-oz organic cotton sherpa. It measures 20" x 30". Price: $40, www.giggle.com.

Holy Lamb Organics: You can use these covers with a Holy Lamb Organics changing pad or over another pad. The wool cover is eco-grown wool and is strapless. The flannel cover is made out a two-layer quilted organic cotton with straps on the four corners to secure it to the changing table pad. Price: $50 to $75, www.holylamborganics.com.

EcoBedroom: An organic sherpa fleece cotton changing pad cover surrounded by elastic for a snug fit to standard changing pads. Size: 20" x 30". Price: $39.95, www.ecobedroom.com.

DIAPER SPRAYER

A nifty little sprayer that you install onto your toilet (simple to do). You can spray solid waste off the diaper and into the toilet where it belongs. You can use this with disposables and cloth diapers. This sprayer can also be used as mini-bidet for adults and children. Jennifer uses her diaper sprayer for rinsing little potties as well.

bumGenius Diaper Sprayer: A chrome high-pressure spray that comes with sprayer, fixtures, hose and mounting clip. Price: $39.95, www.bumgenius.com.

MiniShower: A white high-pressure diaper sprayer that comes with the sprayer, solid brass chrome-plated tee adapter, adjustable hose, wand holder. Price: $44.95 to $79.95, www.minishower.com.

feeding

• • •

For many moms deciding what and how you feed your child is one of the most important areas for thinking "green." You will have many choices to make regarding how you feed your child.

Right off the bat, let me say that we encourage all mothers to try breast-feeding and making homemade food when baby starts solids. We offer some great resources for breastfeeding support and yummy cookbooks to help you make your own baby food. As real moms, we know that how you feed your child changes as they grow and your situation also changes. We offer you a range of green feeding options, so that you can pick the combination that feels right and works well for both you and your growing family.

According to the EPA and National Academy of Sciences, "standard chemicals are up to ten times more toxic to children than adults, depending on body weight." (EPA 175-F96-001, National Academy of Sciences, "Pesticides in the Diets of Infants and Children.") Also, babies in the womb and small children are perhaps more at risk from the harmful effects of chemicals in food because of their developing organs.

In choosing organic food and related products, pay attention to the ingredient label. Yes, going green does take a lot of label reading! Is the product certified organic? Read our Green Labels chapter to better grasp organic certification and different certifiers' standards. Different organic certifiers follow different standards. In general, choosing organic means that the product in question should be grown without toxic chemicals such as synthetic growth hormones, antibiotics, synthetic herbicides, pesticides or chemical fertilizers. Organic certification is the only way to ensure that organic standards have been met.

So, does organic food taste better? Many organic connoisseurs feel that

EPA FISH GUIDELINES

Women who may become pregnant, are pregnant or nursing, and small children are urged to follow EPA guidelines for fish consumption. The EPA acknowledges that fish and shellfish contain quality protein, omega-3 fatty acids, essential nutrients and are low in saturated fat. These qualities promote heart health and brain-growth development in children. Therefore, eating fish and shellfish is part of a well-balanced diet. However, nearly all fish and shellfish contain traces of mercury that can harm the developing nervous system of a baby.

EPA Recommendations:
- Do not eat shark, swordfish, king mackerel or tilefish. They are known to contain high levels of mercury.
- Eat up to 12 oz (two average meals) a week of a variety of fish and shellfish that are lower in mercury.
- Five of the most commonly eaten fish low in mercury are shrimp, canned light tuna, salmon, pollock, and catfish.
- Another commonly eaten fresh fish, albacore ("white") tuna, has more mercury than canned light tuna. So, when choosing your two meals of fish and shellfish, you may eat up to 6 ounces (one average meal) of albacore tuna per week.
- Check local advisories about the safety of fish caught by family and friends in your local lakes, rivers, and coastal areas. If no advice is available, eat up to 6 ounces (one average meal) per week of fish you catch from local waters, but don't consume any other fish during that week.

As this book goes to print, the most recent guidelines are from 2004. The guidelines can change slightly. Please see the EPA website for any updates, www.epa.gov/waterscience/fish/advice/index.html.

organic food does taste better. Many groups believe that (a) using natural practices growing food, practices that enhance the soil's nutrients, has a wonderful side effect: it also enhances taste; (b) organic food is healthier because of the lack of potentially harmful chemical ingredients used to

cultivate the food; and (c) organic agriculture is better for our environment because toxic chemicals are not disrupting the eco-system. In some
organic products, it's easy to tell a difference. Crack an organic egg and a
non-organic egg and you can't help but notice the difference in yolk color
and size. Even better, find a source for locally-produced eggs. You'll never
buy eggs at the supermarket again.

Which brings us to another point—life-cycle analysis. Debate is growing
about which is better for the environment—an organic product grown
elsewhere and shipped to a faraway destination, or a non-organic locally
produced product. While one product is grown organically in another
hemisphere, much energy is expended bringing that product to consumers in another hemisphere, often out of their local season. You will
have to decide your preference based on your local area and product
availabilities. We try to buy local organic food and focus on in-season
products when possible. We also love to shop at local farmers' markets
and get to know the people growing our food.

PLASTICS AND FEEDING

If you are reading this book, you have probably heard all the recent news
about toxic plastic baby bottles. It probably scared you, as it did us.

At some point in feeding your child, you will run into plastic. We have
been using non-toxic feeding gear for quite some time now, before it
went mainstream. We are so happy that news of these potentially toxic
chemicals is making national headlines—it is about time! Since you have
already read our Green Choices chapter in which Alicia Voorhies, the
founder of The Soft Landing (a great online boutique for PVC-, BPA- and
phthalate-free shopping), gives her advice on potential toxins lurking in
baby products. Here is a quick recap:

- **Bisphenol A (BPA)**, a chemical that makes plastic shatterproof and is
  found in polycarbonate plastic, is dangerous because it may cause
  adverse health effects, such as: increase in obesity and diabetes, interference with the normal development of unborn babies, stimulation
  of mammary gland development (a risk factor for breast cancer), and
  early onset of puberty. Polycarbonate plastic is usually marked with the

number seven recycling symbol.

- **Phthalates** are also a plastic softener or "plasticizer." These can be dangerous because they may disrupt hormonal balances. The European Union Parliament banned or partially banned the use of certain phthalates in children's toys. Phthalates can also be found in household products, personal care products and medical supplies. In animal tests, phthalates have been linked to reproductive and neurological damage.

- **Polyvinyl Chloride (PVC)** is widely used in plastics—think shower curtains, pipes and toys. Researchers believe that over time PVC releases toxins, such as mercury, dioxins, and phthalates. PVC products are often found to contain lead, which is added as a stabilizer. PVC plastic releases carcinogenic dioxins when produced or burned. PVC is usually marked with the number three recycling symbol and it is also one of the most difficult plastics to recycle.

Plastic Research

Our favorite resources for plastic research.

- **Center for Environmental Health:** Studies on lead in plastic-based products, www.cehca.org.
- **Center for Health, Environment & Justice:** Informative BPA and PVC guides, www.chej.org.
- **Environment California:** Great research and guide on toxic baby bottles, www.environmentcalifornia.org.
- **Environmental Working Group:** www.ewg.org.
- **Safe Mama:** www.safemama.com.
- **The Soft Landing:** Research the "learn" section, www.thesoftlanding.com.
- **ZRecs BPA Survey:** www.zrecs.blogspot.com/2008/02/z-report-on-bpa-in-infant-care-products.html.
- **ZRecs Mobile Product Check:** Use your phone and text messaging to check products while shopping, www.zrecs.blogspot.com/2008/02/use-z-report-at-store-with-text.html.

- **ZRecs BPA-Free Wallet Card:** Print out this handy shopping guide, www.zrecs.blogspot.com/2008/03/bpa-wallet-card.html.

BREAST, PUMP OR BOTTLE

Breastfeeding your baby is just about *the* greenest choices you can make as a mother. We encourage all mothers to try breastfeeding. Health professionals all agree that breast milk is the best food for your baby. The composition of your breast milk changes to meet the needs of your growing baby. Breastfeeding doesn't require constant bottle washing and preparation, therefore uses less energy—though, as many moms know, something that is so natural may take work. Consulting with a lactation consultant helped Melissa overcome some breastfeeding difficulty and develop a feeding plan that worked for her and baby. Jennifer started attending her local La Leche League meeting while she was pregnant and found the women supportive and knowledgeable whenever she had questions about breastfeeding and nutrition.

Our goal is to provide you with options regarding the tools available to help you breastfeed, especially if you are going back to work. And if breastfeeding doesn't work out for you, we also want you to know the safest ways to feed your baby. No matter which method you choose, you will need support and resources for your decision. As with everything in parenthood, choice can be an evolving decision. Staying flexible, keeping an open mind and making conscious choices will allow you to do the best for your baby.

Itsabelly's Recommended Feeding Necessities
- **Breastfeeding:** Burp cloths, nursing bra and pads, nursing pillow and nipple cream.
- **Pumping Breast Milk:** Burp cloths, nursing bra and pads, nursing pillow, nipple cream, breast pump, four 4 to 8 oz baby bottles, bottle drying rack, breast milk storage containers, insulated bottle holder, bottle brush and dishwasher basket for bottle accessories.
- **Bottle-feeding:** six 4 to 8 oz bottles, insulated bottle holder for diaper bag, bottle brush, bottle drying rack and dishwasher basket for bottle accessories.

BURP CLOTHS

Regular cloth prefold diapers are great to use as burp clothes—practical and inexpensive. Sure, it's nice to have a few "cute" burp cloths, but you will need some that you don't mind getting dirty. After their lives as burp cloths (or diapers), prefold diapers make great rags around the house. We recommend three packs.

BabyKicks Hemparoo®: A hemp-based, absorbent prefold diaper that is 55% hemp and 45% cotton fleece. Hemparoos come in sizes from newborn to large toddler. Price: $6.59 to $9.56, www.babykicks.com.

Green Mountain Cloth-Eez: One of the most popular sources for high quality, heavyweight 100% cotton twill diapers. The white prefolds are bleached using hydrogen peroxide, not chlorine, and are dioxin and acid-free. Green Mountain also sells unbleached Indian prefolds. Since unbleached prefolds have not been degummed, they need to be washed in hot water to remove the natural cotton oils more than bleached prefolds. Green Mountain prefolds are offered in nine sizes ranging from preemie to toddler. Price: $14 to $36 per dozen, www.greenmountaindiapers.com.

Pro Services: Many diaper services use these durable 100% cotton twill prefold diapers. Pro Services prefolds are available in five sizes from preemie to toddler. Price: $18.50 to $24.50 per dozen, www.prodiaper.net.

Under The Nile: These prefolds are 100% Egyptian organic cotton made with milton knit and a three-layer terry liner. Price: four for $34, www.underthenile.com.

NURSING BRA

You will get a lot of wear from a nursing bra that is easy to use, supportive and comfortable to wear. Some nursing advocates warn that underwire bras can cause clogged milk ducts. Some moms, however, can't live without an underwire! Jennifer skipped the traditional nursing bra and opted for a stretchy cotton bra that she could easily pull over to one side for nursing. Melissa loved her comfy Bravado nursing bra. It was so easy to use that nursing in it was a snap. We recommend having at least two nursing bras in rotation and three if you wish to do less wash or want a certain style for certain clothing.

Blue Canoe: While not marketed specifically as nursing bras, nursing mothers often use the Jane Bra Top and the Cross-over Bra, organic cotton bras that provide gentle support and contain no elastic or latex. The fabric is 90% organic cotton and 10% Lycra, so they have just the right amount of stretch and provide easy access for nursing. Both bras are available in natural and a variety of low-impact-dyed colors. Made in the USA. Price: $24 to $32, www.bluecanoe.com.

Essential Nursing Bra Tank with Bamboo: Bravado makes this eco-friendly nursing tank with a built-in nursing bra. Bamboo is an eco-friendly fabric option offering breathability and wicking properties. A bamboo nursing bra will soon be released, according to telephone customer support. Bravado makes perhaps the best and most supportive nursing bras in a wide range of styles. We hope they begin to offer more organic and eco-friendly options. Price: $30 to $45, www.bravadodesigns.com.

Under The Nile: A tank top style with crossover openings for nursing. Soft 100% Egyptian organic cotton and 2% lycra knit make this bra stretchy and comfortable. Price: $16, www.underthenile.com.

NURSING PADS

In the beginning weeks of breastfeeding and during growth spurts, many women need nursing pads to absorb leaks. Some moms find they need to wear nursing pads the entire time the breastfeed. Washable, reusable pads are really simple to use and can reduce your waste. Jennifer was pleased with her cotton and wool nursing pads and threw them in the wash in a lingerie bag. Some moms may prefer to wear disposable pads while they are out on the town.

Danish Woolen Delight: Wool can absorb up to 40% of its weight without feeling wet—perfect for breast pads. We love the softness of these pads and the thoughtfulness of shapes and sizes so that your pads don't show through your t-shirt. The Original is double-layer wool. The Ekstra is felted wool for a greater barrier effect and absorption. To avoid bulk in your bra, the larger sizes of Ekstra have felted wool only in the most needed areas. The Softline, made from untreated organic wool that is mechanically processed with a newly patented method, makes a more economical choice. Danish Woolen Delight nursing pads are offered in mini, x-small, small, medium large and oval (teardrop shaped). Price: $12.99 to $26.99, www.danishwool.com.

Lansinoh: These 100% cotton washable pads aren't organic, but the contour shape worked well for Jennifer. One box contains four pads. Price: $8.99, www.lansinoh.com.

Organic Essentials: Organic cotton disposable nursing pads. One package contains 30 pads. Price: $6.45, www.organicessentials.com.

Under The Nile: Organic Egyptian cotton washable nursing pads with soft flannel knit and one layer of absorbent terry liner. Price: $5, www.underthenile.com.

NURSING PILLOW

A good quality and comfortable nursing pillow is essential to breastfeeding, and comfy for bottle-feeding too! A nursing pillow can have a life beyond feeding time—it is great for baby's tummy time or as a sitting prop. We selected pillows that use organic fabrics and natural fillings. Parents wishing to avoid petroleum-based products should choose a pillow filled with wool or cotton rather than the polyfil of many mainstream nursing pillows.

Nesting Pillow: Organic cotton canvas covers the organic buckwheat hull filling of this nursing pillow by Blessed Nest. Buckwheat hulls interlock to give the pillow stability and flexibility while allowing air to circulate. It is about 30"W x 16"D x 5"H and weighs 6 lbs. The slipcover has a 26" zipper and is easily removable for machine washing. The top and bottom of the slipcover is made of a thick, absorbent terry cloth, and the banding fabrics are 100% cotton. The slipcover is pre-washed and dried to preshrink and to remove any of the fabric's finishes. The pillow is handmade in the USA and most of the materials are from sustainable, organic and/or domestic mills. Price: $79 to $84, www.blessednest.com.

Organic Caboose Maternity/Nursing Pillow: An organic nursing pillow covered and stuffed with pure organic cotton to support your baby during feedings. Organic Caboose's pillow measures 25"L x 16"W x 6"H. It comes in an unbleached natural cotton color. A zippered pillowcase in seven colors is sold separately. Made in USA. Price: $49.99, www.organiccaboose.com.

Organic Cotton & Wool Nursing Pillow: An organic cotton cover that is filled with pure wool to support your baby at the right height for nursing. Pillowcases are available to protect the pillow. This organic nursing pillow comes in natural flannel, natural with shell print or blue flannel. Price $80, www.motherearthnurserydesigns.com.

TOPICAL TREATMENT NIPPLE CREAM

A high quality nipple treatment cream is essential in the first weeks of breastfeeding when chapped and sore nipples can be a hindrance to breastfeeding success. Since you are putting the cream where baby nurses, it is important to choose a cream with high quality, pure ingredients. We give you a vegan and organic option and a more conventional option. Nursing mothers should be aware that lanolin is derived from sheep; therefore it may carry trace pesticide and antibiotic residue or be unsuitable for those with a wool allergy or who are vegan.

eco mom tip:

Breast milk is the best nipple cream—and it's free! It can be applied to soothe sore, cracked nipples.

Lansinoh: The only topical nipple treatment that is endorsed by La Leche League International in the USA. Created with a patented refining process, that removes all allergenic components and brings the lowest level possible of any environmental impurities (including pesticide residues). Lansinoh uses ultra-pure, medical-grade lanolin to help heal sore, cracked nipples. It is the only lanolin available that contains no preservatives or additives. It does not have to be removed before breastfeeding. We should note that this is a lanolin product, therefore not recommended for vegans, vegetarians or those with wool allergies. Some women love this product, while others do not like its thicker-than-honey consistency. Its plastic tube is free from plasticizers including BPA and phthalates. Price: $7.99, www.lansinoh.com.

Motherlove Nipple Cream: Certified organic marshmallow root, calendula, olive oil, shea butter and beeswax make up this popular cream. It does not need to be washed off before nursing. You can also use Nipple Cream for diaper rash or skin irritations. Motherlove claims that Nipple Cream does not contain lanolin, which contains several pesticides, or Vitamin E, which should not be ingested by infants. All Motherlove products are tested for bacteria, lead and heavy metals. Motherlove products do not contain dairy, egg, fish, shellfish, tree nuts, peanuts, wheat or gluten. Price: $9.95 to $15.95, www.motherlove.com.

Nipple Butter: Earth Mama Angel Baby makes the first certified vegan, organic, all natural, plant-based balm created without lanolin. Soothing Nipple Butter is made with cocoa butter, shea butter, mango butter and healing calendula. No need to wash this natural formula off before nursing. Nipple Butter comes in one-ounce and two-ounce sizes. Price: $9.95 to $14.95, www.earthmamaangelbaby.com.

MANUAL BREAST PUMP

A manual breast pump is usually sufficient for occasional use. Although, Jennifer had success with her hand pump to store breast milk for when Vava (Grandma) was babysitting, she would not have wanted to rely on it if she needed to pump full time. If you ever spend the night away from your baby, do not forget to pack your breast pump in mom's suitcase!

Medela Harmony Breastpump: The unique 2-Phase Expression pumping system from Medela gives mom a faster let-down, which reduces pumping time. The let-down mode mimics baby's rapid initial suckling and expression mode simulates baby's slower, deeper nursing. The ergonomic

swivel handle and massaging SoftFit breastshield make this a comfortable hand pump.
Conversion kits allow you to upgrade to
either the Medela Symphony or Medela
Lactina electric pumps. All parts that come
into contact with breast milk are BPA/
DEHP-free. The Harmony breast pump
includes a SoftFit Breastshield, a container
stand, two five-ounce containers and lids.
Price: $35, www.medelabreastfeedingus.com.

ELECTRIC BREAST PUMP

If you are pumping on a regular basis we recommend using a personal
electric breast pump or hospital grade breast pump. While more expensive than hand pumps it is worth the investment. Be aware that many
non-hospital grade pumps are marked as "single-user" products because
of contamination risk—milk can be aspirated into the pump mechanism,
which cannot be sterilized. La Leche League recommends that "if a mother needs to pump to increase her milk supply, provide milk for a premature baby or other situations where the baby is not breastfeeding to
provide stimulation for the mother's breasts, the hospital-grade rental
pumps are the preferred option."

Medela® Pump in Style Advanced: Melissa and baby Isabella were both
very happy with this efficient and comfortable electric breast pump. All
parts that come into contact with breast milk are BPA/DEHP-free. The
2-Phase Expression pumping mimics baby's nursing rhythms allowing
for maximum milk flow. The let-down mode simulates baby's initial
fast suckling. Expression mode simulates baby's slower, deeper suckling.
Adjustable speed and vacuum control give you a customized pumping
experience. Packaged in a convenient and stylish shoulder bag, other
accessories include a battery pack, removable cooler carrier, four collection containers and lids, two PersonalFit™ Breastshields, two valves, four
membranes and a cooling element. Price $249 to 279,
www.medelabreastfeedingus.com.

BOTTLES

News about toxic baby bottles has splashed the front pages of newspa-pers and held the nightly news headlines. We are so fortunate that many parents are learning about ingredients that are toxic and do not belong anywhere near a baby's bottle. In the past few months of writing this book, the amount of change in the industry is amazing. Environment-alists and mom bloggers have long called attention to the problems of bisphenol A, phthalates and PVC. Companies are waking up and realizing that customers demand safe products. Since we started writing this book, many mainstream companies have made announcements that they are ridding their products of BPA. We look forward to updating our blog with this information. In addition to the consumer out-cry, we think these "big" manufacturers also got a little worried about the stiff compe-tition they are starting to receive from the new-to-the-market, alterna-tive bottle brands we recommend below. We herald the competition and innovation and thanks to all the mamas out there who've spoken up and demanded safe products. Don't forget to read our Green Choices chapter for more information about toxic baby bottle ingredients.

We recommend having at least four bottles for pumping moms and six to eight bottles for bottle-feeding. Moms switching between nursing and bottle-feeding may have more success with wide neck bottles and slower flow nipples. The wider neck seems to provide more of a "cushion" for baby's mouth similar to the breast. Bottle nipples usually flow faster and at a constant rate, which is different from the breast where baby may "work" a little more to get milk that arrives at varying rates. A slower flow nipple may be more similar to mommy's nipple for baby. It often takes a few attempts to find the "perfect" bottle for baby, so prepare for some of your own product testing.

Adiri: This revolutionary bottle design mimics breastfeeding. The bottle is 100% BPA-, phthalate-, vinyl chloride- and polycarbonate-free. The bottle features a unique "Fill, Twist and Feed" system and comes in an 8-oz size. Adiri bottles come in Stage One (newborn to three months), Stage Two (three to six months) and Stage Three (six months old and older). The Adiri Petal™ vent system reduces air ingestion. Price: $11.95, www.adiri.com.

BornFree Bottles: Glass and BPA- and phthalate-free plastic bottles in 5-oz and 9-oz sizes. The plastic bottles are made from a safer alternative plastic, polyethersulfone (PES). BornFree offers a wide selection of nipple sizes and flow rates: slow flow, medium flow, fast flow, y-cut fast flow, variable flow and y-cut wide neck. The bottles feature an inner air valve and vent. Price: $9.99 to $19.99, www.newbornfree.com.

Evenflo Glass Bottles: These classic glass baby bottles are easy to find at baby super stores. Evenflo glass bottles come in four or eight ounce bottles. Evenflo makes latex and silicone nipples. Price: $2, www.evenflo.com.

Green To Grow: Bottles made from the safe, durable and heat-resistant plastic polyethersulfone (PES), which is BPA- and phthalate-free. Green to Grow bottles come in 5-oz and 10-oz options with regular and wide neck versions. The nitrosamine-free silicone nipples come in beginner, intermediate and expert flow rates. As a company, Green to Grow implemented a "Bottles to Babies" bottle recycling and donation program, uses 100% recycled paper and soy inks in packaging and corporate materials, and donates 1% of annual sales to environmental causes. Price: $7.49 to $10.49, www.greentogrow.com.

Think Baby: These bottles are free of BPA, PVC, nitrosamines and lead. The bottles are made from the safe, durable and heat resistant plastic polyethersulfone (PES). Think Baby bottles feature a patented venting system to help reduce colic. They even come in recycled packaging. The bottles come in 5-oz and 9-oz sizes. Silicone nipples come in a slow, medium and fast flow version. Price: $16.99 for two pack, www.thinkbabybottles.com.

Wee Go: A modern take on the glass baby bottle. The bottles are covered with a soft sleeve that helps protect the bottle from breaking. Wee Go bottles are BPA-, phthalate-, PVC- and polycarbonate-free. The non-toxic, plastic-free sleeve comes in six bright colors. Currently, Wee Go sells only Stage 1 silicone nipples (for newborn to six months). Bottle and sleeve are dishwasher safe. Price: $17.95, www.gobabylife.com.

BOTTLE DRYING RACK

If you are using bottles, you will be washing bottles—frequently, and bottles need a place to dry. Conventional dish drainers are not particularly convenient for drying six baby bottles and parts, and you may not want your dish drainer sitting on the counter for hours. Today you can find well-designed drying racks that aren't even an eyesore.

Bottle Tree: Made by L'ovedbaby. This wooden bottle drying rack is a wonderful alternative to plastic drying racks. The unique tree design saves precious countertop space. The Bottle Tree can hold up to 12 baby bottles plus other accessories. It is water-sealed and has an attached drainage plug. Price: $25, www.lovedbaby.com.

Munchkin: The number one drying rack in America holds bottles, nipples, cups, valves, straws and a bottle brush. A built-in reservoir keeps your countertop dry. The patented design folds flat to reduce storage space. Two peg heights hold accessories of all sizes. Price: $7.95, www.munchkin.com.

Prince Lionheart: The Complete Drying Station accommodates all sizes of cups, bottles, nipples and cup parts. It adjusts to fit all sinks and counters. The slanted design allows for thorough drying without puddles of water. Prince Lionheart products are BPA-, PVC- and phthalate-free. Price: $12.99, www.princelionheart.com.

Splash: Melissa didn't mind leaving bottles drying on the counter in her Splash rack. In fact, visitors always commented how hip and stylish it looked. Skip*Hop makes this modern bottle drying rack that is BPA-, pthalate- and PVC-free. The unique circular design saves counter space and has special spaces to accommodate nipples, straws, valves and bottles. A handy bottle brush is even incorporated into the design. The Splash comes in white, poppy, and marine colors. Price: $28, www.skiphop.com.

DISHWASHER BASKET FOR BOTTLE ACCESSORIES

Using a dishwasher basket will save you from searching for that transparent-colored sippy cup valve in the bottom of your dishwasher in the midst of all those bits of leftover food. Melissa was always relieved that she could use her basket to keep all of Isabella's little bottle accessories in one space so they wouldn't get lost. Without it, her dishwasher seemed to enjoy playing the same game our washing machines do with socks.

Dr. Browns: A PVC-, phthalate- and BPA-free dishwasher basket in two different versions—one for standard bottles and another for wide neck bottles. Price: $5.99, www.handi-craft.com.

Luv'n Care: A BPA-free polypropylene dishwasher basket that can hold nipples, pacifiers and other small bottle and sippy cup parts. Price: $4.99, www.nuby.platformtwo.com.

Munchkin: The Deluxe Dishwasher Basket and Mini Dishwasher Basket are both BPA-free. These unique dishwasher baskets have straw cleaning rack that hold items upright. The Deluxe version holds eight straws and the mini holds four straws. Versions also have a nipple-sanitizing lid—the Deluxe holds 14 nipples and the Mini holds six nipples. The baskets have locking lids so everything stays in place. The white baskets even come accented in four different colors—blue, pink, green or yellow. Price: $4.95, www.munchkin.com.

Toddler Dishwasher Basket: Prince Lionheart claims that this is the largest capacity dishwasher basket available. It is top rack safe and fits all dishwashers. A removable sippy cup valve basket is included. Prince Lionheart products are BPA-, PVC- and phthalate-free. Price: $16.99, www.princelionheart.com.

BOTTLE BRUSH

If you are washing bottles, a bottle brush will help you help you do the job right.

Nuby Bottle and Nipple Brush Set: A set designed with soft and durable nylon bristles. The brush has a sponge tip and snap-in nipple brush that makes hard-to-reach areas easier to clean. Price: $3.95, www.nuby.platformtwo.com.

BREAST MILK STORAGE BAGS OR CONTAINERS

You have done the hard work of pumping precious breast milk—high five, mom! Now you need something to store that liquid gold and you don't want your storage container to taint your milk with plastic toxins. Breast milk storage bags take up less space to store because they can lay flat in the freezer. Sometimes storage bags can be messy if you aren't careful pouring the milk into a bottle. Storage bottles take up more freezer space, but can be a wonderful time (and mess) saver when they work with your breast pump or bottle.

Lansinoh: Breast milk storage in freezer bags and 5-oz storage bottles. The storage bags are made of 100% virgin plastic and are 100% BPA-free. The storage bottles are 100% BPA-free and made of polypropylene, a safe plastic for breast milk storage that is chemical additive-free. The bottles come four to a pack. The bags are available in 25 or 50 packs. Price: $7.49 to $9.99, www.lansinoh.com.

Mother's Milkmate: You can pump, freeze and feed—all from the same Mother's Milkmate bottle! The bottles are compatible with most standard pump systems including Medela and Lansinoh. Mother's Milkmate storage bottles are made from polypropylene plastic and are BPA-free. The bottles come with removable freezer labels for freshness dating. Top rack dishwasher safe. The Breast Milk Storage System comes with ten storage bottles, a "First In/First Out Breast Milk Storage Rack™" that keeps the freshest bottle easily available. Price: $13.95 to 28.95, www.mothersmilkmate.com.

STARTING SOLIDS

Some of your most memorable times with baby will be watching his facial expressions as he tries new foods and textures. The transition to feeding your baby solids will be a big step—and it doesn't have to be food from a jar. You can make homemade baby food in the comfort of your own kitchen with the right equipment and the right ingredients. Going organic is even healthier for your baby and better for our environment. Advertising produce as organic means farmers must grow for three years without the application of synthetic pesticides or chemicals. Look for the USDA Certified Organic or QAI labels on each food item to make sure you're buying a certified organic product.

eco mom tip:

If you freeze baby food use foil, freezer paper or freezer bags coded with #4 and stay away from plastic or glass not labeled freezer safe. Always cool your food well before storing it.

Melissa felt that feeding Isabella the healthiest and freshest foods possible when she entered the solid foods stage was critical for her baby's growing little body. She had heard from other moms that making your own baby food instead of buying pre-packaged baby foods was easy and better for the health of baby and the environment. She knew it would take a bit more effort to prepare baby food but it was worth it to her keeping Isabella's good health as a priority. Jennifer was able to cut down on baby food preparation time by serving baby food that was part of the family's meal.

Melissa was given the baby food cookbook titled *Superfoods For Babies and Children* (US edition) written by Annabel Karmel, as a baby gift, and it's become her favorite baby shower gift to give to friends. Melissa substituted organic ingredients in the recipes where she could to make Isabella's meals as nutritious as possible. Preparation took the most time but with the right tools, it was easy! Melissa was also concerned about the premium she had to pay for organic foods so she looked up the list of the most chemical-laden produce. She found it was wisest to narrow down her organic shopping list to the items that were most exposed to toxic chemicals.

Itsabelly's Tips For Choosing Safe Food
The Environmental Working Group recommends buying only organic for the following produce members of the "Dirty Dozen," which have been found to contain the highest levels of pesticides. The "Tempting Twelve" is produce with the lowest levels of found pesticides. If you are watching your budget (and who isn't these days?) or don't have many organic options at your local grocery store, these lists will help you maximize your grocery dollars.

- **Dirty Dozen:** Apples, bell peppers, celery, cherries, imported grapes, nectarines, peaches, pears, potatoes, red raspberries, spinach and strawberries.
- **Tempting Twelve:** Asparagus, avocados, bananas, broccoli, cauliflower, sweet corn, kiwi, mangos, onions, papaya, pineapples and sweet peas.
- Print out the EWG wallet produce guide to make shopping trips a breeze: www.foodnews.org.
- For protein sources, try to buy organic, hormone- and antibiotic-free chicken, turkey, beef. USDA regulations do not allow hormones in pork or poultry. As of March 2008, the USDA is finalizing its standard for meat that would carry a "naturally-raised" claim. The Itsabelly Blog, www.itsabelly.typepad.com will be updated for details.

Itsabelly's Tips For Choosing Safe Food Storage

All the recent news about plastics leaching bad toxins got you worried about how to store your leftovers? If you don't want to go anywhere near plastic, glass or stainless steel is always the safest solution. Here are some options to consider for storing your family's food.

- Anchor Hocking and Pyrex make glass baking, bowls and storage items. www.pyrexware.com, www.anchorhocking.com.
- Stainless steel bowls are easy to find at local cooking stores or online.
- For safe plastics to store your food in, choose containers with recycling codes on the bottom #1 PETE, #2 HDPE, #4 LDPE and #5 PP.
- CorningWare Pop-Ins makes stoneware which can go from freezer to oven or microwave, www.corningware.com.
- Check out *The Green Guide's* comprehensive list of safe plastic food containers by Andreea Matei, www.thegreenguide.com/doc/95/containers.

Itsabelly's Baby Food Cooking Tips

You really don't need any special equipment for preparing food for baby. Here's what we keep handy: food processor, blender or food mill; cutting board; peeler; knife; ice cube tray or plastic freezer containers; measuring spoons and cup; freezer tape; steamer; pot with lid; roasting pan; permanent marker or Dry Erase pen.

- Baby food is pureed, mashed or strained. Have fun and create different tastes for your baby.
- Steam vegetables and fruits. Peel the hard skin off fruits like apples and pears before steaming them. Steaming them will help make the fruit soft and easy to puree.
- Sauteé chicken, beef or turkey with some extra virgin olive oil, chopped onion, tomatoes and garlic to add some great flavor. Then puree the meat with some steamed carrots or sweet potato (use any vegetable you like).
- Do not add sugar or salt—your baby's body doesn't need anything extra in this department.
- You can feed your baby the same food you're eating—before you add the seasonings.
- Neither peanuts or honey should be given to infants under one year of age, longer if you have a family history of food allergies.
- You can make batches of food and freeze them in small portions using an ice cube tray and covering with cellophane wrap. Remove one cube at a time for defrosting when you're ready to feed baby.

- As baby gets bigger you can make larger portions using plastic containers.
- Label the foods you make with the date made and ingredients.
- When warming baby's food, make sure you test it for the appropriate temperature before feeding baby.

ITSABELLY'S PRODUCT RECOMMENDATIONS FOR WHEN BABY STARTS SOLIDS

FOOD MILL

There is no need for high tech gadgets that consume electricity to prepare baby's food. A simple food mill will puree fruits, veggies, even meats, while separating skins and seeds.

KidCo BabySteps Food Mill: An eco-friendly food processor—no electricity or batteries are needed. This hand-operated mill is BPA-, phthalate- and PVC-free. The easy-to-use mill blends and purees fresh foods while separating bone, seeds, skin and other undesirable food parts. The KidCo Food Mill comes with a 4-oz serving cup, serving spoon, removable strainer and medical-grade stainless steel blade. That the KidCo Food Mill can be purchased with a carrying case makes it perfect for travel. Price: $13.95 to $16.95, www.kidco.com.

BABY FOOD COOK BOOK & RESOURCES

Figuring out what to make for your dinner and baby's too can be overwhelming. A good baby-food cookbook will keep you inspired with new recipes (and even some that *you* won't mind either). We feel that introducing our babies to variety and interesting tastes and textures has helped with their willingness to try new foods as they grew older. These cookbooks also provide lots of information on when to introduce certain foods and food allergies.

Superfoods For Babies and Children: Author Annabel Karmel explains how nutritious food benefits your child by promoting growth, boosting energy, improving immunity and helping build strong bones and teeth. She discusses how to avoid food allergies, colic, constipation and eczema, and helps readers learn how to evaluate food labels. Beautiful illustrations and easy-to-read content make this Melissa's favorite baby-food cookbook. Price: $24.95, www.annabelkarmel.com.

Organic Baby & Toddler Cookbook: Lizzie Vann and Daphne Razazan help parents prepare nutritious and appetizing meals for their children. They offer 70 recipes for babies up to preschool age. Essential superfoods are recommended for each age stage. Vann, who founded Organix, a successful English organic children's food company, in 1991, and Razazan give vegetarian and special dietary advice. Price: $15.

Mommy Made Cookbook: Written by Martha and David Kimmel with contributor Suzanne Goldenson. This cookbook is practical and user-friendly and features 40 easy-to-make recipes perfect for introducing your baby to wholesome solid foods. Price: $12.

Wholesome Baby Food: A great resource for nutritious baby food recipes, food/age charts and food allergy information, www.wholesomebabyfood.com.

DISHWARE AND UTENSILS

Choosing non-toxic dishware and utensils is just as important as choosing a non-toxic sippy cup. Your child will appreciate eating his meal out of a bowl that is beautiful. Jennifer feels that how we serve food makes an impression on the child about the quality of the food, and creates reverence around the meal. We recommend having three sets of bowls, plates and utensils on hand. Of course, you can get by with less. Jennifer does. She just washes more frequently.

Baby Björn: The unique three-leaf clover shape and Baby Björn spoon makes scooping food easier for baby. The rubber base and plate design make it difficult for little hands to pick up and throw the plate when mealtime turns into playtime. Dishwasher- and microwave-safe (maximum of 90°C/194°F). Baby Björn does not use chemical additives such as cadmium, lead, bisphenol A (BPA), phthalates, bromine, PVC or chlorine. The plastic is recyclable. Price: $23, www.babybjorn.com.

Bambu: Utensils, bowls, plates and a really cool spork made from bamboo. The utensils are natural bamboo color. The Bambu Mini Me bowl is beautifully coiled by hand and finished with a unique lacquering process. These lovely bowls are available in key lime, blue corn and berry. Bamdino Plates are disposable plates that are compostable, decomposing in four to six months. Bambu is a member of 1% For The Planet and has the Co-op America Seal of Approval. Hand wash. Price: $3.50 to $11.95, www.bambuhome.com.

Boon: Dining options that every modern design-loving parent wouldn't mind having at the table. The Groovy Interlocking Plate and Bowl has four compartments to keep food separated. Two of the bowls are perfect for your toddler's favorite dipping sauces. You can customize the configuration of the bowls. The Boon Catch Bowl has a unique flexible food catcher that helps keep food in bowl, not on the floor, and has a suction cup base to keep the bowl on the table. Boon Benders are really neat utensils with a bendable end. As baby's motor skills develop, you gradually straighten the utensil. Boon ModWare utensils are for the toddler graduating from Boon Benders but not ready for silverware. Boon also makes a great Snack Ball that works well for travel. The Boon items listed here are BPA-, phthalate- and PVC-free. All Boon feeding products are dishwasher-safe. Price: $4.99 to $12.99, www.booninc.com.

Camden Rose Spoon and Bowl: An heirloom-quality cherry wood bowl and spoon sealed with beeswax. Other options include sealing with an all-natural wood finish or leaving the item unsealed/unfinished. Spoon and bowl are designed, manufactured and packaged in the USA. Price: $24.99, www.camdenrose.com.

TreBimbi: An Italian-made collection that includes plates, cups, spoons, forks and kid-friendly knives. Each utensil has a stainless steel body and a colored, non-toxic polypropylene handle. The plate is also made from non-toxic polypropylene. Pieces snap together for storage and have fun and bright mix-and-match colors. Price: $19.95 to $45, www.trebimbi.co.uk.

Traditional Lacquerware Children's Set: This beautiful set is made from Urushi wood in a traditional Japanese method in which several coats of lacquer are applied to the carved piece. The results—a durable and water-proof piece that resists strong acids and high temperature. Imported from Japan, this handcrafted set includes one bowl, one cup and cutlery in a gift box. The more expensive set includes the same as the lower-priced set, along with a plate. Price: $69.95 to $89.95, www.lifewithoutplastic.com.

BABY FOOD STORAGE

It doesn't take much cooking ability or preparation to make homemade baby food. The last thing you want to do is store your homemade creations in toxic containers. These baby food storage containers are safe and make storing and freezing baby food a breeze. Sectioned storage containers allow you to prepare bulk individual servings of baby food. When you are ready to feed baby, defrosting a cube at a time is a snap and keeps waste to a minimum.

Baby Cubes: We like Baby Cubes because each individual portion has its own lid. Baby Cubes are made of a non-toxic polypropylene virgin raw material that is BPA- and phthalate-free. Baby Cubes are microwave, dish-washer and freezer-safe. Eight 2-oz Baby Cubes per package. The cubes fit neatly into stackable trays, and have a dry-erase writing surface so you can note the date and meal prepared. Price: $7.95, www.babycubes.com.

Baby Steps: KidCo makes these BPA- and phthalate-free baby food storage trays. Each tray holds seven 2-oz serving sections. The tray comes with a locking lid to seal the food tightly inside. You can use a dry erase marker to label the tray contents and date. The serving size works well with the Baby Steps serving dish. The Baby Steps tray is dishwasher-safe. Price: $9.99, www.kidco.com.

Fresh Baby Food Storage Trays: These food storage trays simplify feedings and reduce waste. Each tray makes 12 pre-portioned servings of about 1 oz each. The trays are FDA-approved food-safe plastic #4 (Low Density Polyethylene) and #2 HDPE (High Density Polyethylene). The trays do not contain PVC, bisphenol A or plasticizer. Fresh Baby also sells the "So Easy Baby Food Kit." This award-winning all-in-one kit teaches how to prepare fresh, natural meals for your baby in less than 30 minutes a week. The kit includes a cookbook with over 40 recipes, instructional DVD, freezer trays and nutritional tip cards. Price: $14 to $35, www.freshbaby.com.

SIPPY CUPS

To best find a sippy cup that meets your needs, we offer recommendations for both metal containers and plastic that is free from bisphenol A (BPA), DEHA and phthalates. Stainless steel and aluminum make great sippy cups and water bottles because of their durability and longevity. Imagine passing down a sippy cup! Stainless steel cup interiors are typically not lined; aluminum bottles usually have a lining to make the bottle taste neutral. Stainless steel, used in food processing, dairy and brewery operations, is resistant to stain and rust because of its chromium content. Metal sippy cups are a bit more expensive than their non-toxic plastic cousins.

We recommend having at least two sippy cups in rotation, but three is better, just in case you leave one in a shopping cart (Jennifer hates to count the number of times she's done this!). Don't buy a lot at once. All sippy cups are different and your child will definitely have a preference of cup.

BornFree: This BPA-, phthalate- and PVC-free no-spill training cup comes in four colors. You can choose from training cup soft spouts or drinking cup hard spouts. The "drinking cup" spout allows a greater liquid flow, but is not no-spill. The cup has a grooved design that is easy to hold when the handles are removed. The cup is made from a polyamide (PA) plastic. Price: $10, www.newbornfree.com.

Fluid: The unique, ergonomic two-handed grip design of this sippy cup by Boon allows your child to hold it easily. Plus, the angled spout requires less head tipping while drinking. The Fluid sippy is BPA-, PVC- and phthalate-free, and is recommended for babies nine months and older. As a company, Boon contributes 10% of profits to children's charities. The cup can hold 9 oz and is dishwasher-safe. Price: $6, www.booninc.com.

....
ZRECS SIPPY CUP SHOWDOWN

The ever-savvy Zrecs blog conducted a sippy cup showdown. Check out the reviews here: www.zrecs.blogspot.com/2007/05/sippy-cup-show-down-safer-bpa-free-sippy.html.
....

Foogo: One of our favorites, Thermos makes vacuum-insulated sippy cups and straw bottles in stainless steel accented with fun colors. Foogo is for children ages six months and older. All Foogo products use no plastics containing bisphenol A (BPA). The soft drinking spout is made from "food contact safe" thermoplastic elastomer (TPE). The valve plate and lid are made from polypropylene (PP#5). The Foogo sippy cup is available with blue and yellow accents or pink and purple accents. The Foogo sippy holds 7 oz and is available with or without handles. The Foogo line also includes a 12-oz straw cup and a food jar, perfect for packing zero-waste preschool lunches. Price: $14.95, www.thermos.com.

Klean Kanteen: A 12-oz non-leaching, taste-neutral stainless steel bottle that comes with a sippy adapter made from non-leaching polypropylene (#5 plastic) and two sippy spouts, made by Avent. Increase the lifetime usage of the Klean Kanteen sippy by replacing the sippy adaptor with a sport-drinking spout. On hot summer days, you will love the wide spout that lets you add ice cubes to the sippy. Klean Kanteen makes grown-up size bottles also. All of us on Team Itsabelly have matching mother-child sippy cups and water bottles. Price: $17.95, www.kleankanteen.com.

Safe Sippy: Another one of our favorites. The Safe Sippy, is a stainless steel sippy cup with handles and a "fun" design. The plastic cap, independently certified free of BPA, phthalates and DEHA, is made from polypropylene (#5 plastic), the most stable of all plastics. The Safe Sippy uses a non-toxic silicone straw-shaped spout, which they say is better for developing mouths. As your child grows, you may remove the handles on this cup. When you do so, the cup features a tapered waist for holding ease. Melissa loved that the Safe Sippy body is covered in thermoplastic rubber sleeve—no dents when Isabella decided to play toss with her cup!

The Safe Sippy is offered in vibrant blue, pink and green, and holds 11 oz. Price: $14.95, www.thesafesippy.com.

Sigg: Popular with parents and children both, these eco-friendly sippy cups are available in a wide variety of fun colors and designs. Sigg bottles are lined with a water-based, non-toxic, crack-resistant coating baked into the interior walls. The only downside about Sigg bottles is that their narrow neck makes cleaning a pain, unless you use one of their special brushes. The lining is non-leaching and taste-neutral. Reusable sippy cups are offered in three different sizes: baby (0.3L), kids (0.4L) and big kids (0.6L). They even make sizes with hip designs for mom and dad. Jennifer has to resist the temptation to buy more Siggs than she needs just because they look really neat. Sigg's blue or red handles make the baby or kids' bottle easier to hold. Sigg bottles are recommended for age two and older. The bottles are 100% recyclable. As a company, Sigg donates 1% of annual sales to environmental causes. Price: $5.99 to $19.99, www.mysigg.com.

Think Baby: These 9-oz training cups are free of BPA, PVC, nitrosamines and lead. Think Baby training cups are made from PES (polyethersulfone), a durable and heat resistant plastic. The sippy spout is made from non-toxic silicone and has a travel cap to reduce risk of spillage. The cup has easy-to-grip handles. All Think Baby bottle and training cup parts are interchangeable and dishwasher-safe. Price: $8.99, www.thinkbabybottles.com.

BIBS

We understand that sometimes your messy little eater needs a bib that is both waterproof and wipeable. We've found two options that are lead, PVC-, BPA- and phthalate-free, so that convenience doesn't have to be hazardous. If your child's bib is labeled "polyvinyl chloride", or "vinyl," or "PVC," it may contain lead. As you know, lead is harmful to developing brains. For the green purist, we also found some organic cotton bib options. If you buy cloth bibs, we recommend having six to seven bibs on hand. If you are buying wipeable, waterproof bibs you can buy less because cleaning them is easier. Melissa washes her Bumkins in the sink and leaves them to air dry.

• • •

IS MY BIB SAFE?
By Michael Green, Executive Director, Center for Environmental Health,
www.cehca.org.

During the 2007 shopping season, news reports of dozens of toys and other children's products found with high levels of lead demonstrated that industry is not taking enough care to keep health hazards out of their products, and that the government is not doing enough to protect our children.

Stepping into this void, action by the nonprofit Center for Environmental Health (CEH) has changed the way entire industries produce children's products, eliminating health threats from arsenic, lead, and other unnecessary chemical threats to children. Since 1996, the Center's groundbreaking work has eliminated health hazards from dozens of baby and children's products, including diaper creams and powders, children's medicines, vinyl lunchboxes, metal and vinyl jewelry, wooden playground structures, imported candies, and many more.

One focus of the Center's work has been in eliminating lead hazards to infants and children. Lead is a stunningly toxic metal. A long list of problems has been linked to lead exposure, including:
• lowered intelligence
• behavior problems
• cancer
• kidney problems
• delayed puberty

Children exposed to high lead levels score lower on IQ tests, are more impulsive and have shorter attention spans. But even low-level exposures can cause problems: recent research from Duke University showed that low levels of lead exposure in early childhood were linked to lower test scores when children reach fourth grade.

Given the well-known effects of lead on children's learning and behavior, a Chicago-area grandmother was stunned when she found high lead levels in her grandson's vinyl baby bib. Marilyn Furer had seen news reports on the CEH work to end lead threats from vinyl children's lunchboxes, so she called CEH when she found lead in Wal-Mart vinyl baby bibs. CEH commissioned independent lab testing, which found that the Wal-Mart bibs had lead levels that were as much as 15 times higher than lead levels allowed in paint.

Since infants and toddlers will often touch their bibs and put their hands in their mouths, or even chew on their bibs, CEH knew that vinyl bibs posed a serious threat. The nonprofit surveyed the marketplace and in addition to Wal-Mart, found high lead levels in bibs sold at Toys"R"Us and Babies"R"Us stores. CEH notified the media and the companies that the lead levels in the baby bibs posed a health hazard, and within days the companies pulled the products from store shelves nationwide.

What You Can Do

Vinyl is often called a "poison plastic," because it is often made with lead and other toxic chemicals that can pose health threats during the production, use and disposal of vinyl products. Especially when shopping for children, avoid vinyl products. For example, look for all-cotton baby bibs, made from organically grown cotton whenever possible. The Center for Environmental Health has tips for protecting infants from chemical threats in the home at www.cehca.org/protect-your-home-and-family.

• • •

ITSABELLY'S BIB RECOMMENDATIONS

Baby Björn Soft Baby Bibs: A durable and ergonomically designed bib with a unique adjustable fastener to fit your child's body perfectly. This bib is also unique because it has a deep pocket to catch food spills. Baby

Björn does not use chemical additives such as cadmium, lead, bisphenol A (BPA), PVC, phthalates, bromine or chlorine. All Baby Björn plastics are recyclable. Price: $6.99, www.babybjorn.com.

Bumkins Organic Cotton Bibs: These premium, 100% organic unbleached cotton fabrics are finished with delicate coordinating satin or cotton trims. The fabric is plush, absorbent terry that is gentle next to baby's skin. Bumkins organic bibs come in a Chin or Everyday size. Bumkins Chin bib is a great size for teething babies. The Chin bib pack comes with two bibs. The Everyday Bib pack comes with one cotton trimmed bib and two satin trimmed bibs. Price: $6.95 to $10.95, www.bumkins.com.

Bumkins Waterproof Bibs: A waterproof, odor- and stain-resistant bib that comes in six different sizes and styles. Bumkins uses a proprietary waterproof fabric that is PVC-, BPA-, phthalate- and lead-free. Melissa loves the "catch-all" pocket on Bumkins bibs. These bibs, made in the USA, are machine washable. The Starter Bib fits babies three to six months and measures 8" across and 6.5" from the neck down. Bumkins' SuperBib and Reversible SuperBib measures 10" across and 9" from the neck down, and fit babies three months to over two years. The Reversible SuperBib reverses to absorbent terry fabric. The Sleeved Bib sports long sleeves, making it great for messy eaters and little artists. It measures 13.5" across chest, 12.5" from the neck down, and 32" cuff to cuff. The Sleeved Bib is sized to fit youngsters from six months to over two years. Bumkins' Junior Bib has more shoulder coverage and fits children from one year to over three years. The Junior Bib measures 14.5" across, 14" from the neck down, and 17" sleeve to sleeve. The SuperSized SuperBib fits children six months to over three years. Its unique length and angled design works well for car snacks. The SuperSized Bib measures 18" across and 18" from the neck down. Price: $7.95 to $19.95, www.bumkins.com.

Silibib: Silikids produces this hypoallergenic food-grade silicone bib. This bib is waterproof, bacteria-resistant and dishwasher-safe, and is available in four vibrant color options with a modern circle design. The Silibib fits babies three months and older. It measures 5.5" from the neck down and 7" across. Price: $19.95, www.silikids.com.

Under The Nile Organic Cotton Bibs: Under the Nile offers a traditional style bib along with a wider style bib with a stretchy ribbed neck and also terry or knit 100% organic cotton fabric. Some of the bibs come screen-printed with designs such as snails, or eco sayings like "Plant a seed for the future." Price: $6 to $9, www.underthenile.com.

HIGH CHAIR

There are many wonderful and family friendly wooden high chair options that are comfortable for baby and will actually look attractive at your dining table. We focused on wooden high chairs because we feel their durability gives them a long lifespan. Many of these chairs can grow with your child—morphing from a high chair to an "at the table" chair for children and teens. We love chairs that allow baby to dine with the family at the table. Just because a baby doesn't have proper manners yet doesn't mean they need to be sidelined. Inclusive family meals are important. At the table is where baby will learn her manners, practice conversation and bond with family. For those of you who love trays, we found some wooden high chairs with trays and ones that also convert to table chairs for older children. Check out our Green Choices and Green Labels chapters to understand labels that you may read in researching wooden high chairs.

Babylon Toddler High Chair: A wooden high chair for babies 12 months and older that can work in modern interiors as well as with classic décor. Argington manufacturers this high chair made from durable Forest Stewardship Council (FSC) certified sustainable birch wood with a 100% non-toxic, water-based finish. The high chair has an adjustable seat and footrest accommodating nine different height positions ranging from countertop or bistro table all the way down to coffee table. The chair has a three-point harness and can support up to 200 lbs. An Infant Tray Kit is available separately. JPMA Certified. Price: $199, www.argington.com.

Geuther Family High Chair: Another European chair that will last throughout childhood. This chair is made in Germany of durable, high quality wood. Unique knobs let you quickly adjust the chair without tools. The adjustable tray and footrest can be removed and turned into a big kid chair. The chair has a safety strap and is intend for babies over six months. This chair is available in ten colors and coordinating trims. A chair pad is sold separately. Price: $198, www.euro-baby.us.

Tripp Trapp: One of the first "at the table" wooden high chairs from Europe (since 1970). This chair allows children of all ages and sizes to share a meal with their family without being separated by a plastic tray. Stokke can be used from six months with a baby rail (sold separately) and five-point harness. The angled design of the chair allows you to move the chair to any table height up to 32" and the multiple height adjustment settings give your child a wide range of seat and footrest settings, insuring a long lifespan of usage. According to Stokke, the chair is "ergonomically designed to provide stability, comfort and confidence." Jennifer's children love sitting and eating comfortably at the table in their Tripp Trapp chairs. This cultivated beech wood is available in nine formaldehyde-free color finishes and with colorful cushions that are sold separately. According to Stokke, the wood is cultivated in a natural and balanced process. The Tripp Trapp chair comes with a seven-year warranty on all wooden components. JPMA certified. Price: $229, www.stokkeusa.com.

Svan High Chair: Starting at six months, your little one can enjoy this great European-designed birch wood highchair. The wood is harvested using environmentally friendly practices. This ergonomic chair is fully adjustable to grow with your child. Its removable safety guard may be taken off after three years. It comes with a removable phthalate-free and BPA-free plastic tray cover that can go in the dishwasher, and is available in five lead-free stain finishes. The tray comes off to seat a child at the table and grows to an adult sized chair. The Svan is truly multi-functional because it is a high chair, booster chair, and full-sized chair all-in-one. Machine-washable cushions, which are PBDE-free, are sold separately in a wide range of colors. JPMA certified. Price: $199 to $249, www.svanusa.com.

bathing & skincare

• • •

For our families, this was one of the most important categories to choose eco-friendly and natural products. Ever try deciphering the back label of a lotion or shampoo bottle? We're sure you will agree that it is also one of the most confusing categories to understand what makes a product safe or not.

As we have seen with recent studies from the Environmental Working Group and Organic Consumers Association, even some products toting "organic" and "natural" labels can be deceptive. Recent studies have confirmed what environmentalists have been saying for a long time. Toxins used in baby products appear to enter the systems of infants—as well as any human! It makes sense—your skin is your body's largest organ, after all. And since babies and children are so much smaller than adults their exposure rate is greatly multiplied.

We recommend those products that we have used and which met our families' requirements for safety. You may wish to adopt different practices for your family. No one product or brand fits everyone's needs, so we have tried to recommend a variety of products. Most of the products we recommend are available over the internet. We're real moms—we know what it feels like to realize during bath time that you are out of shampoo —so we also recommend products that you can find at your local drugstore or big box superstore.

When you are doing your product research, remember that product formulations may change over time. The rating you find on the Environmental Working Group's Cosmetic Database may be based on an older formulation. Yes, it means more work, especially when you baby is squirming in his sling, but it's best to **always** read the label before you buy. We've tried to make it easier on you by including some links to product cheat sheets you can print and take shopping with you.

While you are scanning the label, you will want to keep an eye out for these toxic ingredients. Unfortunately, some won't even be listed.

- **1,4-Dioxane:** In skincare products, you won't see 1,4-dioxane listed on the ingredient label, as it is a byproduct of the ethoxylation process. A recent study by the Organic Consumers Association found 1,4-dioxane can even be found in products listed as natural and organic. 1,4-dioxane is dangerous because it is both a known carcinogen in animals and a known eye and respiratory tract irritant. It also may cause damage to the central nervous system, liver and kidneys. 1,4-dioxane is primarily used in manufacturing solvent applications, fumigants and automotive coolant.
- **Avobenzone (Parsol 1789, Eusolex 9020, Escalol 517):** A chemical sunscreen shown to degrade significantly in light, resulting in less protection over time.
- **Diethanolamine (DEA):** A synthetic agent added to skincare and bathing products to create foaming action and creamy texture. It may react with other product ingredients and form nitrosamines, which are known carcinogens. Other names or synonyms are bis(hydroxyethyl) amine, diethylolamine, hydroxydiethylamine, diolamine, and 2,2'-iminodiethanol. Variants of DEA include lauramide diethanolamine, coco diethanolamide, cocoamide diethanolamine or coconut oil amide

of diethanolamine, lauramide DEA, lauric diethanolamide, lauroyl diethanolamide, and lauryl diethanolamide.

- **Lanolin:** Some of the products we recommend contain lanolin. If you are vegan or vegetarian, you may want to avoid lanolin. It is a substance extracted from wool sheared from sheep, so you want to make sure the sheep was treated humanely. Make sure that the lanolin is cleaned to remove pesticides and herbicides. If you have allergic reactions to wool, you may want to think twice about using lanolin.
- **Oxybenzone:** A synthetic sunscreen that can be absorbed into your skin and may be an endocrine disruptor. Oxybenzone is dangerous because it can affect the nervous system, has been linked to cancer in some laboratory studies, and creates harmful free radicals when exposed to the sun.
- **Parabens:** A group of synthetic preservatives used in cosmetics, skincare and pharmaceuticals. Parabens can also be used as a food additive. Parabens are dangerous because they are potential endocrine disruptors. Some studies have found parabens in breast tumors. You will find parabens listed as methylparaben, ethylparaben, propylparaben, butylparaben, isobutylparaben, isopropylparaben and benzylparaben.
- **Petroleum-based chemicals:** If you wish to avoid petroleum byproducts, avoid petrolatum, mineral oil and paraffin. Petroleum is a non-renewable byproduct of crude oil and may have potentially dangerous impurities.
- **Phthalates:** Chances are that you won't actually see "phthalates" listed on the ingredient list. Phthalates are often found in fragrance, which can be listed as "fragrance" rather than the individual components that make up the fragrance. Phthalates are added to cosmetics and skincare products to bind the product and fragrance. Phthalates can also be used in polyvinyl chloride (PVC) plastic to improve flexibility. According to Environment California, phthalates have been found to cause early puberty in girls, impaired sperm quality in men, genital defects and reduced testosterone production in boys, genital defects and testicular cancer. Phthalates can be listed as diethylhexyl phthalate (DEHP), dibutyl phthalate (DBP), butyl benzyl phthalate (BBP), di-isodecyl phthalate (DIDP), di-isononyl phthalate (DINP), di-n-octyl phthalate (DNOP), and others.
- **Polyethylene Glycol (PEGs or PPGs):** A family of synthetic ingredients

processed with ethylene oxide. PEGs and PPGs are used as surfactants, cleansing agents, emulsifiers, skin conditioners, and humectants. The National Toxicology Program's Eighth Annual Report on Carcinogens found that ethylene oxide exposure increases the incidence of uterine and breast cancers, leukemia and brain cancer. PEG compounds are often contaminated with the carcinogen 1,4-dioxane.

- **Propylene Glycol:** A thickening and filling agent derived from glycerin. Propylene glycol can be found in many products—even those listed as natural. The FDA determined that propylene glycol is "generally safe for use" for both food and cosmetics. However, it may raise your risk of cancer and carry toxins that affect the reproductive and immune systems. Propylene glycol is an allergen and eye irritant.
- **Sulfates:** Listed as sodium lauryl sulfate and sodium laureth sulfate. Sulfates are synthetic cleansing agents found in shampoos, shaving foams, bubble baths and even toothpaste. Sulfates remove oils from the skin and may potentially damage the lipid layer of your skin.
- **Triethanolamine (TEA):** The Organic Consumers Association and Cancer Prevention Association label TEA as a "hidden carcinogen" which releases a precursor of a highly potent nitrosamine carcinogen. TEA is often used as a pH balancer in skin lotion, eye gels, moisturizers, shampoos and shaving foams.

ITSABELLY'S BATHING AND SKINCARE RECOMMENDATIONS

BABY BODY WASH / SHAMPOO

Sodium lauryl/laureth sulfate and or other sulfate products are synthetic cleansing agents that are commonly used in soaps and baby washes and can irritate sensitive skin. Many fragrances use phthalates that can harm baby's reproductive system. Unfortunately, you are not off the hook if you buy a fragrance-free product either. Often times, manufacturers add a fragrance to neutralize the smell of the product. The founder of Earth Mama Angel Baby, Melinda Olson, wrote an informative article in our Green Choices chapter. Melinda gives a quick run-down of the ingredients you should be on the look out for in skin care products.

We love baby body washes that double as shampoo. There is no need to buy two bottles—soon your bathtub will be full of bath toys anyway!

Baby Bee Shampoo and Wash: An all-in-one baby shampoo and wash that smells wonderful. Cleansing and moisturizing coconut and sunflower oils are combined with soy protein that will leave baby's hair and skin silky soft. Burt's Bees make this sodium laureth sulfate-, paraben- and phthalate-free baby wash. Price: $7 to $9, www.burtsbees.com.

California Baby Shampoo and Body Wash: Their product line does not contain sodium lauryl sulfate (SLS) or DEA. Since this wash does not contain numbing agents, it is naturally no-tears. The California Baby Wash line includes Super Sensitive™, Calming™ and Swimmer's Defense™. Price: 8.5 oz, $9.95, www.californiababy.com.

Angel Baby Shampoo and Body Wash: A gentle, certified vegan castile soap made with organic and natural ingredients. Because no foaming agents are used, it is packaged in a self-foaming bottle which, by the way, Jennifer's kids love pumping themselves, covering themselves with "shaving cream" during their bath. Contains no sodium lauryl sulfate, pthalates, parabens, artificial fragrance or dyes. If you love this body wash as much as we do, you can buy a gigantic one-liter refill bottle— an eco-friendly way to reduce packaging. Price: $7.95 to $69.95, www.earthmamaangelbaby.com.

La La Baby Wash & Shampoo: Melissa loved this Mama Rose's Naturals baby wash that is naturally tear-free, naturally antiseptic and anti-inflammatory.

The addition of lavender, chamomile, calendula, rose, orange blossom, witch hazel, aloe, grapeseed oil, jojoba, shea butter and vitamin E also make this wash soothing and calming. This wash does not contain sodium lauryl sulfate. Price: $9, www.mamarosesnaturals.com.

BABY LOTION / OIL

Many traditional baby oils and lotions may contain potentially harmful ingredients such as parabens, mineral oil, fragrance and phthalates. Why take a risk with your baby's lotion? Choose a product that is free from these chemicals.

Angel Baby Lotion: One of Melissa's favorite baby lotions because of its irresistible smell. A certified vegan lotion made with organic rooibos, soothing to eczema, skin allergies and diaper rash. Angel Baby Lotion comes in a 2-oz travel size, 4-oz and 8-oz bottles. All Earth Mama Angel Baby products are phthalate- and paraben-free. Price: $7.95 to $19.95, www.earthmamaangelbaby.com.

Baby Bee Apricot Oil: Jennifer loved to put a few drops of Apricot Oil in bathwater for a sweet smelling bath. Apricot, grapeseed, vitamins and wheat germ oils will keep baby's skin soft and glowing. This product contains lanolin. Burt's Bees makes this product, and it is phthalate- and paraben-free. Price: $8 to $9, www.burtsbees.com.

Baby Tata Oil: A 100% organic massage oil that soothes and protects your baby's skin. Baby Tata blends organic sweet almond oil, apricot kernel oil, and grapeseed oils. Price: $15.95, www.babytata.com.

Buttermilk Lotion: Burt's Bee's baby lotion moisturizes baby's sensitive skin with soothing, real buttermilk, aloe and sunflower oil. Buttermilk Lotion is phthalate- and paraben-free. Price: $7 to $9, www.burtsbees.com.

Sweet Nectar Baby Oil: We love Mama Rose's Naturals baby oil! It contains calendula, lavender, chamomile, and oils of grapeseed, meadowfoam seed, sweet almond, apricot kernel, jojoba, rosehip seed, eveningprimrose and vitamin E, and no mineral oil. You can even add a few drops to your

INFANT MASSAGE

Infant massage is a great way to ease colic and bond with baby, and calm *both* mommy and baby. At the beginning of every infant massage, Jennifer poured a little oil into the palms of her hands, rubbed her hands together near baby's ear and asked, "Would you like a massage?" After a few massages, her wee ones would get so excited as soon as she poured the oil in her hands because they loved their massages so much! Melissa's hubby, Randy, cherished the special bonding time he experienced during his daughter's infant massage.

Great Infant Massage Books & DVDs:
- **Baby Tata:** Recipient of the 2006 *Parenting* magazine Best DVDs of the Year. This DVD combines infant massage, exercise and play. www.babytata.com.
- *Baby Massage: The Calming Power of Touch* by Alan Heath and Nicki Bainbridge.
- *Infant Massage—Revised Edition: A Handbook for Loving Parents* by Vimala Schneider Mcclure.

Don't forget your favorite natural baby oil and some relaxing music.

hair before shampooing for extra conditioning. Price: $12, www.mamarosesnaturals.com.

Weleda Baby Calendula Oil: A soothing and protective oil made purely from calendula, sesame oil and chamomile. Jennifer loved using this oil after baby's bath—it almost seemed to warm the skin. Calendula Oil can be used for the daily care of baby's skin and baby massage. Price: $13, www.weledababy.com.

DIAPER CREAMS

We found it helpful to have a variety of diaper creams on hand because you never know what formula may work best for baby's rash—different rashes call for different treatments. Check with your healthcare practitioner before treatment, especially if baby has never experienced that particular type of rash before. Many traditional diaper creams are mixed with questionable "inactive" ingredients such as mineral oil, parabens and phthalates, to name just a few.

Angel Baby Bottom Balm: A certified vegan balm infused with organic olive oil, herbs, shea butter and naturally antibacterial and anti-fungal essential oils. It helps heal existing diaper rash and protect against flareups. You can also use this balm to soothe itchy cradle cap, bug bites, scrapes, chicken pox, minor rashes, burns and scrapes. All Earth Mama Angel Baby products are phthalate- and paraben-free. Price: $9.95 to $14.95, www.earthmamaangelbaby.com.

Angel Baby Diaper Rash Soap: Both a certified vegan diaper rash treatment and a first aid soap. Made with organic oatmeal, olive oil, organic palm oil, organic coconut oil, organic calendula, chickweed, plantain and pure essential oils of tea tree and lavender, it doubles as an effective and safe first-aid soap for the whole family. Earth Mama Angel Baby products are phthalate- and paraben-free. Price: $7.95, www.earthmamaangelbaby.com.

Baby Bee Diaper Ointment: Burt's Bees makes this zinc-based ointment that contains vitamins A and E, sweet almond oil, beeswax and chamomile to act as natural barriers to help protect baby's sensitive skin. Burt's Bees products are now free from phthalates and parabens. Price: $7.50 to $8.50, www.burtsbees.com.

Calming™ Diaper Care: California Baby's Calming Diaper Rash Cream has a relaxing essential oil blend of French lavender and organic tea tree, and is naturally anti-bacterial and anti-fungal. California Baby also makes a Calendula Cream and an Aloe Vera Cream to sooth baby's bottom. The product line contains no nut oils, gluten, soy, oat or dairy. Price: $10 to $11.50, www.californiababy.com.

Magic Touch Skin & Diaper Balm: Mama Rose's Naturals makes this great non-zinc diaper balm. It contains certified organic herbal infusions and pure essential oils, which can help promote the formation of new skin cells and relieve diaper irritation. Melissa used this balm to soothe other skin irritations and insect bites. Magic Touch includes tea tree, lavender, chamomile, calendula, chickweed, echinacea, grapeseed oil, jojoba, meadowfoam seed oil, shea oil, rosehip seed oil and vitamin E. Price: $12, www.mamarosesnaturals.com.

Sunshine Spray Skin & Diaper Care: An aromatherapeutic, antiseptic, anti-bacterial, and anti-inflammatory spray that can help ease anxiety and relieve skin irritation, insect bites and diaper rash. Sunshine Spray won a 2006 iParenting Media Award. Sunshine Spray is alcohol-free and contains rose, lavender, chamomile, orange blossom and witch hazel floral waters. Made by Mama Rose's Naturals in Oregon. Price: $12, www.mamarosesnaturals.com.

Weleda Calendula Diaper Care: One of Jennifer's favorite zinc-based creams. Weleda Calendula Diaper Care cream contains zinc oxide, lanolin, and beeswax to bring relief and nourishment to sore skin. This cream adds a protective and water-resistant layer to the skin to protect against moisture. Calendula and chamomile extracts help soothe and heal the diaper area. The lanolin in this product has been cleaned to remove any pesticide residue. Weleda products do not contain synthetic preservatives, fragrances, colorants or raw materials derived from mineral oils, as well as genetically modified organisms (GMO's). Price: $10.49, www.weledababy.com.

SUNBLOCK

Direct sun exposure should be avoided for children under one year of age. If sun exposure is unavoidable and clothing cannot be used to cover the infant, it is acceptable to use sunblock after applying a small test patch first. The AAP also recommends that if infants under six months must use sunblock, it should be a non-chemical sunscreen.

Many traditional sunblocks use chemical ingredients, such as parsol 1789 and oxybenzone to block harmful sun rays. Chemical sunblocks filter the sun and can get absorbed by the skin and cause hormonal imbalance. The sunblocks we recommend use minerals that remain on the top of the skin to scatter and reflect UV rays. Sunblock should block both UVA and UVB sunrays. UVB rays cause sunburn, while UVA rays cause more skin damage over time because they penetrate the skin more deeply.

You also want to make sure baby's sunblock (and yours too!) is paraben- and phthalate-free. And don't forget—baby needs sunblock year-round. Skin can be damaged even on cloudy days.

Badger SPF 30 Sunblock: A 30 SPF broad-spectrum sunblock that works well for both children and parents! Badger Sunblock is one of the Environmental Working Group's highest-ranking sunblocks for ingredient safety. This sunblock uses micronized zinc oxide for a natural, physical barrier to the sun's harmful rays. Olive oil, beeswax, jojoba oil, cocoa butter and shea butter provide moisturizing qualities. Essential oils of lavender, Moroccan blue tansy, lime and orange and ylang ylang add a dreamy scent. Price: $16, www.badgerbalm.com.

California Baby: Their line of suncare products are non-chemical and tear-free. California Baby uses micronized titanium dioxide as a chemical sun filtering agent and offers UVA-UVB broad-spectrum protection. The Citronella sunscreen lotion is SPF 30+ and provides natural bug repellent in addition to sunscreen. The No Fragrance sunscreen is available in SPF 30+ and SPF 18+. The Everyday/Year-Round formula uses Japanese Green Tea for its anti-oxidant properties and a beautiful essential oil blend. All California Baby suncare products are PABA-free. Convenient travel sticks are available in the Everyday/Year-Round and No Fragrance formulas. Their product line contains no nut oils, gluten, soy, oat or dairy. Price: $12.99 to $17.99, www.californiababy.com.

Earth's Best by Jason Mineral-Based Sunblock: A PABA- and fragrance-free sunblock that provides SPF 30+ and high UV protection for baby. Organic calendula extract, oat oil and organic marigold extract are added to fight sun damage and soothe skin. Earth's Best by Jason products are 70% organic and free from parabens, lanolin, mineral oil, petrolatum and waxes. Price: $12.49, www.jason-natural.com.

NAIL SCISSORS OR CLIPPERS

Cutting baby's nails is often an anxiety-filled experience for new parents. Well-sharpened tools will make cutting baby's delicate nails easier.

Tweezerman Scissors and Clippers: Tweezerman is a socially responsible company that offers free product lifetime sharpening services. The scissors feature stainless steel blades with safe rounded tips. Rubberized handles provide extra grip for even the shakiest hands. The baby nail clipper has a large handle that provides better control; its sharp blades will cut without tearing baby's nails. It even includes a nail file for smoothing nail edges after cutting. We never got around to using the nail file though—we were just happy for a quiet moment to cut baby's quickly growing nails! Price: $25, www.tweezerman.com.

TOWELS AND WASHCLOTHS

We recommend buying three soft hooded towels (baby will look so cute in the hood after bath) and two packs of washcloths.

Buchic Bamboo: The hooded towel measures 30" x 30" and is made from soft bamboo fiber. The washcloths come in a pack of five, also made from soft bamboo fiber. Bamboo is highly absorbent, fast drying and antibacterial. The hooded towel and washcloth comes in natural, pale pink, sprout green or Tahiti blue. Price: $10 to $29, www.buchic.com.

Under The Nile: Both Under the Nile's hooded towels and washcloths are 100% handpicked Egyptian organic cotton terry, grown and produced without the use of pesticides or chemicals throughout the entire production process. Price: $5 to $28, www.underthenile.com.

BATHTUB

Most baby baths are made out of plastic, which means you have to worry about plastic toxic ingredients—again! No mama wants her baby bathing in chemical-laden bathwater. Plastics and toxins expert Alicia Voorhies from *The Soft Landing* wrote a helpful article on understanding plastics in our Green Choices chapter.

We only recommend bathtubs for baby, not bath seats that supposedly adhere by suction onto the bathtub floor. These seem to be a safer alternative to bathing baby. If you don't have a counter top that is wide enough to be safe (remember you will be bathing a wiggly, slippery baby), place the tub on the floor and sit to bath baby. Many babies have accidents in bath seats. Remember that a baby can drown in an inch of water! Always keep hold of baby in the tub.

We love the European bath buckets that are finally making their way to the States. Popular in Europe, these bath tubs look like big buckets that snuggly fit baby for a bath. Baby will bathe in the comfortable fetal position in warm water—a close reminder of the womb. Don't worry; you will be able to clean all of baby when they are sitting in a bath bucket. Baby doesn't need to be outstretched in an open bath to get clean. And, really, how dirty is your baby if he isn't crawling around the dirt outside? A baby's bath is all about comfort and relaxation. These bath buckets make a great eco-friendly tub, using less water because of their vertical compact design. The water stays warmer longer, about twenty minutes, because of the smaller surface area. And when baby's outgrown her bath bucket, reuse it as a bucket for washing the car or gardening.

EuroBath: Made by Primo this two-position baby bath is for ages newborn to 24 months. As Melissa found out, you really can use it that long—she used it until Isabella was a full two years old! Babies under six months are bathed in a reclining position, while toddlers can sit up on the other side. A larger bathtub, it measures 36"L x 21"W x 10"D. It is made from polypropylene, a non-toxic plastic, with a hole at the end of the tub rim so that you can hang the tub to dry. The EuroBath comes in pearl white, pearl mint green and transparent blue. Price: $34.99, www.primobaby.com.

Spa Baby Tub: An upright baby bathtub with a non-slip base for stability. The smooth curved rim makes it easy to hold onto the tub. It comes in a soothing transparent sea green color. You can use the Spa Baby Tub from birth to ten months. Made of safe non-toxic polypropylene #5, the Spa Baby Tub is BPA-free. Price: $44.95, www.spababytubs.com.

TummyTub: A European favorite baby bath, designed in the Netherlands. The TummyTub has an anti-skid base and low center of gravity for safety and stability, is made of polypropylene and is fully recyclable. TummyTub also sells a convenient bath stool that allows you to use the Tummy Tub while sitting in a chair. The bath stool also works well as a stepping stool for older children. The TummyTub website has an online video displaying how to use the Tummy Tub. Baby can use the TummyTub from birth to three years. (Maybe we have big three-year-olds, but a three-year-old seems a *little* big for a bath bucket.) Price: $60, www.tummy-tub.com.

Prince Lionheart WashPOD: Prince Lionheart just released their WashPOD, which provides "a safe and secure environment, similar to that inside a mother's womb." In addition to the base of the tub, the WashPOD has an outer support system that wraps around the tub. Age: zero to six months. Prince Lionheart products are BPA-, PVC- and phthalate-free. Price: $25, www.princelionheart.com.

SOFT HAIRBRUSH AND COMB

A soft brush is a must for baby's fine hair and sensitive scalp. Make hair brushing more green by choosing a brush made from sustainable wood and made to last a long time.

Ambassador Baby Hairbrush: The wood on this brush is not endangered wood. The boar bristles are sheared humanly from farm-raised animals. Price: $7.95, www.amazon.com.

Kost Eco-Friendly Baby Brush: The soft goat hair bristles on this brush will be gentle on your baby's skin. This fair-trade brush is made with sustainable beech wood. Price: £9, www.allthingsgreen.net.

Widu Baby Brush: A soft natural bristle brush hand set in ash wood and made in Italy. The wood is finished with purified linseed oil. No toxic chemicals or lacquers are used. Price: $25, www.widu.com.

health & baby care

• • •

When baby is not feeling well, you want to take care of your baby the best way you can. As a new mommy, you worry about the ingredients in medications and wonder if there is a natural alternative. But then you also wonder if that natural alternative will be as effective as your mom's old stand-bys.

Consult with your pediatrician and don't be afraid to ask for alternative care methods. A good doctor will be willing to address your concerns and suggest a range of treatments. For example, many doctors now recommend that using home remedies such as a saline nasal spray, bulb syringe, steam showers and a humidifier can be effective solutions to treating a cold. You can sometimes supplement traditional medicine with a homeopathic formula. Always discuss treatment methods, including home and natural remedies, with your doctor before use.

DIGITAL THERMOMETER / RECTAL THERMOMETER

Melissa found that using a digital thermometer made taking Isabella's temperature painless and quick. Besides speed, another benefit of digital thermometers is that there is no mercury to worry about if the thermometer is damaged or breaks. You can find oral, ear, underarm and rectal digital thermometers. According to *Consumer Reports* (April 2007) the oral thermometers fared better overall and are recommended for children over the age of three. Most doctors recommend taking temperatures rectally as the most accurate for very young children. Ear digital thermometers may work the fastest, but getting an accurate read can be difficult due to improper ear positioning of the thermometer.

FIRST AID ESSENTIALS KIT

Some people experience allergies to latex, which can range from irritation to severe reactions. Some bandages may use adhesives that can also cause allergic reactions or irritation to the wearer's skin.

All Terrain First Aid Essentials: Latex-free bandages that are not tested on animals and use water-based adhesives (no solvents, alcohol or EMK). These bandages use natural, food-grade colors and pigments and are made from recycled or recyclable material. Price: $3.99, www.allterrainco.com.

NASAL ASPIRATOR

A nasal aspirator removes mucus from your child's nose. While using a nasal aspirator is never a fun job, it is a simple method for treating baby's cold without using medication. Of course, any time your baby is under the weather, consult with your doctor to determine the appropriate level of care for your little one.

Nosefrida: Invented in Sweden by ear, nose and throat specialists, has been used by Swedish moms and dads for years. The Nosefrida was recently spotted on the shelves of Whole Foods in the USA. Dr. Sears likes this product because nothing needs to enter baby's nose. Parents have found that babies tolerate the Nosefrida better than other nasal aspirators. Nosefrida is effective and hygienic and has been clinically tested. Nosefrida is BPA- and phthalate-free. Price: $15, www.nosefrida.com.

COTTON PADS / SWABS

Choosing an organic cotton ball or swab will ensure that you are cleaning baby with cotton that is free from chemicals. Plus, your organic cotton purchase supports sustainable and pesticide-free agriculture, which is better for our environment.

Organic Essentials Balls / Pads / Swabs: Organic Essentials offers a complete line of soft certified organic cotton personal care products. The cotton is whitened with hydrogen peroxide. The organic cotton swabs have a biodegradable stick. Price: $3.19 to $5.29, www.organicessentials.com.

GRIPE WATER / GAS PAIN RELIEVER

Gripe water is a popular natural remedy in Europe that is becoming more accepted and available in the United States. Jennifer and Melissa found that gripe water was a great help for their babies with gas and pain.

Melissa even added it to her daughter's milk when she had a tummy ache. Unfortunately, some gripe water formulas contain alcohol—a big no-no in our book for a baby formula! It is also important to note that some gripe water may use essential oils and herbal extracts sold under dietary supplement guidelines, which receive looser FDA regulation. However, the FDA regulates and registers homeopathic formulas, although not in the same manner as conventional over-the-counter drugs. Homeopathic medicines contain tiny amounts of natural remedies designed to stimulate the body's own self-healing properties.

Baby's Bliss GripeWater: An all-natural herbal supplement used to ease gas and stomach pain often associated with baby's colic, hiccups, and teething. It is made with organic ginger extract, organic fennel extract, grapeseed extract, sodium bicarbonate, fructose, citrus bioflavonoid extract, citric acid, deionized water and vegetable glycerin. Baby's Bliss also makes a GripeWater Travel Pack with two 1.5-oz bottles with droppers, and apple flavored GripeWater. It is not recommended to give this product to a child with a history of kidney failure or renal problems. Price: $11.99, www.blissbymom.com.

Colic Calm: Homeopathic gripe water that helps calm baby's irritation due to colic, infant gas, stomach pain, hiccups, teething and reflux. Colic Calm is a homeopathic blend of chamomile, fennel, caraway, peppermint, ginger, aloe, lemon balm, blackthorn and vegetable charcoal. Colic Calm can be used as early as two weeks of age, according to the manufacturer. Completely free of alcohol, sugar, simethicone, sodium bicarbonate (baking soda), herbal oils and extracts, citric acid, wheat, gluten, soy, dairy, and animal products. Price: $18.95, www.coliccalm.com.

Wellements: A formula made with certified organic ginger, fennel and chamomile to help ease baby's discomfort due to gas and stomach upsets, hiccups and teething. Formula also contains sodium bicarbonate, glycerin, organic agave fructose and purified water. Wellements contains no parabens, alcohol, sucrose, fillers, binders, artificial flavors, artificial color, yeast, wheat, gluten, soy, dairy, GMO ingredients or starch. Price: $10.95, www.wellements.com.

PAIN-AND-FEVER REDUCER

We recommend that you have a bottle of infant pain-and-fever reducer that has been recommended by your doctor on hand for emergencies. Conventional medicines probably do not have the most natural ingredients. However, some fever reducers have been used for quite some time and found to be effective. In the case of a high fever, we would err on the conventional side, along with natural treatments; your doctor should be able to recommend some natural techniques to reduce baby's fever or pain in addition to traditional medication. Dr. Sears' website on fevers gives simple and easy to follow advice to evaluating your child's fever, www.askdrsears.com/html/8/T082100.asp. In addition to treating a fever with traditional medicine, Dr. Sears' also recommends giving your child a lukewarm bath or drinking cool liquids to bring the fever down. Dr. Sears insists, and so do we, that you trust your "gut" instinct in treating the fever and deciding to call your doctor. Your baby's doctor should be available to address your concerns. In addition to a conventional fever reducer, we like this homeopathic treatment for little bumps and bruises.

Hyland's Bumps 'n Bruises™ Tablets and Ointment: A natural, homeopathic formula first aid treatment that comes in tablet or ointment form. You apply the ointment or take the tablet when accidents that may result in bruising, swelling and pain occur. The formulas contain *Arnica montana,* a commonly used homeopathic medicine for relieving bumps, bruises, swelling and pain. Jennifer even took single ingredient *Arnica* tablets after both of her deliveries and found it helpful for a speedy recovery. Both products are aspirin-free. Bumps 'n Bruises is recommended for toddlers and older children. Price: $6.99 to $12.95, www.hylands.com.

mama care

• • •

As new mothers, we often focus so much energy on our baby's well-being that we neglect our own. Jennifer and Melissa both felt that if they took time to keep themselves healthy, happy and yes, a little pampered, they had more energy as mothers. Many conventional products for mama carry the same toxin concerns as those for baby. We selected our favorite products for taking care of mama during the new transition to motherhood.

PREGNANCY BODY PILLOW

A comfortable body pillow is almost essential to getting a good night's rest in the later months of pregnancy. A pregnancy pillow offers support where you need it. You can often position these special pillows to support your growing belly and hips. We must admit that sometimes it feels a little silly snuggling up to such a large pillow. Trust us, though—you will thank us in the morning! Many traditional pillows use polyester to stuff their pillows. If you cannot buy a natural fiber stuffed pillow, check into making or buying an organic cotton cover for your pillow.

Holy Lamb Organics Body Pillow: You can buy this body pillow in two sizes to better fit your body type and needs. The Body Pillow is great for full-body pregnancy support. The Mini Body Pillow is better for petite moms or those wishing for less bulk. Both pillows are filled with eco-grown wool and covered with an organic cotton sateen cover. The Body Pillow measures 20" x 58" and the Mini Body Pillow measures 11" x 58". Zippered pillow covers or pillowcases are sold separately. Price: $125 to $170, www.holylamborganics.com.

Holy Lamb Organic Body Pillow Covers: Holy Lamb recommends protecting your body pillows by using a zippered pillow cover and a pillowcase. Place a zippered cover over your pillow and then slip on a pillowcase. Both covers and cases are made with organic Sateen 250-thread-count cotton fabric. Price: $45 to $55, www.holylamborganics.com.

Organic Caboose Cotton Body Pillow: A body pillow covered and stuffed with 100% American grown organic cotton. The size is 20" x 56" with about six lbs of cotton. The pillowcase is sold separately in several colors. Price: $110.00, www.organiccaboose.com.

TresTria Pillow: A versatile pillow that can be used as a pregnancy pillow, family bed pillow, nursing-in- bed pillow and reading pillow. The pillow is made with certified (Eco Umwelt Institut) 100% natural latex, which means no petroleum products are used. The pillow is covered with a 100% organic cotton sateen cover certified by Control Union Certifications and Fair Trade Labeling Organization. TresTria pillow measures 36"L x 11"W x 5 1/2"H. Price: $129.95, www.betterforbabies.com.

PRENATAL VITAMINS

Many multivitamins may contain the same levels of important vitamins, but their differences lie in the quality and sources of those vitamins and other filler ingredients. You may want to check that your vitamin is from non-genetically modified (GMO) sources. If you are vegetarian or vegan make sure your vitamins are plant-derived. Before taking any vitamins or supplements, please discuss your choices with your healthcare practitioner.

MORNING SICKNESS REMEDIES

Some new moms find out that morning sickness can really happen at any hour of the day or night. Fortunately, there are many natural alternatives to help ease mommy's tummy. Because herbs can interact with your medication or pregnancy, be sure to consult with your healthcare practitioner before taking any natural supplement.

Morning Sickness Magic: Mommy's Bliss, famous for their Gripe Water, created an herbal supplement created to help ease nausea during pregnancy and support a healthy pregnancy. Key ingredients are ginger, vitamin B-6, red raspberry leaf and folic acid. One package contains sixty capsules. Price: $14.99, www.blissbymom.com.

Morning Wellness Tea: A certified organic tea made with ginger root, spearmint, chamomile, lemon balm, peppermint and red raspberry leaf.

Sip this soothing, minty tea first thing in the morning, and throughout the day when needed. Made by Earth Mama Angel Baby. Price: $7.95 to $12.95, www.earthmamaangelbaby.com.

Tummy Aid Herbal Supplement: Mama Rose's Naturals recommends using this tincture to help relieve stomach upset, morning sickness, nausea, indigestion and heartburn prevalent during pregnancy. Tummy Aid tincture contains a blend of peppermint, catnip, ginger and marshmallow. Mama Rose's tinctures do not contain alcohol, sugar or preservatives. Price: $12, www.mamarosesnaturals.com.

Tummy Aid Tea: An organic and caffeine-free tea to help relieve stomach upset, morning sickness, nausea, indigestion and heartburn prevalent during pregnancy. Mama Rose's Naturals Tummy Aid Tea contains certified organic red rooibos, red raspberry leaf, meadowsweet, peppermint, marshmallow root, ginger, and cinnamon. Price: $8, www.mamarosesnaturals.com.

PREGNANCY SUPPLEMENTS AND TEAS

Herbal tinctures are a concentrated mixture of herbs that is typically taken in water. Many midwives belief that herbs, used correctly, can help prepare a woman's body for labor. If nothing else, enjoying a hot cup of tea or sipping an herbal tincture gives you a moment to rest your sore feet and enjoy a break! Since herbs can interact with medication and your pregnancy, please read the warning label before consuming. And, as always, ask your healthcare provider for his or her advice first.

Organic Pregnancy Tea: Prepare your womb for childbirth using herbs women have used down through the ages. Raspberry leaf, strawberry leaf and nettle leaf along with other herbs tone uterine muscles, provides nourishment. A certified organic tea by Traditional Medicinals. Price: $4.99, www.traditionalmedicinals.com.

Peaceful Mama Tea: Drink a cup of this relaxing tea before bedtime to help you sleep when your growing belly seems to get in the way of a full night's rest. Earth Mama Angel Baby uses a 100% certified organic blend of chamomile, lemon balm, oatstraw and lavender blossoms to help calm and relax expectant mamas. We have even heard of new daddies drinking a cup to relax! Price: $7.95, www.earthmamaangelbaby.com.

Third Trimester Tea: Earth Mama Angel Baby recommends that drinking this tea during the end of your pregnancy will help prepare your body for birth. 100% certified organic herbal tea contains red raspberry leaf, a traditionally used uterine tonic. Organic nettles, organic alfalfa, organic oatstraw, organic chamomile, and organic rose hips pack the tea with vitamins and minerals. Please contact a professional practitioner experienced with herbs before taking any herbal tea. Price: $7.95, www.earthmamaangelbaby.com.

Welcome Womb Tincture: Wish Garden Herbs are a favorite of midwives! An herbal tincture that helps strengthen the womb and discourage miscarriage and premature labor. Jennifer's midwife prescribed this tincture when she was on bedrest. Wild yam root, black haw bark and false unicorn root quiet and calm the uterus. Please contact a professional practitioner with experience in herbs before taking any tinctures. Price: $10.99, www.wishgardenherbs.com.

Womb Support Herbal Supplement: An alcohol-free tincture full of essential nutrients to help support the uterus and reproductive system. Pregnant women may begin taking this tincture four weeks before due date to help prepare their body for birth. Red raspberry, squaw vine, alfalfa and wild yam make up this herbal tincture that can be taken in water. Please note that this tincture should not be taken during the first few months of pregnancy, as the herbs may stimulate the uterus. Please contact a professional practitioner experienced with herbs before taking any tincture. Made by Mama Rose's Naturals in Oregon, this tincture contains no sugar or preservatives. Price: $12, www.mamarosesnaturals.com.

Womb Support Tea: An organic and caffeine-free birth preparation tea that helps to support the uterus and reproductive system. Pregnant women may begin taking this tincture four weeks before due date to help prepare their body for birth. Mama Rose's Naturals blends certified organic red rooibos, red raspberry leaf, nettle leaf, squaw vine, alfalfa, dandelion root and lemon balm. Please note that this tea should not be taken during the first few months of pregnancy, as the herbs may stimulate the uterus. Please contact a professional practitioner experienced with herbs before taking any herbal tea. Price: $8, www.mamarosesnaturals.com.

POSTPARTUM SITZ BATH HERBS

For years, women have found postpartum relief with the use of herbs that have traditional healing properties. You can add your sitz bath herbs to your bathtub or to a traditional sitz bath that fits on your toilet. After delivery of both her children, Jennifer found that a daily sitz bath as recommended by her midwife greatly helped in her healing.

Herbal Sitz Bath: A sachet of calendula, comfrey leaf, chamomile, plantain leaf and other healing herbs help soothe discomfort from childbirth. Mama Rose's Naturals includes a reusable cotton muslin tea sachet to add to your warm bath. Price: $7, www.mamarosesnaturals.com.

Postpartum Bath Herbs: A soothing blend of salts, oatmeal and organic herbs used historically to heal postpartum women. Earth Mama Angel Baby Bath Herbs use wound-healing, styptic and antibacterial organic yarrow, wild harvested witch hazel, organic calendula, marshmallow and plantain. It comes with a reusable muslin bag to fill with the bath herbs. Price: $8.95, www.earthmamaangelbaby.com.

POSTPARTUM MENSTRUAL PADS

You will need some postpartum pads for both vaginal and C-section births. It is estimated that over 14 billion pads, tampons and applicators go into North American landfills every year. Many mainstream feminine care products are made with fibers bleached with chlorine. This process releases dangerous toxins, dioxin one of them, into our environment. Over time, our bodies may absorb these chemicals. Conventional pads and even some more "eco-friendly" pads may contain super absorbent polymers similar to disposable diapers. Switching to cloth pads not only helps the environment by requiring fewer materials for production and less consumption. It can also save you money!

GladRags: One of the two most popular cloth pad brands. Reusable cloth pads come in regular or organic cotton. We like that their organic cotton pads can come in dyed or undyed colors. Gladrags suggests using their night pads for postpartum use. GladRags uses a three-part envelope design; you insert the pads into a liner that snaps around your panties. GladRags sells introduction, sampler and deluxe kits. The organic cotton pads are available in color-dyed and un-dyed versions. The dyes used in the organic pads are Oeko-Tex Standard 100 certified. GladRags are made in Portland, Oregon. Prices: $8.99 to $188.99, www.gladrags.com.

Lunapads: Reusable cloth pads made from 100% cotton fleece in hip and colorful fabric choices. 100% organic cotton fabric in a cream color is also available. Lunapads' design places the liner pad on top of the main pad, which means you change the liner throughout the day. Lunapads makes a great postpartum kit, a pad and pantyliner introduction kit, a heavy flow kit and a deluxe kit. All Lunapads Kits purchases include a free washable nylon pouch for carrying pads while out of your home. Lunapads also makes a Lunablanket that you place on your bed during postpartum to absorb any leaks and protect your sheets. Price: $14.99 to $152.99, www.lunapads.com.

Seventh Generation Disposable Pads: A full line of chlorine-free disposable feminine care products. Some of the pads use wood pulp for the absorbent material, while others use super absorbent natural polymer. Seventh Generation discloses all materials and ingredients, so check their website for the complete listing. Price: $4.29 to $5.69, www.seventhgeneration.com.

NEW MAMA LOTIONS, TINCTURES AND CREAMS

Our favorite potions for new mamas. Many natural and organic herbs can be used to help women heal after birth and adjust to motherhood. As with all skin care products, check labels for parabens and pthalates. If you are vegan or vegetarian, be on the look-out for products that use animal by-products, such as lanolin or beeswax. If you wish to avoid petroleum products stay clear of mineral oil, PEG compounds and propylene glycol.

Blossoming Belly Lotion Bar: Mama Rose's Naturals convenient packaging makes this belly bar great for travel. Itsabelly clients love that they can just roll this on their belly to relieve itching and stretch marks without having to get their fingers messy. Packed full of hydrating coconut oil, shea oil, avocado butter, mango butter, cocoa butter, jojoba, calendula and vitamin E. Price: $12, www.mamarosesnaturals.com.

Happy Mama Spray: Earth Mama Angel Baby's uplifting aromatherapy spray is made with lime and ginger pure essential oils and flower essences to help relieve pregnancy nausea, "baby blues" and "toddler rampage." Spray it on bed linens as part of baby's goodnight routine. Whenever Melissa needed an uplifting moment after stressful time a few Happy Mama spritzes brought her right out of her slump. She also uses it as a bathroom freshener instead of using toxic fragrance sprays. Happy Mama spray is phthalate-, 1,4-dioxane- and paraben-free. Price: $14.95, www.earthmamaangelbaby.com.

Earth Mama Bottom Balm: Store this balm in the refrigerator and use it to soothe hemorrhoids, postpartum vaginal swelling and bruising and episiotomies. The balm soothes and cools with an organic olive oil base infused with healing organic herbs: St. John's wort, yarrow, witch hazel, calendula and shea butter. Certified vegan, Bottom Balm is phthalate-, paraben-, 1,4-dioxane- and toxin-free. Price: $8.95 to $13.95, www.earthmamaangelbaby.com.

Maternal Balance Herbal Supplement: An alcohol-free herbal tincture to help ease common new motherhood emotional fluctuations of anxiety and depression. Motherhood is an ever-changing emotional state; this tincture can help bring you balance. Mama Rose's Naturals uses a herbal extract blend of motherwort, skullcap, chaste tree berry and wild yam Please note that this herbal tincture should not be used during pregnancy. Price: $12, www.mamarosesnaturals.com.

Natural Stretch Oil: Another great product from Earth Mama Angel Baby. The plant-based oils used in this natural, vegan-friendly formula are cold pressed without solvents to ensure purity. Organic calendula, organic chamomile, borage oil, vitamin E and neroli essential oil nourish and soothe itchy skin and help deter stretch marks. You can also use this oil in your bath or perineal massage. It contains no nut oils and is toxin-free. Price: $8.95 to $24.95, www.earthmamaangelbaby.com.

New Mama Bottom Spray: Earth Mama Angel Baby makes this cooling and soothing perineal mist to help ease postpartum discomfort. It is made with all-natural ingredients: astringent witch hazel, antibacterial lavender, and cooling peppermint pure essential oils. Jennifer credits this spray for her quick healing after the natural births of both of her children. Bottom Spray is vegan-friendly and free from phthalates, 1,4-dioxane, parabens or artificial preservatives. Price: $14.95, www.earthmamaangelbaby.com.

Rhoid Balm: We wish Motherlove could have created a different name for this balm—perhaps it might have stopped the weird glance from the Whole Foods male cashier. Strange looks aside, this balm is well worth the embarrassing purchase moment. A blend of witch hazel leaf, plantain, yarrow, calendula, olive oil and beeswax helps shrinks hemorrhoids and relieves itching. Price: $8.50 to $13.50, www.motherlove.com.

NEW MAMA TEAS

Herbal teas are not only a wonderful way to relax; they have also been created to provide benefits essential to a new mother. Many women swear by nursing teas to increase milk supply. Jennifer couldn't believe how a cup of nursing tea before bedtime could increase her milk supply the next day. Midwives swear by the ingredients in the postpartum recovery teas. Before enjoying your hot cup of mama tea, be sure to read the warning label on the package. Some postpartum teas, if used during pregnancy, can stimulate labor. And since teas can have ingredients that may interact with your medication or pregnancy, we suggest consulting with your healthcare provider before drinking any special teas.

MilkMaid Tea: A delicious nursing tea that you can enjoy iced or hot. Earth Mama Angel Baby blends 100% certified organic galactagogues and other herbs traditionally used to help increase milk supply. Milkmaid Tea is not for use during pregnancy. Price: $8.95 to $13.95, www.earthmamaangelbaby.com.

Organic Mother's Milk Tea: A sweet and spicy nursing mother's tea that combines anise, fennel and coriander to help promote healthy lactation and to increase breast milk production. Jennifer drank this tea a couple of days before she needed to pump milk to store while she'd be away from baby. Traditional Medicinals makes this certified organic tea that contains fenugreek seed along with other herbs traditionally used to increase milk supply. Price: $4.99, www.traditionalmedicinals.com.

Postpartum Recovery Tea: A delicious blend of herbs that is soothing and healing after childbirth. The astringent herbs help tone the uterus while others nourish, calm and balance brand new mamas. We also like using this tea to ease monthly PMS symptoms. Made by Earth Mama Angel Baby, this tea is a combination of 100% certified organic herbs rich in iron, calcium, magnesium and phosphorus. Herbs include: cinnamon bark, red raspberry leaf, lady's mantle leaf, nettle leaf, lemon balm leaf, lavender flower, oatstraw and alfalfa leaf. Price: $7.95, www.earthmamaangelbaby.com.

Recovery Tea: A wonderful organic and caffeine-free tea for postpartum ease. A calming blend of herbs nourish the body, support the uterus, and balance hormone levels and emotional distress. An herbal blend of certified organic red rooibos, red raspberry leaf, lavender, chamomile, hibiscus, peppermint, cinnamon, lemon balm, passion flower, partridge berry, cramp bark, hops, motherwort and skullcap. Please note that Recovery Tea should not be used during pregnancy. This tea may also be used during your menstrual cycle. Made by Mama Rose's Naturals in Oregon. Price: $8 to $15, www.mamarosesnaturals.com.

teething

• • •

Teething can be just as stressful for mom and dad as it is for baby. It is heart-wrenching to see baby in pain. You want to help stop the pain as quickly as possible. But wait and do some research before running down to the local pharmacy.

Choosing to use natural products becomes even more important when you are considering putting that product directly into your baby's mouth. Conventional teething gels use ingredients that numb rather than relieve. And there are other ingredients lurking in the gel to worry about. Plastic teethers are of course welcome to all the worries about toxic plastic ingredients, such as PVC, pthalates and BPA. We searched for natural teething remedies, pacifiers, teethers and even a cute necklace that worked well for our children.

NATURAL TEETHING REMEDIES

Fortunately, there are several all-natural and homeopathic alternatives to Benzocaine teething gels that leave baby's mouth numb. According to some doctors, there is a small risk of allergic reactions and decreased gag reflex to Benzocaine. As always, use good judgment and consult with a healthcare practitioner before administering teething tablets to your baby.

Amber Teething Necklace: Amberizon makes a beautiful selection of teething necklaces for baby to wear (not chew) that are sized to be close to baby's neck and knotted in between each bead. Teething necklaces are a very popular teething remedy in Europe and worked well for Jennifer's children. Price: $9.99 to $72.50, www.amberizon.com.

Boiron Camilia: This homeopathic treatment is for children four months of age and older. It is packaged as a single dose of liquid offering quick relief of teething symptoms. Jennifer felt that her children were calmer and relieved after taking Camilia. Each dose contains a formula of *Chamomilla vulgaris, Phytolacca decandra* and *Rheum officinale*. One box has 20 doses. Price: $6.99, www.boironusa.com.

Hyland's Teething Tablets: Homeopathic pills with a combination of natural substances that are known to relieve the restlessness and irritability associated with teething. This is a small 1-grain tablet that melts instantly on baby's tongue. The Moog family called these the magic pills because they eased Isabella's teething pains and saved their eardrums from a crying baby. Hyland's Teething Tablets include calcarea phosphorica, chamomilla, coffea cruda and belladonna. Price: $9.69, www.hylands.com.

PACIFIERS

Plastic pacifiers may contain toxic ingredients such as pthalates and BPA, and some babies may be allergic to latex pacifiers. As a result of parents' demand, many conventional brands are changing their product ingredients. Check our Resources for BPA-free online stores and blogs for updated safe product lists.

EcoBinky: A 100% natural pacifier made from pure rubber from the rubber tree, *Hevea brasiliensi*. EcoPiggy claims that there is no risk of latex allergy because the protein that on rare occasions can provoke a latex allergy has been removed. EcoPiggy manufacturers this pacifier in Denmark. The gals at EcoPiggy are working hard to increase distribution beyond Whole Foods, baby boutiques and online stores to more conventional chain stores. Price: $7, www.ecopiggy.com.

Evenflo: The Mimi Soft Touch and Neo One-piece pacifiers are BPA- and phthalate-free. The Mimi Soft Touch has an orthodontic nipple and comes in sizes for newborn to six months and for older than six months. The Mimi Neo has a rounded nipple and comes in one size. Both versions come in a two pack. Price: $4.95, www.evenflo.com.

Natursutten: All Natursutten pacifiers are made from pure natural rubber, and are softer than silicone. Melissa loved the one-piece design because it had no cracks or crevices where water and bacteria could get in and was easier to clean. These pacifiers are also free from chemical softeners, parabens, PVC or phthalates. The protein that on rare occasions can provoke a latex allergy is removed from the rubber mass used for these pacifiers. Natursutten come in two shapes—a rounded nipple or orthodontic nipple. The rounded nipple pacifier comes in four sizes, ranging from newborn to over 12 months old. The orthodontic nipple comes in two sizes—one for newborn to six months and another for over six months. Made in Europe and CE certified. We list the manufacturer's website, which is in Danish. To buy the pacifier our Resource Directory lists online boutiques specializing in BPA-free products. Price: $6.95, www.natursutten.com.

TEETHERS

Many moms will be surprised to find these colorful wooden baby toys from Europe listed as teethers. Yes, they really are teethers. They are safe for baby and baby will love them. For those who may worry about giving baby a wood toy for teething, we selected a natural all-rubber teether that has been quite popular in Europe for some time. Conventional teethers may contain BPA, phthalates and PVC. As a result of parents' demand, many conventional brands are changing their product ingredients. Check our Resources for BPA-free online stores and blogs for updated safe product lists.

Camden Rose Maple Teether: Designed to stimulate sight and touch with beautiful organic shapes and the soothing comfort of hardwood. It is easy to grasp and soothing to rub on tender gums. Each teether is made from maple wood and finished with beeswax, and is recommended for three months and older. Price: $10.99 to $12.99, www.camdenrose.com.

Chewable Jewels: Dentist Dr. Helen Bloom along with her sister Joy Wright and their friend Mary Wheeler Settlemier knew that when a baby teethes, anything is fair game, so jewelry wearing is usually off limits for mama. These three smart mamas created these lovely teething necklaces, bracelets and key chains that mommy wears and baby chews. Chewable Jewels can also be used as a nursing necklace to help keep babies' attention when they enter the nurse-and-look-around stage. With colors from blue topaz to chili pepper to smoky quartz and many jewel colors in between, you are sure to find a few to add to your wardrobe. Chewable Jewels are made from FDA-approved silicone and FDA-approved colorings and are free from phthalates, latex, BPA and lead. Price: $15.95 to $19.95, www.docbloom.com.

Haba Wooden Teethers: Haba is a well-known German manufacturer of wood and cloth baby toys. Haba offers a wide assortment of colorful and engaging baby teethers made from beech wood with a non-toxic finish. Price: $8.99 to $17.50, www.haba.de.

Vulli Teethers: Popular since 1961 in France, Vulli makes teethers from all natural rubber and non-toxic food-quality paint. We love Sophie the Giraffe's retro look. Vulli also makes a "Chan Pie Gnon" line of teethers that look like cute forest mushrooms. Price: $13.95 to $19.95, www.vulli-toys.com.

safety & babyproofing

• • •

This is one of the categories where it is necessary to buy plastic. Most baby-proofing items are usually not made from eco-friendly materials. Another great way to practice eco-friendly consumption is to recycle the plastic or pass the item onto a friend if the item is still in good condition.

BABY GATE

If you have stairs in your house, baby gates are a must. You can also use them to keep baby out of areas you do not want baby to enter, like around a fireplace or wood-burning stove. Baby gates will be up for quite a while so invest in high quality, durable gates. Once baby starts to roll and wiggle, it is time to put up baby gates if your house requires them for safety. Pressure-mounted gates should never be used on the top of stairs. A toddler can conceivably push through a pressure-mounted gate, as there is no hardware securing the gate to the wall. You can use a pressure-mounted gate at the bottom of the stairs, in doorways and hallways. Hardware-mounted gates are typically more durable than pressure-mounted gates and, again, *must* be used at the top of stairs.

KidCo: Manufactured in Denmark, these gates are made to EU standards, which exceed US standards. These gates are PVC-, phthalate- and BPA-free. KidCo baby gates are made from thick virgin steel, furniture-grade hardwood (including environmentally friendly, certified sustainable wood), glass-reinforced resins and certified non-toxic (no lead) paint. KidCo makes a variety of gates to fit your house—pressure- or hardware-mounted gates, fireplace and wood-burning stove gates, irregular shape or extra-wide area gates and freestanding play area gates. KidCo's website has a great baby gate finder to help you select the right gates for your house. JPMA certified. Price: $24.99 to $164.99, www.kidco.com.

Babyproofing Necessities: If you are near an Ikea, it is a great place to buy affordable babyproofing items. Ikea is famous for their socially responsible manufacturing and business practices. Depending on your house and

furniture, you may need the following items, all of which Ikea sells
(www.ikea.com): outlet covers, cabinet locks, door stops, window catches,
multilocks, finger guards, baby gates, and stove guard or stove control covers. Prince Lionheart, www.princelionheart.com, also makes babyproofing
items. Prince Lionheart products are BPA-, PVC- and phthalate-free.

BABY MONITOR

A model with rechargeable batteries will save a lot of money—baby mon-
itors are famous for quickly using batteries.

Graco Baby iMonitor: An Energy Star approved digital baby monitor that
has clear reception and is sensitive to sounds. The private signal means
you don't have to worry about your neighbor's eavesdropping on your
nighttime lullabies to baby. Melissa loved the compact size, rechargeable
batteries and extended range (2000 ft). Price: $79.99,
www.gracobaby.com.

MobiCam Ultra: Another of Melissa's favorites. We offer this baby monitor because of its unique product features and Mobi's green efforts. A
large color display on the parent unit allows you to
view your baby sleeping. The Mobi Cam has a
300-ft range during the day and night vision
with up to a 25-ft range. Mobi is eliminating BPA from products and switching to
rechargeable batteries; check with Mobi
for completion date. Environmentally
friendly switching AC power supplies do
not use any electricity unless the power to
the unit is actually turned on. Price: $169.99,
www.getmobi.com.

eco mom tip:

Use your cordless phone's
room-monitoring function for
your baby monitor and cross one
item off your "to buy" list.

—*Laura Lafayette,*
Portland, OR

nice-to-haves

• • •

Here is a short list of some of our favorite eco-friendly little extras. While these are not essential for a healthy baby, they may help in entertaining baby when you need a few moments to do something for yourself. And trust us, you will appreciate those few moments—especially when you haven't showered in a few days!

Everywhere you look you find children's toys, bouncy seats and other fun "nice to haves" made out of plastic. Obviously these items have the same toxin concerns as other plastic items. Before purchasing anything plastic, check with the manufacturer about the ingredients. Ask if the product is free from BPA, phthalates and PVC. Your baby will probably chew on his toys. Exersaucers and bouncy seats will also fall victim to baby's gnawing instincts —not to mention that baby will be sitting in the plastic contraption.

It really is true that children are more fascinated by the box the toy came in than the toy. Jennifer believes that this is because the box provides open-ended imaginative play. Often the toy itself provides the child with more limited, scripted play. We love wooden toys because they are usually simpler and leave more to the child's imagination. Also, wooden toys typically last longer than plastic toys because they don't have small parts to break. And when they do break, wooden toys can often be repaired with some carpenter's glue and sand paper.

We recommend some non-plastic-based bouncy seats, playmats and toys. These days you can even find quality wooden toys at Target! With a Google search of "wood baby toys" you will find an online shopping extravaganza. We also recommend some of our favorite wooden and natural toy manufacturers. You'll find our favorite online toy boutiques in our Green Resource Directory.

ITSABELLY'S MOMMY-AND-ME RESOURCES

Finding baby and mommy focused classes and playgroups in your local community will help you connect with other moms with children the same age as yours. You can learn some new songs or even get in shape—all with baby at your side.

- Find local playgroups and mom groups at www.matchingmoms.org and www.playgroupsusa.com.
- Read local parenting magazines or newspapers for infant sign language classes, infant massage and baby yoga classes.
- University child development centers often have mommy-and-me classes.
- Check out these national organizations for a local class:
  - **Baby Signs:** Take a class to learn to communicate with your baby using baby sign language, www.babysigns.com.
  - **Baby Bootcamp:** This innovative stroller-fitness program helps moms regain or enhance pre-pregnancy fitness levels and meet the physical challenges of parenting by emphasizing strength training in a supportive environment, www.babybootcamp.com.
  - **Gymboree Play and Music:** Seven levels of developmentally appropriate art, music and play classes for child and caregiver. Classes begin from newborn until five years old, www.gymboreeclasses.com.
  - **Healthy Mom Fitness:** A wide variety of classes to help pregnant and new moms prepare for the physiological changes, develop stamina and strength for labor and delivery and restore muscle tone after the baby is born, www.healthymomsfitness.com.
  - **Music Together:** Since 1987, Music Together is a fun early childhood music program for babies, toddlers, preschoolers, kindergartners, and their caregiver, www.musictogether.com.
  - **Kindermusik:** Classes are based upon Kindermusik's music and movement curricula for caregivers and their children, ages newborn to seven years old, www.kindermusik.com.
  - **Stroller Strides:** Fun and rewarding fitness classes where you exercise with your baby in a stroller at outdoor or indoor venues, www.strollerstrides.com.

BOUNCY SEAT

There are several brands of baby bouncy seats that are not plastic eye-sores and will actually look lovely in your living room.

Baby Björn BabySitter: Jennifer's babies loved bouncing in their Babysitter and playing with the cute wooden bears on the simple toy bar. A great bouncer roomy enough to fit a growing baby, the Babysitter makes it easy for the baby to learn how to bounce. The seat has three adjustable seat positions for play, rest and sleep. When baby is older, remove the restraint to use as a toddler chair. The Babysitter can be used from birth to 24 months (up to 29 lbs). The seat cover is also reversible and washable. The seat fabric is made in accordance with the Oeko-Tex Standard 100, class 1, eco-certification. Price: $99.95, www.babybjorn.com.

Oeuf Baby Lounger: Another great minimalist design from this socially responsible manufacturer. The Lounger's padded, machine-washable, canvas seat is supported by its steel frame. We must note that while the outside fabric of the seat is 100% cotton, the padding inside is polyester. The Oeuf Baby Lounger can be used from birth until the child can sit up unassisted or reaches 18 lbs. Price: $98, www.oeufnyc.com.

Svan Bouncer: A beautiful and slim design that converts from a nearly full-recline to an upright position. It has an ergonomic backrest fitting babies from six to 30 lbs. Great for babies and also for early pre-high chair feedings. No bells and whistles, but loops are included so you can attach your own toys. The bouncer is made from bent birch wood with a PBDE-free padded seat. JPMA certified. Price: $119.99, www.svanusa.com.

PLAYTIME

Who wants to surround baby in an exersaucer made out of possibly toxic plastic? Besides the plastics being hazardous to baby, some doctors/psychologists believe that a baby can become over stimulated in those contraptions. Here are some alternatives that are simple, space-saving and entertaining for baby.

Haba Dangle and Drape Activity Center: Haba is a German manufacturer well known for their colorful wood and cloth baby toys. An extremely simple yet versatile activity center. A clutching toy can be dangled from the wooden frame and when baby is a toddler, the set converts into a play tent by draping cloth over the sturdy frame. The height is adjustable and the set folds for easy storage. Includes a washable tent cover and clutching toy with bell. Price: $101, www.haba.de.

Haba Dream Meadow Activity Center and Playmat: A colorful and soft playmat that can also be converted into a travel bed or diaper changer by flipping up the sides of the playmat. You can hang different toys from the play gym bar. The activity center also includes a squeaker and rustling and glitter foil pockets. You can also buy a rocker attachment for the bottom of the play center. Price: $149.99, www.haba.de.

Merry Muscles Jumper: Designed by an occupational therapist to protect your baby's bone structure and body alignment. Baby bounces using the soles of his feet, instead of the tiptoes, to avoid permanent damage to baby's toes. Also, baby's hips are cradled, preventing baby from bouncing with stiff legs, eliminating the possibility of bone or joint injuries caused by impact. The back section of the jumper protects the spine and head. Adjusts to fit age two months to two years. Price: $69.95 CAD, www.babyloveproducts.com.

LULLABY CD
Calming music can be a wonderful addition to baby's bedtime routine. Used consistently it can become a sleep cue for baby.

Putomayo Dreamland Series—Asian, Celtic and the Original CD: Putomayo creates wonderful collections of children's world music that their parents will also enjoy. For each Putumayo Kids release, at least one percent of Putumayo's proceeds benefits relevant non-profit groups that support children, families, schools and other charities. Price: $13.99, www.putumayo.com.

Bengali Lullaby: A meditative chant sung in English, Spanish and the original Bengali version. Great for rocking baby or infant massage. Price: $9.99, www.joserubendeleon.com.

ITSABELLY'S FAVORITE TOY BRANDS

Check out these manufacturers for great baby clutching toys, rattles, blocks, playsilks, stuffed lovelies and rolling cars.

- **BlaBla:** www.blablakids.com
- **Camden Rose:** www.camdenrose.com
- **Chelona:** www.chelona.gr
- **Haba:** www.haba.de
- **Plan Toys:** www.plantoys.com
- **Sarah's Silks:** www.sarahssilks.com
- **Selecta:** www.selecta-spielzeug.de
- **Vilac:** www.vilac.com

the green r's: reducing, reusing & recycling your baby gear

So, you've heard of the green Rs, right? No, we're not talking about reading, writing and 'rithmetic. The *green* three Rs are: **reducing, reusing** and **recycling**. Accomplishing these three Rs can seem like a daunting task when planning for a baby. How do you reduce consumption when you have a mile-long list of items you need to buy before baby arrives?

REDUCING

Conscious planning to reduce consumption and planning your baby purchases go hand in hand. Your mile-long list of things to purchase gives you the opportunity to sit back and evaluate all your needs and to purchase only necessary items. Thankfully, humans don't have the 33-day gestation period of a rabbit. We get nine months to plan our baby's arrival!

To start, take a good, hard look at that long list of everything baby needs. Every family has a different lifestyle and different needs. Our Green Registry List offers several different sleeping options for baby—a Moses basket, cradle, crib, or co-sleeper. Surely, you don't need all of them, and we aren't suggesting you buy all of them! Since every family is different, we want to give our readers options from which they can choose what's going to work best for them.

Study each item on your list: is it really a need—or a want? Are you getting caught up in the must-have frenzy that seems to pave the way to parenthood today? Are you in a 10k race to keep up with the Smiths next door?

When Malena, Jennifer's first daughter, was born, reducing consumption was not only a green goal but also a spatial necessity. Their two-bedroom South Florida bungalow simply didn't have enough space for an elaborate nursery or lots of baby gear. Jennifer planned to change diapers on the crib, which was never actually used for more than diaper changes and the occasional nap. Because she had an empty closet in the office/nursery, she realized she didn't need a dresser. She planned to use her soft structured-carrier and sling for walks to the park and running errands. Without a garage to store a bulky stroller, she bought a Snap N' Go stroller for longer walks to the beach.

But it wasn't only about space. Friends were always surprised when their children came over for a playdate and found no swings or exersaucers filling every spare corner. Personally, Jennifer felt that many of these baby entertainers were too stimulating for babies. She felt it was *okay* for her baby to stare at some blank space once in a while. She worried that babies who constantly relied on externals for their entertainment would not be able to entertain themselves. We need quiet time for ourselves to think and relax—why wouldn't a baby appreciate the same?

REUSING

Many baby products have a short window of usefulness. Babies outgrow clothing fast, and since infants generally don't get dirty beyond a little spit-up, their clothes are often in great condi-tion. What does this mean for the green baby? The perfect opportunity for buying secondhand baby gear and reselling the baby gear you no longer need.

eco mom tip:

Get to know your consign-ment shop's schedule for putting out new clothes on the floor. Great bargains can often be found at season's end.

—*Maureen Moog*
Seattle, WA

Most communities have several baby and maternity consignment stores, often run by moms for moms. Check your yellow pages or do an internet search, then get out there and start browsing. You will be amazed at the affordable prices of clothing and gear at consignment shops. The deal gets even better when you sell you own items there; you can usually use your balance toward the purchase of new items at an even greater discount.

Melissa was lucky to have Cindy, her generous sister-in-law who not only helped her decide what products she needed and what was a waste of time and/or money, but who also gave her lots of hand-me-down baby gear. Melissa also received lots of maternity clothes from friends who had already had their babies. When Melissa was finished with the items, she continued the tradition, passing them along to other friends.

First, when you buy baby clothing or gear, select gender-neutral items. Even if you know you are having a girl, your next child could very well be a boy. You can increase your opportunity for reusing the item if it is gender-neutral.

The second thing to consider is quality. If you buy high-quality products for your first baby, those items should be able to last through the needs of your next baby.

When our little ones outgrow baby gear and clothing, we find it helpful to separate it into different categories—donations, consignment or saving for the next baby. The donation pile can either be given to a local charity or to a friend. There will always be a mom with a new baby in your local mom's group or preschool.

We usually reserve items that still have the tags on them for the consignment shop so that we can get a higher dollar value. Consignment shops are also a great option for those baby gifts that don't match your lifestyle. And don't forget to let friends and family know your preferences, since many of your newborn items will be gifts.

Itsabelly's Guide To Safe Secondhand
- Some baby products should **not** be used secondhand. Always check the quality and safety of secondhand products.
- We do not recommend secondhand cribs because of safety hazards such as space between spindles, cutouts, decorative trim, the possibility of lead paint, missing parts and lost assembly instructions. You don't want to assemble a crib incorrectly—one missing screw can bring the whole crib down!
- We do not recommend using secondhand car seats, apart from with the special exception of your older child's seat if the car seat meets these conditions: it has not been in an accident, has no cracks and is complete with parts and manual. Please call your manufacturer to find out the expiration date of your car seat.

- If the item doesn't come with an owner's manual, see if you can download one from the brand's website.
- Keep up to date with product recalls, www.recalls.gov.

RECYCLING

Before kids, when we cleaned out our closets and switched clothing for the season, we collected items to donate to the local big box thrift store. Sure, it was easy—just throw everything in a bag, drive up to the drop-off center, give them your bag and leave with a tax receipt. After having kids, we began to wonder if this type of donation was the best way to help families in need. As stay-at-home moms, we understood the sacrifice that mothers make to take care of their families. If we struggled sometimes at the cost of raising children, how would someone manage who wasn't as fortunate as we are?

Melissa had been a volunteer for her local Dress for Success chapter. She knew the great value of organizations that offer clothing and supplies for free, along with counseling and coaching to overcome difficulties.

Jennifer had read stories about how some donations to big box thrift stores actually get shipped overseas and resold to local residents. Some countries have banned the import of used clothing, claiming that these imports take away jobs from the domestic market. In her article on the subject, reporter Molly Bloom states that textile recycling is a billon dollar industry. She also reports that for-profit recyclers may even pay charities to use their logos to operate clothing drop off bins.

On the other hand, some research shows that some of these organizations recycle and find markets for donated items rather than see them go into a landfill. (Clothing that is too worn can be recycled into fiber for rags and old shoes into rubber.) Economist Pietra Rivoli, claims that many countries that import used clothing mainly manufacture clothing for the export market, which is not affordable to local residents.

The bottom line: this one has to be your call.

CAN CHARITABLE DONATIONS HURT PEOPLE ABROAD?

For more information on how your charitable donation to a big thrift store can do more harm than good when shipped overseas:

- "When donations go farther than you think," by Molly Bloom, *Newark Star Ledger*, www.mollybloom.net/bins.html.
- "Where the used shoe fits," by Kelly Kearsley, *The News Tribune*. dwb.thenewstribune.com/business/story/5583524p-5021353c.html
- EnviroMom Blog: www.enviromom.com/2007/10/ avoiding-goodwi.html.
- Pietra Rivoli, a finance professor at Georgetown University, studied the second life of clothing for her book, *The Travels of a T-shirt in the Global Economy: An Economist Examines the Markets, Power, and Politics of World Trade.*

Both mamas decided to do some research. They wanted to find organizations that would pass donated clothing along for free to families in need, that offered more than just free shopping, that took an "it takes a village" approach to help families get back on their feet. They wanted to find organizations that had valuable programs for young children. It wasn't an easy quest.

Through our research, we decided to support local family shelters. We visited our local organization when we dropped off items to see firsthand how our donations would be used and witness the assistance and services these organizations provide to help families in need. We were surprised at the wealth of services these shelters can offer with limited funds. Bigger charities receive more donations because of their "brand name" and media exposure. However, with a little research you can find good local alternatives.

Itsabelly is committed to encouraging the donation of items to family-friendly charities. Check out our blog, www.itsabelly.typepad.com, for recommendations, sign up for Itsabelly news and don't forget to let us know about your favorite local charity.

Finding a Family-Friendly Charity
- Internet searches: Use the following phrases plus your location—women's shelter, family shelter, children's shelter, donate baby items, family charity, family services center, donation, family, baby items.
- Questions to ask before donating:
    - What type of programs do you offer local families?
    - How will my donation be used?
    - Do you resell unsold clothing to textile recyclers?
    - Check the organization's website or call for a wish list of needed and not-needed items.
    - Call before dropping off large items.
    - Due to legal restrictions, many charities cannot accept car seats.

eco mom tip:
Donate your cloth diapers and slings to charity. Miracle Diapers, www.miraclediapers.org, accepts cloth diapers and natural family living items to pass on to families in need.

green resource directory

• • •

Here's a list of some of our favorite resources when it comes to the latest in books, websites, magazines and blogs. Every day we find new sites that focus on green living, so many that it's a real challenge to keep up with all the information that's now out there. We will be highlighting our favorite sources on our blog, www.itsabelly.typepad.com, so check there for updates and our latest finds. These resources were also used for research in writing our book. Sprinkled throughout each section, we added our favorite stores for buying related items. Our recommended brands can be found in the Green Brand Directory.

BABYWEARING
- **Attached to Baby:** A comprehensive babywearing store with great customer service, www.attachedtobaby.com.
- **KellyMom Sling Sewing:** A listing of many sling sewing patterns and websites, www.kellymom.com/parenting/sling.html#sewing.
- *Mothering* **Magazine BabyWearing Issue Reprint:** Comprehensive babywearing articles, www.mothering.com/shop/index.php?target=products&product_id=29888.
- **Peppermint:** A babywearing store with a great carrier comparison chart, www.peppermint.com.
- **Safe BabyWearing Blog:** www.babyslingsafety.blogspot.com.
- **Sling Rings:** The only source for safe sling rings, www.slingrings.com.
- **SoBeBabies:** A selective babywearing boutique that also sells unique diaper bags, strollers, European children's furniture and clothing, www.sobebabies.com.
- **The BabyWearer:** Everything you need to know about babywearing, product reviews and active online forum, www.thebabywearer.com.
- **Wear Your Baby:** An amazing wealth of information on baby wearing including videos and printable illustrations to learn carrying positions and a helpful comparison chart of carriers and position advantages, www.wearyourbaby.com or www.mamatoto.org.

BIRTH / PREGNANCY

- **American Pregnancy Association:** Helpful pregnancy information and tips, www.americanpregnancy.org.
- **Binsi:** Did you know you don't have to wear a hospital gown? Binsi makes beautiful and functional skirts that you can wear during labor. Binsi also makes matching tops that work well for nursing. www.birthinbinsi.com.
- **Birthing from Within:** Childbirth preparation classes based on self-discovery, creative self-expression and parents' individual needs. Birthing From Within views birth partners as birth guardians who also need support, not just as someone coaching mom, www.birthingfromwithin.com.
- **Bradley Method:** Natural childbirth preparation that stresses the importance of Healthy Baby, Healthy Mother and Healthy Families. Classes emphasize partner coach education. Classes also cover pregnancy and postpartum issues, www.bradleybirth.com.
- *The Business of Being Born:* A documentary on the way American women have babies by Ricki Lake and Abby Epstein, www.thebusinessofbeingborn.com.
- **Doulas of North America** (DONA): Find a local birth or postpartum doula, www.dona.org.
- **Earth Mama Angel Baby:** Wonderful natural skincare and herbal products. Earth Mama's website provides a complete birth plan customizable template and an educational reading room, www.earthmamaangelbaby.com.
- **HypnoBirthing:** A unique method that allows women to use their natural instincts to have a safe, relaxed, natural birth education enhanced by self-hypnosis techniques, www.hypnobirthing.com.
- *Ina May's Guide to Childbirth:* Written by leading midwife Ina May Gaskin. An inspiring book that helps women reduce their fear of childbirth by regaining confidence in their body's ability to birth. Gaskin also covers birthing's practical side with information such as avoiding standard medical interventions that may be harmful to mother and baby, www.inamay.com.
- **International Childbirth Education Association:** Since 1960, promotes family-centered maternity care. Find a local childbirth preparation class.

Lists all types of classes, www.icea.org.

- **Lamaze:** Childbirth preparation classes that give access to information on the health and safety benefits of normal birth to mother and baby. Lamaze focuses on confident woman choosing a normal birth, www.lamaze.org.
- **Mother Tree Birth Services:** Doula services in Portland, OR, and Vancouver, WA, www.mothertreebirth.com.
- *The Birth Book:* Dr. William and Martha Sears help you in selecting the right birthing environment and team, preparing physically and emotionally, and lessening discomfort and speeding the labor process, www.askdrsears.com.
- **The Bump:** The ultimate guides to pregnant local living, www.thebump.com.
- *The Pregnancy Book:* Written by Dr. William and Martha Sears and Dr. Linda Hughey Holt. A month-by-month guide that steers you through every decision and issue relating to pregnancy, www.askdrsears.com.
- *Pushed:* A book about the current state of maternity care and a blog that covers uncensored, unsweetened information about U.S. childbirth care. Both are book and blog by journalist Jennifer Block, former editor for *Ms.* magazine, www.pushedbirth.com.

BLOGS / MAGAZINES

- **5 Minutes for Mom:** A mom community blog that helps you make the most of your "mom" time, www.5minutesformom.com.
- *Baby Bargains:* by Denise and Alan Fields. A great book for product reviews of conventional baby gear, registry recommendations and how to save money on baby products.
- **Baby Tool Kit:** Interesting parents' tips and gear reviews with both a geek *and* green twist, www.babytoolkit.blogspot.com.
- *Babble:* Blogs, magazine and online community for a new generation of parents, www.babble.com.
- *Cookie* **Magazine:** A hip and fashionable family magazine, www.cookiemag.com.
- **Cool Mom Picks:** Blog highlights unique products and services and writes great gift giving guides, www.coolmompicks.com.
- *Fit Pregnancy:* A popular pregnancy magazine that focuses on health,

nutrition and exercise, www.fitpregnancy.com.

- *Get Organized Guide for New Moms:* by Stacey Crew gives helpful organization that every mother can use, www.clearvisionorganization.com/gopack/gopack_moms.shtml.
- **Itsabelly Blog:** Melissa's informative parenting blog that covers many green topics, www.itsa-belly.com.
- *Mother Jones:* An independent nonprofit magazine and website committed to social justice and investigative reporting, www.motherjones.com.
- *Mothering* **Magazine:** You can also read articles online and join lively discussions in their forum, www.mothering.com.
- **Sparkplugging:** Work at home resources and online community. Itsabelly's Melissa Moog writes the Simply Green Living Blog, www.sparkplugging.com.
- **The Cradle:** A parenting lifestyle destination site that also has an Eco Cradle section, www.thecradle.com.
- **Urban Mamas:** An on-line community of Portland moms focused on sharing tips, reviews, ideas and fun activities for families, www.urbanmamas.com.

BREASTFEEDING

- **Breastfeeding.com:** A website dedicated to breastfeeding information and support. Also has other parenting information. For a fun break, check out the breastfeeding celebrity section, www.breastfeeding.com.
- **Breastfeeding Online:** Information to empower women to choose to breastfeed and to educate society about the importance and benefits of breastfeeding. Also has a breastfeeding store, www.breastfeedingonline.com.
- **KellyMom:** A comprehensive website on breastfeeding and parenting, www.kellymom.com.
- **La Leche League:** Experts in breastfeeding knowledge and support. Find a local La Leche League chapter for breastfeeding support. The LLL store features nursing apparel, pumps and breastfeeding accessories, www.lalecheleague.org.
- *Medications and Mothers' Milk:* Written by renowned clinical pharmacologist, Dr. Thomas W. Hale. A comprehensive reference book on

medications impact on breastfeeding mothers and infants. Includes information on more than 1000 drugs, vitamins, herbs, and vaccines.

- **Mocha Milk:** All things related to breastfeeding and the African-American woman. Mocha Milk provides support, research and encouragement, www.mochamilk.blogspot.com.
- **Motherwear:** A catalog and online store that sells nursing wear, pumps and breastfeeding accessories, www.motherwear.com.
- **Safety of Commonly Used Drugs in Nursing Mothers:** An informative chart of drugs to avoid and ones that are safe to take during breastfeeding by Philip O. Anderson, PharmD, FASHP, FCSHP, Director, Drug Information Service at the University of California San Diego Medical Center, www.health.ucsd.edu/pharmacy/resources/breastfeeding.htm.
- *The Nursing Mother's Companion*: Author Kathleen Huggins, R.N., M.S. provides easy to use information on breastfeeding and solving nursing issues.
- *The Womanly Art of Breastfeeding*: The definitive guide to breastfeeding by La Leche League, www.lalecheleague.org.
- **World Alliance for Breastfeeding Action:** A global network of individuals and organizations concerned with the protection, promotion and support of breastfeeding worldwide, www.waba.org.my.
- **Worldwide Network of Lactation Professionals:** Find a board certified lactation consultant, www.ilca.org.

DIAPERS AND ELIMINATION COMMUNICATION

- **Born To Love:** Lots of how-to and frugal cloth diapering information along with an online shop, www.borntolove.com.
- **Cotton Babies:** A complete cloth diapering boutique. Cotton Babies also sells baby gear, apparel for baby and mom and natural family living products, www.cottonbabies.com.
- **Diaper Decisions:** A good cost comparison chart, www.diaperdecisions.com.
- **DiaperFree Baby:** A network of free support groups promoting a natural approach to responding to babies' elimination needs. There is also an online store that sells potties and elimination communication necessities, www.diaperfreebaby.com.

- **Diaper Hyena:** An online cloth diapering and natural parenting resource. Diaper Hyena has a WAHM cloth diapering directory, cloth diaper folding instructions and cloth diapering educational articles, www.thediaperhyena.com.
- **Diaper Jungle:** A comprehensive resource for cloth diapering parents, diaper sewing information and directory of WAHM diaper businesses, www.diaperjungle.com.
- **Diaper Pin:** Cloth diapering product reviews, community forum, comparison of cloth diapering systems, savings calculator and cloth diapering dictionary, www.diaperpin.com.
- **Green Mountain Diapers:** Online shop selling everything you need for cloth diapering. Green Mountain Diapers focuses on natural fiber items, www.greenmountaindiapers.com.
- **National Association of Diaper Services:** Find a local cloth diaper service, www.diapernet.org.
- **Real Diaper Association:** Provides support and education to parents for the use of cloth diapers. Also provides information for advocacy and finding a local cloth diapering group, www.realdiaperassociation.org.
- **The EC Store:** Gear devoted to elimination communication or potty learning anytime, www.theecstore.com.
- **Tidee Didee Cloth Diaper Service:** A cloth diapering service serving the greater Portland, Oregon metro area and Southwest Washington, www.tideedidee.com.
- **Tiny Tots:** Since 1966, a popular diaper service in the California Bay Area. Even if you aren't in the Bay Area, you can shop at Tiny Tots' online boutique. Tiny Tots Togs is an adorable boutique full of products for all your natural family living needs—diapering supplies, slings, potty training, skin care, breast pumps, clothing and even toys. They offer a diaper cover exchange forum. Tiny Tots provides informative data and tips on cloth diapering, www.tinytots.com.
- **University of Minnesota Waste Education:** An analysis of diaper options, www.extension.umn.edu/distribution/housingandclothing/DK5911.html.
- **Zoom Baby Gear:** Cloth diapers for modern babies. Zoom Baby focuses handpicked local, small company and mama-owned brands. They also sell gently used diapers, www.zoombabygear.com.

ENVIRONMENTAL RESEARCH AND GROUPS

- **About Organic Cotton:** An informative, engaging and simple description of the benefits of organic cotton and danger of conventional cotton, www.aboutorganiccotton.org.
- *An Inconvenient Truth:* The book and movie by Al Gore that helped the public reach the tipping point on interest in going green, www.climatecrisis.net.
- **Center for Environmental Health:** Studies on lead in plastic-based products, www.cehca.org.
- **Center for Health, Environment & Justice:** Informative BPA and PVC guides, www.chej.org.
- **Co-op America:** Great online directory of green businesses, www.coopamerica.org.
- **Demeter:** Information on biodynamic farming, www.demeter.net.
- **Eco-Cycle:** Information on building zero waste communities, www.ecocycle.org.
- **Environment California:** Great research and guide on toxic baby bottles and toxic flame-retardants, www.environmentcalifornia.org.
- **Environmental Defense Fund:** Since 1967, the EDF has addressed environmental concerns through strong science, innovative markets, corporate partnerships and public policy, www.environmentaldefense.org.
- **Environmental Media Association:** The EMA uses television, film, music and the entertainment community to increase environmental awareness, www.ema-online.org.
- **Environmental Working Group:** The "mission of the EWG is to use the power of public information to protect public health and the environment." Informative product buying guides and database for checking safety of skincare products, www.ewg.org.
- **Greener Choices:** Easy to understand information on green products from Consumers Union, the people behind *Consumer Reports,* www.greenerchoices.org.
- **Hemp Industries Association:** A trade association that encourages research and development of hemp products, www.hempindustries.org.
- **Institute for Children's Environmental Health:** A nonprofit educational organization that aims to create a healthy, just and sustainable future for all children. ICEH's primary mission is to reduce and eliminate

environmental exposures that can harm our young and future generations, www.iceh.org.

- **Kids for Saving Earth:** Child-friendly information and advocacy for environmental issues and education. A network of over 7,000 schools and environmentally concerned kids and adults, www.kidsforsavingearth.org.
- **Laurie David:** Global warming activist, producer and author. She produced *An Inconvenient Truth.* Her book *Down To Earth Guide on Global Warming* explains global warming in a simple manner and teaches children that they can make a difference. She also writes an informative blog on global warming, www.lauriedavid.com.
- **National Resources Defense Council:** An environmental action group that combines "the grassroots power of 1.2 million members and online activists with the courtroom clout and expertise of more than 350 lawyers, scientists and other professionals," www.nrdc.org.
- **Organic Consumers Association:** Advocates for health, justice, and sustainability and promoting the interest of organic and socially responsible consumer, www.organicconsumers.org.
- **Organic Exchange:** A charitable organization working with farmers, brands and retailers to increase the production and use of organically grown fibers, www.organicexchange.org.
- **Stop Global Warming:** Join the Stop Global Warming march "to declare that global warming is here now and that it is time to demand solutions," www.stopglobalwarming.org.
- **Sustainability Institute:** Focuses on understanding the causes of unsustainable behavior through biology, social science, dynamic modeling, systems analysis and research, www.sustainer.org.
- **TransFair USA:** A nonprofit organization that is a third-party certifier of fair trade products, www.transfairusa.org.
- **Washington Toxics Coalition:** Aim is to protect public health and the environment by eliminating toxic pollution. Don't miss their recent study on Phthalates in Toys, www.watoxics.org.

FEEDING

- **Annabel Karmel:** Well-known for her cookbooks, her site offers food and nutrition information for baby and child. Lots of great recipes and a community forum, www.annabelkarmel.com.

- **Life without Plastic:** Online store featuring cool non-plastic products, www.lifewithoutplastic.com.
- **Local Harvest:** Proponent of community supported agriculture. Find a local farm share, www.localharvest.org.
- **Marine Stewardship Council:** Learn about sustainable fishing, seafood recipes and where to find certified seafood, www.msc.org.
- **Reusable Bags:** A large selection of reusable cloth grocery and lunch bags and non-toxic water bottles for kids and adults, www.reusablebags.com.
- *The Green Guide:* Check out their comprehensive list of safe plastic food containers, www.thegreenguide.com/doc/95/containers.
- **The Soft Landing:** Non-toxic feeding gear that is free from BPA, PVC and phthalates. Owner Alicia Voorhies also writes an informative blog, www.thesoftlanding.com.
- **Wholesome Baby Food:** Recipes and nutrition information for feeding babies and making your own baby food, www.wholesomebabyfood.com.
- **Zrecs BPA-Free Wallet Card:** Print out this handy shopping guide, www.zrecs.blogspot.com/2008/03/bpa-wallet-card.html.
- **Zrecs BPA Survey:** Detailed information rates brands based on their products with BPA, www.zrecs.blogspot.com/2008/02/z-report-on-bpa-in-infant-care-products.html.
- **Zrecs Mobile Product Check:** Use your phone and text messaging to check products while shopping, www.zrecs.blogspot.com/2008/02/use-z-report-at-store-with-text.html.

GREEN HOME

- **Ecohaus:** Green building supplies and household products. Learning section of website has practical and environmental issues regarding building materials, www.environmentalhomecenter.com.
- **Green Building:** Everything you need to know about designing and creating a green home, www.greenbuilding.com.
- **Green Home Guide:** A community-based resource of tips, case studies, expert articles and regional product and service directories for creating green homes, www.greenhomeguide.com.
- **Healthy House Institute:** A resource for healthier indoor environment.

Lots of educational articles, tips and reviews,
www.healthyhouseinstitute.com.

GREEN LIVING

- **Baby Wit:** An online and bricks-and-mortar boutique that sells really unique organic baby clothes made by Light and Gravity, which are hand-screened and hand-dyed with eco-friendly water-based inks in Portland, OR, www.babywit.com.
- **Baby Works:** For 18 years, Baby Works has carried the top brands in cloth diapers and accessories as well as many green products that are gentle on the earth and baby, www.babyworks.com.
- *Big Green Purse:* Author Diane MacEachern believes the fastest way to create environmental change is through changing our spending habits. Her book gives you the background and product reviews to do so. Online you will find green news, reviews of eco-friendly products, www.biggreenpurse.com.
- **Child Organics:** A great selection of eco-friendly and fair trade diapers, toys, clothing, mama coats, handknits, baby care items, bedding and homeopathic remedies, www.childorganics.com.
- **Clementine NW:** Owned by a mom entrepreneur, this on-line green boutique carries great baby and mama products made with the highest quality of safe ingredients, www.clementinenw.com.
- *E/The Environmental Magazine:* A magazine and website that gives you the news and resources to make a difference for the environment, www.emagazine.com.
- **Eco Chick:** A place for women who care about the earth, www.eco-chick.com.
- **EcoChildsPlay:** A blog dedicated to "green parenting for non-toxic, healthy homes," www.ecochildsplay.com.
- **Eco Fabulous Blog:** A blog about sustainable, sexy, stuff, www.ecofabulous.blogs.com.
- **EnviroMom Blog:** Popular Portland, OR, blog about raising green kids that moms everywhere will love, www.enviromom.com.
- **Gaiam:** A healthy lifestyle catalog and online shopping, www.gaiam.com.
- **Go Natural Baby:** An online boutique selling green baby gear and their

own Zah Collection of beautiful and well made certified organic cotton baby clothing, www.gonaturalbaby.com.

- **Great Green Baby:** A shopping blog that features environmentally friendly products for you and your baby, www.greatgreenbaby.com.
- *Green Babies, Sage Mamas:* Written by Lynda Fassa, creator of Green Babies organic cotton apparel. Fassa shares how to have a greener pregnancy and baby through product recommendations and background environmental issues, www.greenbabies.com.
- **Green Baby Guide:** Blog with tips and reviews for green parenting, www.greenbabyguide.com.
- **Green Girl Guide:** The hottest environmentally and/or socially conscious people, places and things in beauty, fashion and lifestyle, www.greengirlguide.com.
- *Green Living:* An easy-to-read handbook that helps you make informed product choices, www.emagazine.com.
- **Green Mom Finds:** A green family blog that features great green products, www.greenmomfinds.com.
- **Green Mommy Guide:** Helping moms go green and stay fabulous, www.greenmommyguide.com.
- **GreenNest:** Everything you need for your green home and family, www.greennest.com.
- **Grist:** Environmental news with a dash of humor, www.grist.org.
- *Healthy Child Healthy World—Creating a Cleaner, Greener, Safer Home:* Written by Christopher Gavigan. Everything you need to know about creating a non-toxic environment for your family. Website has valuable articles on healthy living. Content from leading medical experts and personal stories from green celebs, www.healthychild.org.
- **Ideal Bite:** Receive daily emails of easy green living tips and eco-friendly products and services, www.idealbite.com.
- **Itsabelly Boutique:** Natural and non-toxic skincare, pregnancy snack bars and candles to pamper and nourish mama and baby, http://store.itsa-belly.com.
- *Kiwi* **Magazine:** A magazine that focuses on raising natural and organic families, www.kiwimagonline.com.
- *Lazy Environmentalist:* Book and blog that highlights easy and convenient ways to be greener, www.lazyenvironmentalist.com.

- **Little Urbanites:** A modern boutique carrying the hippest and most stylish environmentally safe products for children from birth to six years old, www.littleurbanites.com.
- **Milagros:** Named after the word "miracles" in Spanish, this store offers an array of natural, fairly-made, and recycled products for your little miracle, www.milagrosboutique.com.
- **Mindful Mama:** A blog about living a green and healthy life, www.mindfulmomma.typepad.com.
- **Mother Nature's Baby Store:** A store focused on providing earth friendly baby products to parenting families, www.mothernaturesbabystore.com.
- *Natural Health:* A green living magazine and website, www.naturalhealthmag.com.
- **Nature Mom's Blog:** Green and natural parenting information and product reviews, www.naturemoms.com.
- *Organic Baby—Simple Steps for Healthy Living:* Interior designer and mother Kimberly Rider shares how to create an eco-friendly environment for your baby, www.atmospherahome.com.
- **Organic Mania:** A blog gives you simple steps to healthy green living, www.organicmania.com.
- **Pauper's Candles:** Beautiful 100% natural soy wax candles that are hand poured and manufactured in the USA, www.pauperscandles.com.
- *Plenty*: A magazine and blogs dedicated to giving a voice to the green revolution, www.plentymag.com.
- **POSH:** A boutique located in the hip and popular Pearl District in Portland that features modern and eco-friendly products. If you can't make it to Portland, no worries—they have you covered with their online shopping, www.poshbabyllc.com.
- *Raising Baby Green:* Written by green pediatrician Alan Greene, MD. Information to make healthy product and lifestyle choices for your pregnancy, birth and baby. Greene's website also has loads of valuable parenting and medical information, www.drgreene.com.
- **Sprig:** *Washington Post*'s Glamour in Green Site: www.sprig.com.
- *The Complete Organic Pregnancy:* Written by Alexandra Zissu & Deirdre Dolan. Learn how to minimize exposure to toxins during your pregnancy.
- *The Green Guide:* Run by National Geographic, this magazine and

website is great green resource, www.thegreenguide.com.
- **The O'Mama Report:** Selected content from the Organic Trade Association for women to understand organic agriculture and organic products, www.theorganicreport.com.
- **Treehugger:** A cutting edge environmental site with informative blogs and green guides for green news and product information, www.treehugger.com.
- **Zenana's Maternity Spa & Wellness Center:** If you are lucky enough to be in Portland, Oregon or visiting, you have to check out this spa for some mommy or daddy pampering time. They have a babysitter on site! www.zenanaspa.com.
- **Zoe B Organic Weekly:** A blog with organic and eco-friendly finds, www.zoeb-organic-weekly.blogspot.com.
- **ZRecs:** A popular blog about what's fun, what's safe and what's smart. ZRecs has great non-toxic buying guides, www.zrecs.blogspot.com.

PARENTING & MEDICAL INFORMATION
- **American Academy of Pediatrics (AAP):** An organization of 60,000 pediatricians that sets the medical standard for children's health and medical guidelines. Invaluable medical information and articles, www.aap.org.
- **Attachment Parenting International:** Information to educate and support parents in raising children in a secure, compassionate and gentle way. Find a local API group, www.attachmentparenting.org.
- **Deirdre Imus Environmental Center for Pediatric Oncology:** Part of the Hackensack University Medical Center, this center researches the link between environmental toxins and childhood disease and illness. The Center uses research, education and advocacy to rid our environment of toxins. Imus is also the author of several green living books, www.dienviro.com.
- **Dr. Greene:** *Parenting* magazine refers to Dr. Greene as the "Al Gore of Pediatrics." Greene's website focuses on medical information with a green twist. Dr. Greene wrote a book on green family living, *Raising Baby Green*, www.drgreene.com.
- **Dr. Karp:** Famous for his teaching of the secrets to making children happy. His book, *The Happiest Baby on the Block* is widely popular,

www.thehappiestbaby.com.

- **Dr. Sears:** The wonderful practice that started with Dr. William Sears and his wife Martha Sears, R.N. has grown to include two of their sons, Dr. Jim Sears and Dr. Bob Sears. Bill and Martha raised eight children and practiced pediatric medicine for over 30 years. The Sears' Family Library covers all your parenting needs with a loving, thoughtful and knowledgeable approach to raising children. Their website is a wealth of medical information. We love their medicine cabinet and "what to do if" articles, www.askdrsears.com.
- **Holistic Moms Network:** A non-profit support and resource organization bringing likeminded moms together to learn more about holistic health and parenting. Find a local group near you, www.holisticmoms.org.
- **Just the Facts Baby:** A website written by professional journalist that does what it says—it gives just the facts from experts on all areas relating to pregnancy, babies and parenting, www.justthefactsbaby.com.
- **National Institute of Child Health and Human Development:** The NICHD conducts and supports research on all stages of human development, from preconception to adulthood, www.nichd.nih.gov.

PLAYGROUPS
- **Baby Signs:** Take a class to learn to communicate with your baby using baby sign language, www.babysigns.com.
- **Find Other Moms:** Register and search for like-minded moms in your area, www.findothermoms.com.
- **Gymboree Play and Music:** Seven levels of developmentally appropriate art, music and play classes for child and caregiver. Classes begin from newborn until five years old, www.gymboreeclasses.com.
- **Healthy Mom Fitness:** A wide variety of classes to help pregnant and new moms prepare for the physiological changes, develop stamina and strength for labor and delivery and restore muscle tone after the baby is born, www.healthymomsfitness.com.
- **Kindermusik:** Classes are based upon Kindermusik's music and movement curricula for caregivers and their children, ages newborn to seven years old, www.kindermusik.com.
- **Music Together:** Since 1987, Music Together is a fun early childhood

music program for babies, toddlers, preschoolers, kindergartners, and their caregivers, www.musictogether.com.

- **Play Group USA:** Find local playgroups and mom groups at www.playgroupsusa.com.
- **Portland Early Learning:** A great educational group helping to develop your child's early language, learning, and literacy skills while always keeping focused on the importance of the parent-child relationship. The center is located in Portland, Oregon. The center also provides an informative newsletter and resource page for non-Oregonians, www.portlandearlylearning.com.
- **Stroller Strides:** Fun and rewarding fitness classes where you exercise with your baby in a stroller at both indoor and outdoor venues, www.strollerstrides.com.

RECYCLING, REUSING AND REDUCING

- **Craigslist:** Browse local classifieds and forums, sell you used baby gear and find secondhand gear for sale, www.craigslist.org.
- **Ebay:** Buy and sell secondhand goods at auction, www.ebay.com.
- **Freecycle:** Online forums to post your stuff to give away or search for something you want, www.freecycle.org.
- **Lime's Guide to Recycling:** A simple-to-use menu lets you select the item you want to recycle and then gives you the information to do so, www.lime.com/features/limes_guide_to_recycling/story/11485/ how_to_recycle_everything.
- **Miracle Diapers:** An organization that collects gently used cloth diapers and donates them to families in need who want to cloth diaper.
- **No Mother Left Behind:** All mothers should babywear; donate your old sling so that they all can, www.nomotherleftbehind.com.
- *The Travels of a T-shirt in the Global Economy: An Economist Examines the Markets, Power, and Politics of World Trade* by Pietra Rivoli. A finance professor at Georgetown University, Rivoli studied the second life of clothing for her book.
- **"When donations go farther than you think,"** by Molly Bloom, *Newark Star Ledger*, www.mollybloom.net/bins.html.
- **"Where the used shoe fits,"** by Kelly Kearsley, *The News Tribune*, dwb.thenewstribune.com/business/story/5583524p-5021353c.html.

SAFETY

- **Austin Baby Proofing:** A wide selection of baby proofing products, www.austinbabyproofing.com.
- **Consumer Product Safety Commission:** Sign up for email notification of product recalls, www.cpsc.gov.
- **CPSC Safe Crib Tips:** Follow these requirements for evaluating that you are using a safe crib, www.cpsc.gov/CPSCPUB/PUBS/5030.pdf.
- **Consumers Union:** An expert, independent nonprofit organization that receives no outside funding. Consumers Union tests and researches products to protect, inform and empower consumers to protect themselves, www.consumerreports.org.
- **Environmental Protection Agency (EPA):** Information on lead, www.epa.gov/ebtpages/emerpoisoningleadpoisoning.html or www.epa.gov/lead.
- **EPA Toxicity and Exposure Assessment for Children's Health:** Summaries of scientific literature and US federal regulations relevant to children's environmental health. TEACH focuses on 18 chemicals of concern, www.epa.gov/teach/index.html.
- **Health Home Test:** At home tests for water, heavy metals, allergens and mold, www.healthhometest.com.
- **Homax LeadCheck:** Easy to use home lead tests. Buy on their website or find it at your local hardware store, www.leadtesttoys.com.
- **Hybrivet Systems:** Heavy metal testing kits that give fast results and are easy to use, www.leadcheck.com.
- **Juvenile Products Manufacturer Association (JPMA):** A national trade organization that includes over 300 companies that manufacturer or import infant products in the US, Canada and Mexico. JPMA certification is recognized by a JPMA product seal, www.jpma.org.
- **Keeping Babies Safe:** An organization dedicated to keeping babies safe from preventable injuries and deaths associated with unsafe cribs, dangerous children's products and unsafe sleep environments. Helpful tips and information for preventing injury from children's products, www.keepingbabiessafe.org.
- **Kids in Danger:** Advocates for safer children's products. Sign up for children's safety email alerts, www.kidsindanger.org.
- **Recall Information:** Website posts recalls from six federal agencies with

different jurisdictions. Sign up for email notification of government recalls, www.recalls.gov.

- **Safe Kids USA:** A global network of organizations that work to prevent accidental childhood injury, www.usa.safekids.org.
- **Safe Mama:** A well-written blog for information on product recalls, child safety, health. Safe Mama has several great product guides, www.safemama.com.
- **The Smart Mama:** A blog on safe products and tips written by an attorney specializing in consumer product labeling. The Smart Mama also offers personal consultations about going green, reducing chemical exposure and testing for lead and other metals, www.thesmartmama.com.
- **The Soft Landing Blog:** An informational blog about safe feeding gear with product reviews and research on the latest non-toxic feeding products for babies/toddlers, http://thesoftlanding.wordpress.com.
- **ZRecs:** Fun, smart and safe product recommendations, www.zrecsblogspot.com.

SKIN CARE

- **AAP Sun Recommendations:** Read about the AAP's guidelines for sun exposure and protection, www.aap.org/family/protectsun.htm.
- **Coalition for Consumer Information on Cosmetics:** Their Leaping Bunny Program sets a cruelty-free standard for cosmetic, personal care, and household products. Use their Compassionate Shopping Guide to find skincare and household products that have no new animal testing, www.leapingbunny.org.
- **EWG Parent's Guide:** A one page buying guide for skin care products, www.cosmeticdatabase.com/special/parentsguide/EWG_parentsguide.pdf.
- **EWG Sunblock Guide:** Print out a sunblock product guide to take to the store with you, www.cosmeticsdatabase.com/special/sunscreens/summary.php.
- **Mountain Rose Herbs:** A catalog and website with a wide selection of organic herbs and herbal products, www.mountainroseherbs.com.
- **Safe Mama's Skincare Users Guide:** Print out an extensive cheat sheet on safe skincare products, www.safemama.com/2008/04/11/

baby-skin-care-products-a-quick-users-guide.

- **SafeMama's Sunblock Cheat Sheet:** www.safemama.com/sheets/ sunscreen_sheet3.pdf.
- **Skin Deep:** Search the Environmental Working Group's database of skincare products to find the safety rating and product ingredient information, www.cosmeticsdatabase.com.
- **The Campaign for Safe Cosmetics:** A coalition of women's, public health, labor, environmental health and consumer-rights groups that works to eliminate the use of chemicals linked to cancer, birth defects and other health problems. Find out which manufacturers have signed the Compact for Safe Cosmetics, www.safecosmetics.org.

SLEEP

- **First Candle:** An organization determined to advance infant health and survival. First Candle focuses on reducing Sudden Infant Death Syndrome (SIDS), miscarriage and stillbirth, www.sidsalliance.org.
- *No Cry Sleep Solution:* Sleep expert Elizabeth Pantley will help you get your baby or toddler to sleep with gentle, effective and loving parenting. Pantley wrote one book that addresses the needs of babies and another for toddlers and preschoolers. Download sleep logs from her informative site. Pantley has also written *No Cry* books on discipline and potty training, www.pantley.com/elizabeth.
- **Safe Bed Sharing:** Learn how to share a family bed safely, www.safebedsharing.org.
- **The Sleep Lady:** Kim West, a sleep expert and author, gives a gentle approach to helping your baby sleep, www.sleeplady.com.

TOYS

- **China Berry:** A wonderful selection of positive and uplifting books and other treasures, www.chinaberry.com.
- **For Small Hands:** A unique selection of real-life child-sized products for imaginative play and daily life based on Montessori philosophy. Kids will love pouring juice from kid-sized glass pitchers, using real brooms and playing with their classic toys, www.forsmallhands.com.
- **Magic Cabin:** Toys that focus on open-ended, kid-powered and imaginative play, www.magiccabin.com.

- **Maukilo:** Largest stock of Haba toys online. A wide selection of toys, many from Europe, with bright colors, textures and quality craftsmanship, www.maukilo.com.
- **Nico and Zoe:** For uncommon, artisan-made toys at a great value Nico and Zoe offers a fun selection of items for your little one through their on-line boutique, www.nicoandzoe.com.
- **Nova Natural:** A family in Vermont created Nova Naturals to feature imaginative toys, beautiful children's books and other beautiful natural products for children and their families, www.novanatural.com.
- **Oompa:** Toys that are natural, non-violent and from manufacturers who provide safe and nurturing environments for their employees. You won't find any battery-operated, cartoon themed, blinking light toys here, www.oompa.com.
- **Rosie Hippo:** Well made wooden toys, games, books and music to inspire creativity and exploration in children and parents, www.rosiehippo.com.
- **Willow Tree Toys:** Run by an Attachment Parenting family. Quality European-style wooden toys, natural organic toys and arts and craft kits that are consistent with the Waldorf educational philosophy, www.willowtreetoys.com.
- **ZRecs Safe Bath Toy Guide:** Make sure bath time is safe with this handy guide, www.zrecs.blogspot.com/2008/04/zrecs-guide-to-safer-bath-toys.html.

TRAVEL & TRANSPORTATION
- **AAP Car Seat Recommendations:** Child seat guidelines based on age and weight, car seat installation tips, www.aap.org/family/carseatguide.htm.
- **Car Safety:** Reviews of car seats' compatibility with car models, usage information and finding a car seat installer, www.car-safety.org.
- **CARES:** An innovative FAA-approved harness restraint device for airplane travel . No need to lug and install a car seat on the plane. CARES can be used for children 22 to 44 lbs, attaching directly to the airplane seat back and augmenting the regular seat belt, www.kidsflysafe.com.
- **Car Seat Lady:** Based in the New York and Baltimore metropolitan area,

the Car Seat Lady will help you choose the right car seat for your car and install the car seat. Website has useful information on traveling in taxis with children, www.thecarseatlady.com.

- **CPSafety:** An online child passenger safety resource for car and airplane travel, www.cpsafety.com.
- **National Highway Traffic Safety Administration:** Visit the "child safety" topic for information on car seat installation, use, ease of use ratings and find a certified installer, www.nhtsa.dot.gov.
- **Seat Check:** Find out your state's car seat laws and a local professional car seat installer. You can also phone 1-866-SEAT-CHECK for locator service, www.seatcheck.org.

VEGAN AND VEGETARIAN

- **People for the Ethical Treatment of Animals:** PETA is the largest animal rights organization in the world. PETA focuses on ending animal suffering in factory farms, laboratories, clothing trade and entertainment industry, www.peta.org.
- **Vegan Action:** A nonprofit organization that certifies 100% vegan products and works to educate the public about the benefits of veganism, www.vegan.org.
- **Vegan Outreach:** A group working to increase education about veganism, www.veganoutreach.org.
- **Vegetarian Times:** Great recipes, wellness information and lifestyle solutions for both vegetarians and "flexitarians," www.vegetariantimes.com.

brand & product directory

• • •

APPAREL & ACCESSORIES
Baby Bambu, www.babybambu.com
Babystar, www.babystar.com
Blue Canoe, www.bluecanoe.com
Bravado Designs, www.bravadodesigns.com
Buchic Bamboo Clothing, www.buchic.com
Disana, www.disana.de/engl/index.html
FlapHappy, www.flaphappy.com
Green Babies, www.greenbabies.com
Hanna Andersson, www.hannaandersson.com
Kate Quinn Organics, www.katequinnorganics.com
L. L. Bean, www.llbean.com
Lands' End, www.landsend.com
Lapsaky, www.lapsaky.com
MamaPoncho, www.mamaponcho.ch
Nuno Organic, www.nunoorganic.com
Patagonia, www.patagonia.com
Pure Beginnings, www.purebeginnings.com
REI, www.rei.com
Sage Creek Naturals, www.sagecreeknaturals.com
Sckoon, www.sckoon.com
SnuggleWool, www.snugglewool.com
Suse's Kinder, www.suseskinder.com
Tragemantel, www.tragemantel.ch
Under The Nile, www.underthenile.com

BABY CARRIERS & SLINGS
BabyHawk, www.babyhawk.com
Beco Baby Carrier, www.becobabycarrier.com
Didymos, www.didymos.de
EllaRoo, www.ellaroo.com
Ergo, www.ergobabycarriers.com

Goo Ga, www.goo-ga.com

Hotslings, www.hotslings.com

Kangaroo Korner, www.kangarookorner.com

Moby Wrap, www.mobywrap.com

New Native, www.newnativeinc.com

Oopa Baby, www.oopababy.com

Sakura Bloom, www.sakurabloom.com

Scootababy, www.scootababy.com

ZoloWear, www.zolowear.com

BABY MONITORS

Graco Baby, www.gracobaby.com

MobiCam, www.getmobi.com

BATHTUBS

EuroBath, www.primobaby.com

Prince Lionheart, www.princelionheart.com

Spa Baby Tub, www.spababytubs.com

TummyTub, www.tummy-tub.com

BEDDING & BLANKETS

BabyStar, www.babystar.com

Buchic Bamboo, www.buchic.com

Danish Woolen Delight, www.danishwool.com

Giggle, www.giggle.com

Nuno Organics, www.nunoorganic.com

Pure Beginnings, www.purebeginnings.com

Robbie Adrian, www.robbieadrian.com

Sage Creek Naturals, www.sagecreeknaturals.com

The Green Robin, www.thegreenrobin.com

BIBS

Baby Björn, www.babybjorn.com

Bumkins, www.bumkins.com

Silibib, www.silikids.com

Under The Nile, www.underthenile.com

BATHING & SKINCARE PRODUCTS
Baby Tata, www.babytata.com
Burt's Bees, www.burtsbees.com
California Baby, www.californiababy.com
Earth Mama Angel Baby, www.earthmamaangelbaby.com
Mama Rose's Naturals, www.mamarosesnaturals.com
Weleda, www.weledababy.com

BOTTLES
Adiri, www.adiri.com
BornFree, www.newbornfree.com
EvenFlo, www.evenflo.com
Green To Grow, www.greentogrow.com
Think Baby, www.thinkbabybottles.com
Wee Go, www.gobabylife.com

BOTTLE DRYING RACKS & BRUSHES
L'oved Baby, www.lovedbaby.com
Munchkin, www.munchkin.com
Nuby, www.nuby.platformtwo.com
Prince Lionheart, www.princelionheart.com

BOUNCY SEATS
Baby Björn, www.babybjorn.com
Oeuf, www.oeufnyc.com
Svan, www.svanusa.com

BREAST MILK STORAGE
Lansinoh, www.lansinoh.com
Mother's Milkmate, www.mothersmilkmate.com

BREAST PUMPS
Medela, www.medelabreastfeedingus.com

CAR SEATS
Britax, www.britaxusa.com

Cosco, www.coscojuvenile.com
Nest Car Seat Covers, www.nestplease.com
Orbit Baby, www.orbitbaby.com

CO-SLEEPERS & FAMILY BED PRODUCTS
Arm's Reach, www.armsreach.com
Baby Bunk, www.babybunk.com
Humanity Family Bed, www.familysleeper.com
TresTria Pillow, www.betterforbabies.com

CRADLES, BASSINETS & MOSES BASKETS
Cariboo, www.cariboo.us
Lillébaby, www.lillebabyusa.com
Little Merry Fellows, www.littlemerryfellows.com
Pure Beginnings, www.purebeginnings.com

CRIBS
A Natural Home, www.anaturalhome.com
Ikea, www.ikea.com
NurseryWorks, www.nurseryworks.net
Oeuf, www.oeufnyc.com
Stokke, www.stokkeusa.com

CRIB MATTRESSES
A Natural Home, www.anaturalhome.com
Natural Mat, www.naturalmatusa.com
Naturepedic, www.naturepedic.com
Pure Beginnings, www.purebeginnings.com
White Lotus, www.whitelotus.net

DIAPER BAGS
Fleurville, www.fleurville.com
LeSportSac, www.lesportsac.com
New Native, www.newnativeinc.com

DIAPER CHANGING PAD & COVERS
A Natural Home, www.anaturalhome.com

EcoBedroom, www.ecobedroom.com

Giggle, www.giggle.com

Holy Lamb Organics, www.holylamborganics.com

Happy Tushies, www.happytushies.com

Organic Caboose, www.organiccaboose.com

DIAPERS — CLOTH
Aristocrats, www.aristocratsbabyproducts.com

BabyKicks, www.babykicks.com

Bamboozles, www.totsbots.com

Blue Penguin, www.bluepenguin.biz

bumGenius, www.bumgenius.com

Bumkins, www.bumkins.com

Bummis, www.bummis.com

BumWare, www.bum-ware.com

Cotton Babies, www.cottonbabies.com

Crickett's Diapers, www.crickettsdiapers.com

Danish Woolen Delight, www.danishwool.com

FuzziBunz, www.fuzzibunz.com

Green Mountain, www.greenmountaindiapers.com

Imse Vimse, www.imsevimse.us

Kissaluvs, www.kissaluvs.com

Kushies, www.kushies.com

Little Beetle, www.betterforbabies.com

Mother-ease, www.mother-ease.com

Pro Services, www.prodiaper.net

Under The Nile, www.underthenile.com

Zany Zebra, www.zany-zebra.com

DIAPERS — DISPOSABLE
Seventh Generation, www.seventhgeneration.com

Tushies, www.tushies.com

DIAPERS — HYBRID
gDiapers, www.gdiapers.com

DIAPER PAILS, WET BAGS & SPRAYERS
bumGenius, www.bumgenius.com
Bumkins, www.bumkins.com
Happy Tushies, www.happytushies.com
MiniShower, www.minishower.com

DISHWARE & UTENSILS
Baby Björn, www.babybjorn.com
Bambu, www.bambuhome.com
Boon, www.booninc.com
Camden Rose, www.camdenrose.com
Lacquer Ware, www.lifewithoutplastic.com
TreBimbi, www.trebimbi.co.uk

DISHWASHER BASKETS
Dr. Browns, www.handi-craft.com
Luv'n Care, www.nuby.platformtwo.com
Munchkin, www.munchkin.com
Prince Lionheart, www.princelionheart.com

DRESSERS, CHANGING TABLES & ARMOIRES
A Natural Home, www.anaturalhome.com
Cariboo, www.cariboo.us
Ikea, www.ikea.com
NurseryWorks, www.nurseryworks.net
Oeuf, www.oeufnyc.com

FOOD MILLS & STORAGE
Baby Cubes, www.babycubes.com
Fresh Baby, www.freshbaby.com
KidCo, www.kidco.com

GLIDERS / ROCKERS
A Natural Home, www.anaturalhome.com
DucDuc, www.ducducnyc.com

GRIPE WATER
Baby's Bliss, Mommy's Bliss, www.blissbymom.com
Colic Calm, www.coliccalm.com
Wellements, www.wellements.com

HAIRBRUSHES & COMBS
Ambassador, www.amazon.com
Kost, www.allthingsgreen.net
Widu, www.widu.com

HEALTH & BABY CARE
All Terrain, www.allterrainco.com
Hyland's, www.hylands.com
Nosefrida, www.nosefrida.com
Organic Essentials, www.organicessentials.com

HIGH CHAIRS
Argington, www.argington.com
Geuther, www.euro-baby.us
Stokke, www.stokkeusa.com
Svan, www.svanusa.com

LULLABY CD
Bengali Lullaby, www.joserubendeleon.com
Putomayo, www.putumayo.com

MAMA CARE REMEDIES, LOTIONS AND OILS
Baby's Bliss, Mommy's Bliss, www.blissbymom.com
Earth Mama Angel Baby, www.earthmamaangelbaby.com
Mama Rose's Naturals, www.mamarosesnaturals.com
Motherlove, www.motherlove.com
Wish Garden Herbs, www.wishgardenherbs.com

MATTRESS PADS
Danish Woolen Delight, www.danishwool.com
SnuggleWool, www.snugglewool.com
White Lotus, www.whitelotus.net

NAIL SCISSORS OR CLIPPERS
Tweezerman, www.tweezerman.com

NEW MAMA TEAS
Earth Mama Angel Baby, www.earthmamaangelbaby.com
Mama Rose's Naturals, www.mamarosesnaturals.com
Traditional Medicinals, www.traditionalmedicinals.com

NIPPLE CREAMS
Earth Mama Angel Baby, www.earthmamaangelbaby.com
Lansinoh, www.lansinoh.com
Motherlove, www.motherlove.com

NURSING BRAS & PADS
Blue Canoe, www.bluecanoe.com
Bravado Designs, www.bravadodesigns.com
Danish Woolen Delight, www.danishwool.com
Lansinoh, www.lansinoh.com
Organic Essentials, www.organicessentials.com
Under The Nile, www.underthenile.com

NURSING PILLOWS
Blessed Nest, www.blessednest.com
Mother Earth Nursery Designs, www.motherearthnurserydesigns.com
Organic Caboose, www.organiccaboose.com

PACIFIERS
EcoBinky, www.ecopiggy.com
Evenflo, www.evenflo.com
Natursutten, www.natursutten.com

PLAYTIME
BlaBla, www.blablakids.com
Camden Rose, www.camdenrose.com
Chelona, www.chelona.gr
Haba, www.haba.de
Merry Muscles, www.babyloveproducts.com
Plan Toys, www.plantoys.com
Sarah's Silks, www.sarahssilks.com
Selecta, www.selecta-spielzeug.de
Vilac, www.vilac.com

PREGNANCY BODY PILLOW
Holy Lamb Organic, www.holylamborganics.com
Organic Caboose, www.organiccaboose.com
TresTria Pillow, www.betterforbabies.com

POSTPARTUM MENSTRUAL PADS
GladRags, www.gladrags.com
Lunapads, www.lunapads.com
Seventh Generation, www.seventhgeneration.com

SAFETY & BABY PROOFING
KidCo, www.kidco.com
Ikea, www.ikea.com
Prince Lionheart, www.princelionheart.com

SIPPY CUPS
BornFree, www.newbornfree.com
Fluid, www.booninc.com
Foogo, www.thermos.com
Klean Kanteen, www.kleankanteen.com
Safe Sippy, www.thesafesippy.com
Sigg, www.mysigg.com
Think Baby, www.thinkbabybottles.com

STROLLERS
Baby Planet, www.baby-planet.com
Orbit Baby, www.orbitbaby.com
Quinny, www.quinny.com
Stokke, www.stokkeusa.com

SUNBLOCKS
Badger, www.badgerbalm.com
California Baby, www.californiababy.com
Earth's Best by Jason, www.jason-natural.com

TEETHERS & TEETHING REMEDIES
Amberizon, www.amberizon.com
Boiron, www.boironusa.com
Camden Rose, www.camdenrose.com
Chewable Jewels, www.docbloom.com
Haba, www.haba.de
Hyland's, www.hylands.com
Vulli, www.vulli-toys.com

TOWELS & WASHCLOTHS
Buchic Bamboo, www.buchic.com
Under The Nile, www.underthenile.com

WIPES & SOLUTIONS
Baby Bits, www.soapsbydenise.com
bumGenius, www.bumgenius.com
Imse Vimse, www.imsevimse.us
Kissaluvs, www.kissaluvs.com
Mama Rose's Natural's, www.mamarosesnaturals.com
Seventh Generation, www.seventhgeneration.com
Small Wonder Wipes, www.smallwonderswipes.com
Tushies, www.tushies.com
Under The Nile, www.underthenile.com

green dictionary

• • •

We wanted to provide a dictionary and glossary of terms in one spot so that you could look up any unfamiliar word or term at a drop of a hat. We know that trying to figure out the world of green can be overwhelming. We know how you feel; our brains were about to explode when we first researched this topic! Our dictionary and glossary are by no means cast in stone but only serve as a reference. We would like to thank The Babywearer (www.thebabywearer.com) for providing us with the baby-wearing-related definitions. We strongly urge you to read labels with a fine-toothed comb and if you're still not sure what a foreign term means call the manufacturer who makes the product. It is your right to make sure whatever your family is exposed to is safe!

ACRONYM CHEAT SHEET

AAP Academy of Pediatrics
ABC Asian baby carrier
AI2 all-in-two
AIO all-in-one
BBP butyl benzyl phthalate
BPA bisphenol A
CBD cannabidiol
CCIC Coalition for Consumer Information on Cosmetics
CHEJ Center for Health, Environment and Justice
CHM Chemical and Heavy Metals
CPSC Consumer Products Safety Commission
CSA Controlled Substances Act
DBP dibutyl phthalate
DEA Diethanolamine
DEA Drug Enforcement Administration
DEHP diethylhexyl phthalate
DIDP di-isodecyl phthalate
DINP di-isononyl phthalate
DNOP di-n-octyl phthalate

DONA Doulas of North America

DSQ Diaper Service Quality

EO essential oils

EMK ethyl methyl ketone

EPA Environmental Protection Agency

EWG Environmental Working Group

FA Food Alliance

FSC Forest Stewardship Council

GMO genetically modified organisms

HDPE high density polyethylene

HIA Hemp Industries Association

JPMA Juvenile Products Manufacturers Association

LATCH Lower Anchors and Tethers for Children

LDPE low density polyethylene

LLL La Leche League

MSC Marine Stewardship Council

NHTSA National Highway and Traffic Safety Administration

NICHHD National Institute of Child Health and Human Development

NOP National Organic Program

OTA Organic Trade Association

PABA para-aminobenzoic acid

PBDE polybrominated diphenyl ethers

PEG polyethylene glycol

PES polyethersulfone

PETA People for the Ethical Treatment of Animals

PPG polyethylene glycol

PUL polyurethane laminate

PVC polyvinyl chloride

QAI Quality Assurance International

SFI Sustainable Forestry Initiative

SIDS Sudden Infant Death Syndrome

SLS sodium lauryl sulfate

SPF sun protection factor

TBT tributyltin

TEA triethanolamine

TEACH Toxicity and Exposure Assessment for Children's Health

THC tetrahydrocannabinol
USDA United States Department of Agriculture
UV ultraviolet light
UVA long wave ultraviolet light
UVB medium wave ultraviolet light
VOC volatile organic compound
WAHM work at home mom
WHO World Health Organization

DICTIONARY

1,4-Dioxane: An accidental byproduct of the ethoxylation process in cosmetics manufacturing. Since it is a byproduct, you won't see 1,4-Dioxane on the ingredient label. 1,4-Dioxane is intentionally used in manufacturing solvent applications, fumigants and automotive coolant. A recent study by the Organic Consumer Association found 1,4-Dioxane in products listed as natural and organic. 1,4-Dioxane is both a known carcinogen in animals and a known eye and respiratory tract irritant. It also may cause damage to the central nervous system, liver and kidneys.

All In Ones (AIO): An all-in-one diaper is a diaper and cover together as one piece. Because the cover is sewn onto the diaper, AIOs do not require a separate cover. An AIO is as easy to use as a disposable diaper.

All In Two (AI2): Similar to an AIO with the diaper and cover sewn together; however the soaker part of the diaper is not completely integrated into the diaper. The soaker may be partially sewn, snapped or placed into the diaper. Because this is the thickest part of the diaper and it is separate from the diaper, AI2s may have a more efficient drying time. An AI2 is similar to using a disposable diaper, except that you may need to place or affix the soaker to the diaper.

Anti-Foaming Agents: Chemicals added to reduce the amount of foam produced, especially when detergents are present in waste-water.

Asian Baby Carrier (ABC): The simplest form of two shoulder baby carriers is essentially a square of fabric with straps at each corner. Two straps tie around the wearer's waist. The other two straps go over the wearer's shoulders (they may or may not cross over), then attach to the carrier or tie to themselves. The Chinese Mei Tai is an example. All Asian-style carriers are unstructured soft carriers.

Avobenzone (Parsol 1789, Eusolex 9020, Escalol 517): A chemical sunscreen shown to degrade significantly in light, resulting in less protection over time.

Backpack Baby Carrier: See Frame Backpack.

Back Carry: Any carry where the baby is worn on the back, almost always facing towards the wearer's back.

Buddha Carry: A carry where the baby sits with his knees up and legs either crossed or tucked underneath; the baby sits on the wearer's front facing out; also called a Kangaroo carry.

Bisphenol A (BPA): A chemical found in polycarbonate plastic that makes plastic shatterproof. It is dangerous because it may cause adverse health effects, such as: increase in obesity and diabetes, interference with the normal development of unborn babies, stimulation of mammary gland development (a risk factor for breast cancer) and early onset of puberty. Polycarbonate plastic is usually marked with the number seven recycling symbol.

Bleach: The third main ingredient in laundry detergents. North American detergents usually contain chlorine-based bleaches that work at lower temperatures. Most detergents for colors contain no bleach.

Borax: A boron compound, a mineral, and a salt of boric acid also known as sodium borate, sodium tetraborate, or disodium tetraborate. Usually a white odorless powder, it dissolves easily in water. Borax is a component of many detergents, cosmetics, and enamel glazes. It is also used as a fire retardant and insecticide. Exposure can cause respiratory and skin irritation.

Ingestion may cause nausea, persistent vomiting, abdominal pain, and diarrhea. See Fillers and Processing Aids.

Builders: The second major component in detergents and are basically water softeners. Builders enhance surfactants' action by deactivating calcium and magnesium and by producing alkaline solutions to aid in cleaning. Most builders are phosphate-based, except in phosphate-free detergents.

Calendula Flowers: An annual plant with flowers known to provide anti-inflammatory, wound-healing and antimicrobial properties.

Carry or Hold: As in the noun "a carry", "hip carry" etc. refers to the position where the baby is worn on the wearer's body. E.g. in the back carry, the baby is carried on the wearer's back.

Cradle Hold: A carry where the baby is lying down on the front of your body as though being cradled. If using a single-shouldered carrier such as a sling, the baby's head is towards the rings. More suitable for newborn and young babies.

Chlorine: A common disinfectant, a toxic gas that can irritate the respiratory system. In the upper atmosphere, chlorine can destroy the ozone layer. See bleach.

Comfrey: A perennial herb commonly used in postpartum sitz baths. Comfrey can be used topically to help heal damaged tissue. The FDA has issued a statement advising against taking comfrey internally because of possible link with liver failure.

Contour / Shaped Diapers: Imagine drawing a line around a disposable diaper that is laying flat and you will have the shape of a contoured diaper. Contour or shaped diapers usually do not have any closure or elastic around the legs. For waterproof protection, you need to use a cover with a contour or shaped diaper. You may need to fasten the diaper with a Snappi or pins before putting on the cover. Contour diapers are more convenient to use than prefolds because they eliminate the need for folding.

Corrosion Inhibitors: Known as water glass or liquid glass, and often sodium silicate. Corrosion inhibitors are generally added to detergents to help reduce corrosion inside the washing machine. See sodium silicate.

Diaper Covers: A diaper cover provides waterproof protection when using prefolds, fitted or contour diapers. Wool or polyurethane laminate (PUL) tend to be the most popular materials for creating a waterproof barrier between the diaper and baby's clothing. Diaper covers are most typically closed with Velcro, APLIX or snaps.

Diaper Doublers / Inserts: Diaper doublers are rectangular pieces made up of layers of absorbent fabric sewn together. If you are using pocket diapers, diaper doublers make trim and convenient stuffers. When you need extra absorbency in other cloth diapers, you can simply add a doubler.

Diaper Liners: A thin material that is placed under baby's tush on the diaper. Liners make solid waste diaper clean up easier. You lift the liner off the diaper and shake the solid waste into the toilet. Some liners are flushable and biodegradable. You can also find reusable liners, such as ones made out of silk. Diaper liners do not add absorbency.

Diaper Sprayer: A sprayer (think of the sprayer attached to some dishwashing sinks) that you install onto your toilet. Installation is usually simple, requiring a minimum of tools. A diaper sprayer allows you to spray solid waste off the diaper and into the toilet where it belongs. You can use a sprayer with disposables and cloth diapers. The sprayer can also be used as mini-bidet for adults and children.

Diethanolamine (DEA): A synthetic agent added to skincare and bathing products to create foaming action and creamy texture. It may react with other product ingredients and form nitrosamines, which are known carcinogens. Other names or synonyms are bis(hydroxyethyl)amine, diethylolamine, hydroxydiethylamine, diolamine, and 2,2'-iminodiethanol. Variants of DEA include lauramide diethanolamine, coco diethanolamide, cocoamide diethanolamine or coconut oil amide of diethanolamine, lauramide DEA, lauric diethanolamide, lauroyl diethanolamide, and lauryl diethanolamide.

Elimination Communication: A system where the baby's caregiver learns the baby's signals, such as body language, for elimination (urination and defecation) and gives the child the opportunity to use the potty rather than their diaper.

Ethoxylation: A chemical process in which ethylene oxide is added to fatty acids in order to make them more soluble in water. For example, sodium laureth sulfate is created from ethoxylated sodium dodecyl. Sodium laureth sulfate is used as a foaming agent in shampoos and toothpastes, and as an industrial detergent.

Fillers and Processing Aids: These are often sodium sulfate or borax and used to absorb water and help powdered detergent flow. Removing most of the filler yields "concentrated" or "ultra" detergents. Alcohols are added to liquid detergents to keep everything in solution and to lower the freezing point.

Fitted Cloth Diapers: Similar in appearance to disposable diapers, fitted cloth diapers have a contour shape and gathered edges around the legs designed to control leaks. Fitted diapers are closed with Velcro, APLIX or snaps. For waterproof protection, you will need to use a cover with a fitted diaper.

Food Mill: A simple food grinder that will puree fruits, veggies, even meats, while separating skins and seeds. You can find both hand-operated and electric food mills.

Frame Backpack: A backpack similar in design to a hiking rucksack but usually with a metal frame, and designed to carry a child.

Front Carrier / Front Pack: A soft carrier specifically designed to be used on the wearer's front. Most suitable for smaller babies. The baby may face in or out. See also soft carrier.

Hemp: A course fiber made from the inner bark of the hemp plant. It is becoming increasingly popular for use in clothing and diapers because of its durability, absorbency and natural anti-microbial properties.

Herbal Tinctures: A concentrated mixture of herbs that is typically taken in water. Many midwives belief that certain herbs, used correctly, can help prepare a woman's body for labor. You can find herbal tinctures for just about any ailment or condition out there. Since herbs can interact with medication and your pregnancy, please read the warning label before consuming. And, as always, ask your healthcare provider for his or her advice first.

Hip Carrier: A single shouldered carrier specifically designed for hip carries.

Hip Carry: A general term for any carry where the baby is against the wearer's hip, either slightly to the front, on the side, or slightly to the back. The baby's legs usually hang out, one to the front and the other behind the wearer with thighs parallel to the floor. Suitable for babies once they can sit unsupported and a popular carry for toddlers.

Hybrid Diapers: The most recent innovation in diapering. A hybrid diaper has an outer cover that is waterproof, reusable and machine washable. The inside contains an absorbent diaper that is flushable or compostable. With a hybrid diaper you'll get the reusability of cloth and the convenience of disposables.

Kangaroo Carry: Usually describes a carry of the wearer's front with the baby facing outwards and the legs inside the carrier (a.k.a. Buddha carry).

Lanolin: A substance extracted from wool sheared from sheep. Some of the products we recommend contain lanolin. If you are vegan or vegetarian, you may want to avoid lanolin. Also you may want to check with the manufacturer that the sheep were treated humanely. Make sure that the lanolin is cleaned to remove pesticides and herbicides. If you have allergic reactions to wool, you may want to think twice about using lanolin.

Lavender: A flowering plant that smells great and can help relieve pain. Lavender flowers are usually added to sitz bath herbs. For some, lavender oil can also be a powerful allergen. Ingesting lavender should be avoided during pregnancy and breastfeeding.

Mineral oil: A colorless, odorless, tasteless oil distilled from petroleum. It can be used as a lubricant and, in medicine, as a laxative. The distillation of petroleum to make gasoline creates mineral oil or liquid petrolatum. Mineral oil is of relatively low value and it is produced in large quantities; therefore it has been widely used. It is a common ingredient in lotions, oils, ointments and cosmetics.

Nursing Hold: A carry where the baby is lying down on the front of your body in a position suitable for nursing. Distinguished from the cradle hold because the baby's head is at the end opposite the rings (in a sling); the baby's legs may stick out the other end. Suitable for newborn and young babies.

Nursing Pads: Absorbent pads that a nursing mother inserts between her breast and bra to absorb milk leaks. Many women only need to wear nursing pads during the beginning weeks of breastfeeding and growth spurts, though others find they need to wear nursing pads the entire time they breastfeed. Nursing pads are available in disposable or reusable forms. Reusable nursing pads can be made from cotton, bamboo, hemp, wool or a blend of those fibers. Nursing pads can be circular or teardrop shaped, and some may even be contoured. Washable, reusable pads are really simple to use and can reduce your waste.

Nursing Pillow: A crescent or semicircular firm pillow that is placed on mommy's (or whoever is feeding baby's) lap. The baby is placed sideways on top of the pillow. The pillow allows for better positioning while feeding baby. A nursing pillow can be used with breastfeeding and bottle-feeding. A nursing pillow can have a life beyond feeding time—it is great for baby's tummy time or as a sitting prop. Parents wishing to avoid petroleum-based products should choose a pillow filled with wool or cotton rather than the polyfil of many mainstream nursing pillows.

Oxybenzone: A synthetic sunscreen that can be absorbed into your skin and may be an endocrine disruptor. Oxybenzone is dangerous because it can affect the nervous system, has been linked to cancer in some laboratory studies, and creates harmful free radicals when exposed to the sun.

Padded Sling: Usually a shaped piece of fabric (something like a pea-pod shape), narrower than an Unpadded Sling. The shoulder end has rings and the opposite end is the "tail". To be considered a padded sling, either the shoulder or the sides of the fabric (rails) are padded. Padding varies in amount from "lightly padded" to "heavily padded". Padded slings usually come in different sizes.

Parabens: A group of synthetic preservatives used in cosmetics, skincare and pharmaceuticals. Parabens can also be used as a food additive. Parabens are dangerous because they are potential endocrine disrupters. Some studies have found parabens in breast tumors. You will find parabens listed as methylparaben, ethylparaben, propylparaben, butylparaben, isobutylparaben, isopropylparaben and benzylparaben.

Phthalates: Chances are that you won't actually see "phthalates" listed on an ingredient list. Phthalates, often found in fragrance, can be listed as "fragrance" rather than the individual components that make up the fragrance. Phthalates are added to cosmetics and skincare products to bind the product and fragrance. Phthalates are also a plastic softener or "plasticizer." Phthalates can be used in polyvinyl chloride (PVC) plastic to improve flexibility. According to Environmental California, phthalates have been found to cause early puberty in girls, impaired sperm quality in men, genital defects and reduced testosterone production in boys, genital defects and testicular cancer. Phthalates can be listed as diethylhexyl phthalate (DEHP), dibutyl phthalate (DBP), butyl benzyl phthalate (BBP), di-isodecyl phthalate (DIDP), di-isononyl phthalate (DINP), di-n-octyl phthalate (DNOP), and others.

Pocket Diapers: These diapers are similar in shape and design to disposables and AIOs. The back top edge of the diaper is left open for you to stuff the soaker into the diaper. The soaker is usually sandwiched between an outer layer of knit PUL and an inner layer of microfleece or cotton. Pocket diapers usually use snaps or hook and loop tape to fasten the diaper. Pocket diapers are simple to use and are great for nighttime and outings.

Podegi (Podeagi): The traditional Korean back carrier is a type of torso carrier. It is like a blanket with long straps that tie around the wearer's chest and waist/hips. The baby rides on your back facing you.

Polybrominated diphenyl ethers (PBDE): A chemical that is used to create fire retardancy on materials such as clothing and mattresses. This flame retardant is a sub-family of the brominated flame retardant group. The three main types are referred to as penta, octa and deca. Studies have found PBDE accumulated in breast milk and other human tissue. The EU has banned some PBDEs. Evidence indicates these chemicals may be toxic to the liver, thyroid, and neurodevelopment.

Polyethylene Glycol (PEGs or PPGs): A family of synthetic ingredients processed with ethylene oxide. PEGs and PPGs are used as surfactants, cleansing agents, emulsifiers, skin conditioners, and humectants. The National Toxicology Program's Eighth Annual Report on Carcinogens found that ethylene oxide exposure increases the incidence of uterine and breast cancers and of leukemia and brain cancer. PEG compounds are often contaminated with the carcinogen 1,4-dioxane.

Polyurethane Laminate (PUL): Typically a waterproof fabric consisting of polyester interlock knit fabric laminated to a thin film of polyurethane. The polyurethane provides the water barrier. Polyurethane is a synthetic resin with varying flexibility that can be used in coatings, adhesives, foams, and electrical insulation. This fabric is often used in waterproof wetbags, cloth diapers and cloth menstrual pads.

Polyvinyl Chloride (PVC): Is widely used in plastics—think shower curtains, pipes and toys. Researchers believe that over time PVC releases toxins, such as mercury, dioxins, and phthalates. PVC products are often found to contain lead, which is added as a stabilizer. PVC plastic releases carcinogenic dioxins when produced or burned. PVC is usually marked with the number three recycling symbol and it is also one of the most difficult plastics to recycle.

Poppable / Poppability: The quality in a babycarrier of being easy to get a baby into and out of, while being easy and practical to wear without a baby. A useful feature for babies who like to be up and down from your arms (or in and out of the babycarrier) frequently, necessitating that the babywearer leave the carrier on in-between times.

Postpartum Menstrual Pads: After birth, you will need some postpartum pads to absorb the lochia or postpartum vaginal discharge. Women typically use higher absorbency menstrual cloth or disposable pads during postpartum.

Postpartum Sitz Bath Herbs: For years, women have found postpartum relief with the use of herbs that have traditional healing properties. You can add your sitz bath herbs to your bathtub or to a traditional sitz bath that fits on your toilet.

Pouch: Essentially a long "tube" of fabric, folded in half lengthwise to create a pocket for the baby. Worn over one shoulder like a sling. Can be used for the same carries as slings. Can be made of woven or slightly stretchy fabrics. Some have a certain amount of adjustability allowing two people of different sizes to use the pouch; this can be achieved by snaps, buttons, zippers or hook and loop closures.

Prefold / Flat Cloth Diapers: These are the same diapers that Grandma used. Prefolds (aka Diaper Service Quality or Chinese Prefolds), have a thick center panel. Flat diapers are a large one-layer piece of cloth that must be folded many times to fit baby. Prefolds save you part of that folding routine. For waterproof protection, you need to use a cover with a prefold. You can fasten the prefold with a Snappi or old-fashioned pins. For some covers, you do not need to fasten the prefold to the baby. You simply fold the prefold in thirds, place it inside cover and then wrap the cover around baby. Cloth prefold diapers are great to use as burp clothes—practical and inexpensive. After their lives as diapers or burp cloths, prefold diapers make great rags around the house.

Pregnancy Body Pillow: A supportive pillow that's either big and long or bean-shaped. You can place the pillow underneath your belly and in between your knees for hip and back support and a comfortable night's rest.

Propylene Glycol: A thickening and filling agent derived from glycerin. Propylene glycol can be found in many products—even those listed as natural. The FDA determined that propylene glycol is "generally safe for use" for both food and cosmetics. However, it may raise your risk of cancer and carry toxins that affect the reproductive and immune systems. Propylene glycol is an allergen and eye irritant.

Snappi: A simple-to-use pinless diaper fastener that offers a practical and reliable way to fasten a cloth diaper. The Snappi is Y-shaped with small claw-like hooks on each end point. You pull the end across the diaper and press it into the cloth to attach it to the diaper.

Rebozo: A traditional, hand-woven Mexican carrier, and used as scarves, pregnancy and birthing aids, and for many other purposes in addition to their use as baby carriers. Similar to an unpadded sling, except that the fabric does not have rings but is knotted together using a slipknot or square knot. Can be used for the same carries as slings.

Soakers: The term soaker is used for two different things. First, this word refers to the middle layer of a cloth diaper, typically an AIO/AI2. Often this layer is made of a different, more absorbent fabric than the rest of the diaper. The term soaker is also used in reference to wool or polar fleece diaper covers. Unlike other diaper covers, wool and polar fleece are water resistant, rather than waterproof. They do allow some wetness to wick through from the diaper but still manage to keep babies' clothes dry. See also Diaper Doubler/Insert.

Shoulder Carry / Burp Position: A position where the baby is held high up on the wearer's shoulder. Can be achieved with a rebozo, wraparound carrier or two unpadded slings.

Sideways Kangaroo Carry: A position where the baby sits sideways in the carrier, usually with knees up and legs inside, or legs poking out the opposite end. Can be achieved with a sling, rebozo, wraparound carrier or pouch.

Sling (or Ring Sling): A piece of fabric, threaded through a pair of metal or nylon sling rings, which goes over one shoulder and around the opposite hip/waist. Adjustable and easy to share between multiple babywearers of different sizes. See also Padded Sling and Unpadded Sling.

Sling Rings: Rings used for adjusting the size and fit of a sling. Metal and nylon are the strongest and the most common. Sizes vary according to the type and width of the fabric used—small enough to offer traction and large enough to be able to adjust the sling easily.

Snuggle Hold or Tummy-to-Tummy: A carry where the baby's front is against the wearer's front, with the baby's head around chest/neck height. Feet can be in or out of the carrier. This position can be used for nursing. Suitable for newborn and young babies (with feet in) and older babies (with feet out).

Sodium Laureth Sulfate (SLS or SLES): A detergent and surfactant found in many personal care products from soaps and shampoos to even toothpaste. While it is an inexpensive and effective foamer it can affect those prone to eczema and other irritants by removing moisture from the top layers of skin. The Environmental Working Group claims that SLES may possibly be contaminated with 1,4-dioxane.

Sodium Polyacrylate: A super absorbent polymer that is used in disposable diapers and disposable menstrual pads. When dry, sodium polyacrylate is like a powder; when wet the powder turns to a transparent gel. Sodium polyacrylate was discontinued from use in tampons due to concern over a link to toxic shock syndrome.

Sodium Silicate: Also known as water glass or liquid glass, available in aqueous solution and in solid form, is a compound used in cements, passive fire protection, refractories, textile and lumber processing. See Corrosion Inhibitors.

Sodium Sulfate: Largely used as filler in powered laundry detergents. It is generally regarded as non-toxic by the science industry, although it should be noted that the dust can cause temporary asthma or eye irritation; See Fillers and Processing Aids.

Soft Carrier: A carrier with straps that go over both of the wearer's shoulders to hold the baby against the wearer's chest and stomach. Most also have a waist strap. The baby may be supported by their crotch or across their entire bottom. Soft carriers with a wide seat area hold the baby's legs up. Soft carriers include front carriers, back carriers and some hip carriers. Some soft carriers can be used on front and/or back and/or hip. See also Structured Soft Carrier, Unstructured Soft Carrier and Asian-style Carrier.

Structured Soft Carrier: This subset of soft carriers includes those that have shape and form even when not being worn. The rigidity is usually achieved with firm fabrics and use of padding.

Sulfates: Listed as sodium lauryl sulfate and sodium laureth sulfate. Sulfates are synthetic cleansing agents found in shampoos, shaving foams, bubble baths and even toothpaste. Sulfates remove oils from the skin and may potentially damage the lipid layer of your skin.

Surfactant: Short for "surface-active agent" and the main ingredient of any detergent. It improves the wetting ability of water, loosens and removes dirt, helps suspends dirt in the water, and prevents dirt from being redeposited on the clean laundry.

Sumo Carry: A carry with the baby on the front of your body, facing forward and with legs out. Babies, especially chubby ones, can look a bit like sumo wrestlers in this position!

Tail: The opposite end of a sling to the rings. A tail may be open or closed. An open tail is the full width of the fabric. Almost all unpadded slings have an open tail. Some padded slings also have an open tail. A closed tail is made narrower or sewn together to make a single piece, common for padded slings. To get a sling to fit really well the tail is pulled through the rings until the sling is quite tight and the baby is held high and firm.

Topical Treatment Nipple Cream: A cream that is applied to nipples to soothe and heal the cracking and chapping that is often experienced in the beginning stages of breastfeeding. Because of ingredient formulations, some creams may need to be removed before nursing. Some creams contain lanolin, a sheep-byproduct, which should be avoided by vegans or those with wool sensitivities.

Torso Carrier: A carrier that ties around the wearer's body and does not pass over the shoulders at all. Can be used to carry a baby on the front or back, in a variety of positions. Can be good for people with neck/shoulder problems. See also Podegi.

Triethanolamine (TEA): The Organic Consumer Association and Cancer Prevention Association label TEA as a "hidden carcinogen" that releases a precursor of a highly potent nitrosamine carcinogen. TEA is often used as a pH balancer in skin lotion, eye gels, moisturizers, shampoos and shaving foams.

Tummy-to-Tummy (TTT or T2T): See Snuggle Hold.

Unpadded Sling: Usually a rectangular piece of fabric around 2m (2.25 yds +) long and 75cm to 110cm (30" to 45") wide, gathered or joined onto two rings at one end. Usually has an open tail. Sometimes offered in various sizes but usually one-size-fits-all. See also Sling.

Unstructured Soft Carrier: This describes a subset of soft carriers that do not maintain their shape when not being worn. The traditional Chinese Mei Tai is an example; also called an Asian-style carrier or Asian Babycarrier (ABC).

Uva Ursi: An herb known for its antimicrobial properties that help fight infection, and its ability to soothe and strengthen inflamed tissues.

Volatile Organic Compound (VOC): A compound with high vapor pressure and low water solubility. This means that under normal conditions, such as room temperature and sunlight, VOCs may evaporate and enter the atmosphere. Many VOCs are human-made chemicals used and produced in the manufacture of paints, pharmaceuticals, and refrigerants. VOCs are common ground-water contaminants. Common VOC sources are paint, dry cleaning solvents and gasoline. VOCs such as formaldehyde may be carcinogenic.

Wet Bag: A bag that is typically lined with PUL for waterproof protection, with a layer of cotton on the outside. Most wet bags are closed with a zipper, although some use a drawstring. Wet bags come in a variety of sizes for storing soiled cloth diapers and cloth menstrual pads, and are great for storing wet clothes while on the go. You can find wet bags that are made by work-at-home moms and can be customized with your choice of fabric.

Wraparound Carrier: A long piece of fabric, 3m to 5.5m L x 45cm to 90cm W, (3.5yds to 6yds L x 18" to 36" W) that is wrapped around the wearer's body (usually over both shoulders), creating a pocket for a baby to sit. For some carries the fabric is doubled lengthwise before being wrapped. Can be used for the same carries as a sling, as well as the Sumo Carry. There are many ways to tie a wrap to achieve a particular carry.

your green registry

• • •

Use this fill-in-the-blanks baby registry to make notes on products you would like to further research or add to your baby registry. There are also spaces to jot down notes on the green topics you want to read more about.

APPAREL
O Baby's Layette
O Summer Babies: Brimmed Hat
O Winter Babies: Bunting, Stroller Blanket, Winter Hat, Mama Coat

TRAVEL & TRANSPORTATION
O Infant or Convertible Car Seat
O Stroller
O Baby Carrier and Sling
O Diaper Bag

NURSERY FURNITURE
O Baby's Sleeping Space: Moses Basket, Cradle, Bassinet, Crib, CoSleeper or Family Bed
O Mattress
O Dresser or Armoire
O Changing Table
O Glider/Rocker

BEDDING
O Bed Linens
O Mattress Pad

DIAPERING
O Baby Wipes
O Wipe Solutions
O Disposable Diapers

- O Hybrid Diapers
- O Prefold/Flat Cloth Diapers
- O Fitted Cloth Diapers
- O Contour/Shaped Diapers
- O Diaper Covers
- O All In Ones
- O Pocket Diapers
- O Diaper Doublers/Inserts
- O Diaper Liners
- O Diaper Pail/Wet Bag
- O Diaper Changing Pad and Cover
- O Diaper Sprayer

FEEDING

- O Burp Cloths
- O Nursing Bra and Pads
- O Nursing Pillow
- O Nipple Cream
- O Breast Pump
- O Baby Bottles
- O Bottle Drying Rack
- O Breast Milk Storage Containers
- O Bottle Brush
- O Dishwasher Basket
- O Food Mill
- O Baby Food Cook Book
- O Dishware and Utensils
- O Baby Food Storage
- O Sippy Cups
- O Bibs
- O High Chair

BATHING & SKINCARE

- O Towels and Washcloths
- O Baby Body Wash/Shampoo
- O Nail Scissors or Clippers

- ○ Baby Lotion/Oil
- ○ Diaper Creams
- ○ Sunblock
- ○ Bathtub
- ○ Soft Hairbrush and Comb

HEALTH & BABY CARE
- ○ Digital Thermometer/Rectal Thermometer
- ○ First Aid Essentials Kit
- ○ Nasal Aspirator
- ○ Cotton Pads/Swabs
- ○ Gripe Water/Gas Pain Reliever
- ○ Pain-and-Fever Reducer

MAMA CARE
- ○ Pregnancy Body Pillow
- ○ Prenatal Vitamins
- ○ Morning Sickness Remedies
- ○ Pregnancy Supplements and Teas
- ○ Postpartum Sitz Bath Herbs
- ○ Postpartum Menstrual Pads
- ○ Postpartum Lotions, Tinctures and Creams
- ○ Postpartum Teas

TEETHING
- ○ Natural Teething Remedies
- ○ Pacifiers
- ○ Teethers

SAFETY & BABY PROOFING
- ○ Baby Gate
- ○ Baby Proofing Necessities
- ○ Baby Monitor

NICE-TO-HAVES
- ○ Bouncy Seat

○ Playtime Gear
○ Lullaby CD

about the company & authors

Itsabelly provides the blueprint to help guide you through the maze of new parenthood successfully. Whether you're expecting, adopting, going through a surrogacy or you're a new parent, we help you navigate the world of all things maternity, newborn and toddler—with an eco twist. For everything from completing your baby registry and baby proofing to finding child care, from pregnancy preparation to back-to-work plans, Itsabelly is your one-stop resource.

As founder and CEO of Itsabelly and one of America's original baby planners, **Melissa Moog** brings enthusiasm and authority to all things maternity and newborn. She reviews products and shares parenting tips on her Itsabelly blog and is the Pregnancy Planning Expert for The Bump, which produces "the ultimate local guides to pregnant living." She also some-how finds time to serve as the President/Founder of The National Baby Planner Association which has set the standard and brought credibility to the industry. Melissa is a featured Green Expert on Sparkplugging.com, the Pregnancy Planning Expert on Bizymoms.com and is the New Mom Editor on Fox12 BetterTV. She is a former corporate HR Director and holds a master's degree in HR/Organizational Development from the University of San Francisco. To recharge, Melissa enjoys cooking, time at the gym, and traveling with her husband, daughter and their two yellow labs.

Jennifer Lo Prete, a writer and marketing consultant, is the marketing manager for Itsabelly. Jennifer holds a Master's in Integrated Marketing Communications from Northwestern University. Prior to becoming a mom, she worked in a congressional press office and managed advertising for both major children's manufacturers and consumer products companies. Seeing firsthand how advertising affects children, she was determined to live a less consumer-driven lifestyle with her family. Raised in a family that made eco-friendly choices both for frugality and practicality, Jennifer expanded these practices when starting her own family in 2003. Jennifer enjoys country living in the California Sierra Foothills with her husband, a preschooler and a toddler. She loves reading, swimming, baking, knitting and sewing. She also writes a blog at onecraftymama.blogspot.com.

index

Buttermilk Lotion, 164